C000213732

Ghosts on the Shore

Travels along the German Baltic coast

Paul Scraton

Influx Press, London

Published by Influx Press

5a Wayland Avenue, London, E8 2HP

www.influxpress.com / @InfluxPress

© Paul Scraton, 2017

First published 2017. Printed and bound in the UK by Clays Ltd., St Ives plc.

ISBN: 978-1-910312-10-0

Editor: Gary Budden

Copy-editor/Proofreader: Momus Editorial

Map: Julia Stone

Cover photograph: Katrin Schönig Design: Austin Burke

for Katrin

Contents

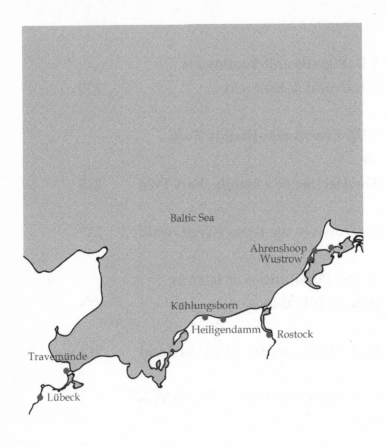

Baltic Sea

Ahrenshoop
Wustrow

Kühlungsborn

Heiligendamm   Rostock

Travemünde

Lübeck

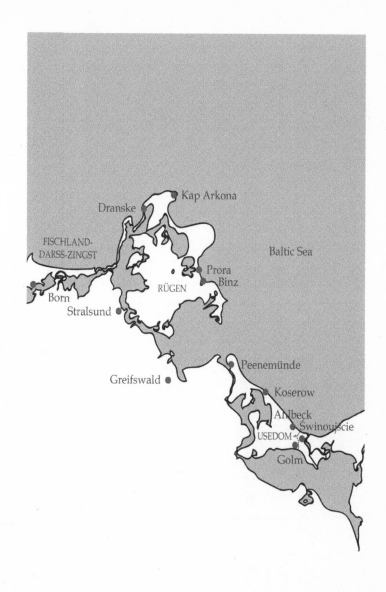

I

North
(Berlin-Lübeck)

Old National Gallery – Heimat – Zinnowitz 1934 – Zentral Omnibusbahnhof Berlin and the contradiction of the coast – Alone on the shore – Service station – Flags on the sand

On a Saturday morning at the beginning of winter I headed out with my daughter from our apartment in the north of Berlin to the city centre. Our destination was the Museum Island, that tribute to ego and royal whim on the banks of the River Spree. The collection of museums was built where once a residential neighbourhood stood, to house the collected art and plundered artefacts of Prussian royalty; a nineteenth-century version of those museum outposts built today on the shores of the Persian Gulf. It remains an unreal place. On that morning, as Lotte and I crossed the stone bridge on to the island, the surrounding streets were quiet. Bewildered tourists killed time as they waited for the city to wake, as the locals slept off the excesses of the night before. We joined a group, recently disgorged from their tour bus, surrounded by the click and whirr of cameras as they captured the bombastic architecture of the museum buildings. This was a place built to impress, and as the museum doors were opened and we were swept inside with the group, the excited chatter fell to a murmur, as if calmed and subdued by the grandeur within.

We climbed the stairs to the very top and then followed a corridor lined with paintings. We did not stop on the way, as we had come for one reason and one room only. In the heart of Berlin we were looking for the Baltic; the German shore captured by the brushstrokes of Casper David Friedrich. He had a room in the museum all to himself, a room filled with his work and yet dominated by the two paintings we had come to see. They had been painted during the same period, between 1808 and 1810, and bought as a pair by the Prussian King, destined to hang together for evermore. And there they were.

Der Mönch am Meer (The Monk by the Sea) on the left. *Abtei im Eichwald* (The Abbey in the Oakwood) on the right.

In the first picture, a monk stands alone on the cliff top, above an uneasy sea and beneath an ominous sky. In the second, a parade of monks makes its solemn progress through the ruins of the abbey that stands just a few hundred metres from the shore. Both these images reflect something of my fascination with the lands along the Baltic coast, a fascination that had developed over the fifteen years I had been living in Germany. The melancholic beauty of the featureless landscape of the cliff top. The ruins of Eldena, hinting at a deeper story. And, as with the lands themselves, the more I looked at the paintings, the more I discovered.

We spent about half an hour in that room, and while Lotte moved between the many different paintings hanging on the walls, I spent most of my time staring at these two.

Which was your favourite? I asked her, as we descended

the stairs, back towards the grey streets that were beginning to wake up to the weekend. She chose a mountain scene – bright, dramatic and heroic – and then skipped ahead. As I followed, I could think only of the monk on the cliff top, and the choppy waters of the Baltic behind.

*

My partner Katrin was born across the river from Museum Island in Berlin, but spent the first eleven years of her life on the Baltic coast. These were also the final eleven years of the German Democratic Republic, that post-war experiment with socialism on German soil, her family moving back to Berlin in the strange eleven-month period between the fall of the Berlin Wall in November 1989 and reunification in the autumn of 1990. Unlike in the West – which had both the North and Baltic Seas – in East Germany the seaside meant the *Ostsee*, as it stretched between the inner-German border at Priwall, just north of Lübeck, and the Polish border on the island of Usedom. During that first decade of her life, Katrin lived first on the island of Rügen, just a few kilometres from where Friedrich's monk had stood on the cliff top, and then in the old Hanseatic city of Stralsund. She spent her summers at camp elsewhere on the Baltic coast. And despite the move back to the city of her birth as Germany was transformed, something about the Baltic remained, and remains, close to her heart.

Germans often speak of the idea of *Heimat*, loosely (but inadequately) translated into English as *Homeland*. Ultimately, it means the place where you feel at home, for many an almost spiritual sense of belonging – a linking of personality and place – that is rooted in culture, in language, in family and in traditions. It might find expression in a phrase of local dialect or the recipe for a particular dish. It might, today, be rooted in support for a football club or a crime literature series specific to a particular region or city. The primacy of *Heimat* in German identity has existed for far longer than there has been a German state, and there was something of a resurrection of the idea – expressed in books and films especially – in the years following the Second World War. If the notion of Germany and German-ness had been tarnished, perhaps for ever, by the crimes of the Nazis, and if it was hard to muster up any kind of feeling of belonging for the two new Germanys imposed from the outside, that were being built out of the ruins of war, there was something comforting in the local patriotism that *Heimat* had to offer.

It is unlikely, and some might say impossible, for an

individual to have two places with which you connect in such a way. And yet for Katrin, who sees herself as a Berliner through and through, there is a split when it comes to her *Heimat*. For all that she is at home in the city, she speaks of a sense of belonging and inner peace whenever she sets foot on a dune path or a sandy cliff top, beneath the big skies that dominate the flat landscape of the Baltic shore, to look out across those waters of her childhood.

For over a decade we had been travelling at least once a year to the coast, travelling north from Berlin to Kühlungsborn and the Fischland-Darß-Zingst peninsula; to the old stomping grounds of Stralsund; the islands of Rügen and Usedom. It was out of these trips that my own fascination with the coast slowly developed, and an idea formed to make a series of journeys to the places of Katrin's childhood and our shared imagination, to search – like beachcombers prodding pebbles with sticks, hoping to discover amber – for the stories of the shore. From this starting point I plotted a route, giving boundaries and limits to my journey. I would travel between the old inner-German border in the west to the Polish border in the east.

This would be the Baltic of my exploration and imagination, the place where Katrin grew up, in that country that no longer exists.

*

The night before I travelled north for the first time in search of the stories to be found among the sands, the wind shook the windows of our nineteenth-century apartment building as it circled the dark courtyard and whipped across the rooftops. My bag was almost packed but there was one more thing I was considering taking with me. A week earlier, we had been to Katrin's parents' apartment, where, as a football match played on the television in the living room, Katrin's mother pressed a collection of photographs into my hand.

Perhaps they are interesting for you, she said.

I smiled my thanks, and yet I did not look at them there and then. I don't know why. Perhaps there had been a goal in Mainz, in Freiburg or in Munich. Perhaps Lotte had asked me a question. Perhaps Katrin's brother had arrived with our nephew. It was only later, as I packed my bag, that I remembered the photographs and dug them out from a cotton shopping bag where they had been left in the hall. I spread them across our kitchen table. Mounted on rough, brown paper, they were of Katrin's family, including her grandmother as a young girl. Some sheets contained two images. Some three or four. On a few of the sheets the photographs were captioned with neat writing in white pencil, but for the most part the images were left to explain themselves. It was clear that Katrin's grandmother had put this collection together, that it was her handwriting on the paper, and that she had done it at some point in adulthood, looking back on her own six- or seven-year-old self a couple of decades after the fact. As I flicked through them, I also became conscious of the fact that no one in the photographs was alive any more.

The rough paper sheets were not bound, but one was clearly the front cover of the collection. It showed a handsome woman in a headscarf, dressed in a flowery blouse and calf-length white trousers, walking down a pier or boardwalk. She held hands with two girls, one of whom was also walking hand in hand with a boy. Both mother and son smiled for the camera while the two girls – including Katrin's grandmother – looked less than impressed. The wind was blowing in from the sea, out of sight behind the camera, pushing their dresses back against their legs and their hair across their faces. Behind the four walking figures the scene on the beach was blurred, the sands filled with shapes, of people and wicker beach chairs. The photograph was in black and white but it was clear that the sun was shining. Outside our apartment, the wind continued to rattle at the windows.

I held the photograph in my hands. It was a nice family portrait, with only one member missing, presumably behind the camera. A summer holiday by the sea, the image was captioned in that neat handwriting that would later, much later, address birthday cards to me. The caption placed the photograph in a specific place, at a specific moment in time:

ZINNOWITZ
1934
AUF DER SEEBRÜCKE

A place. A year. A location. Katrin's grandmother and her family were walking on the pier at Zinnowitz in the summer of 1934. I gathered the collection of photographs and placed them carefully back into the cotton shopping bag. It was the year that did it. It was more than simply family memory. I put the photographs in my bag, to take with me to the coast.

*

The next morning I arrived at the Zentral Omnibusbahnhof Berlin (ZOB) at around seven. The S-Bahn that took me there had been empty apart from a couple who were headed home as I was heading out, but when I arrived at the bus station it was alive with people. Sports teams heading off for the match. A hen night saving money on hotel rooms, preferring instead to sleep off the excesses on their journey back to the provinces. Students standing on the gum-splattered pavement, their oversized rucksacks at their feet. And then there were those for whom the ZOB was a destination in and of itself, patrolling the waiting room with its bolted-down plastic chairs, smoking cadged cigarettes on the concourse beneath the dirty glass roof, amongst the discarded fag ends and crushed paper cups scattered across the concrete.

I bought a coffee from a machine at the newspaper kiosk and watched as the hen party discussed missing members, their agitation levels rising as the departure time for the Dresden bus approached. A police sign warned of pickpockets, another appealed for witnesses to a crime committed a few nights before. I had never taken a bus from ZOB, and yet as I waited for the Lübeck bus I couldn't help but think that I had been here before. The smell of diesel fumes, cheap coffee and stale cigarette smoke took me back to Victoria coach station, a few months after September 11, and an overnight journey between Germany and Lancashire. The incessant security warnings. Pickpockets. Abandoned bags. Eternal vigilance. And then another scene, a couple of weeks earlier than that. The Tito-era station in Zagreb, waiting for a bus to Sarajevo. Concrete floors. Fag ends and coffee cups. Security warnings. One place stimulating memories of others. At Sarajevo bus station, when we finally arrived, I bought a chocolate croissant. Without the taste of machine-weak coffee and the hiss of a bus door opening at ZOB almost fifteen years later, I never would have remembered.

This was my first long-distance coach journey since that journey home at Christmas in 2001. All my other travels in Germany had been by train or by car, but recent deregulation of the buses had opened up numerous new routes that now flickered through on the ZOB's electronic boards, with over ten departures an hour. Darmstadt and Garmisch. Ilmenau and Ulm. Essen and Bottrop. Cheap tickets and free Wi-Fi were pulling cost-conscious travellers away from the train. As my departure time approached the bus arrived at the appointed stop and we climbed aboard. I had about fifteen fellow travellers with me, and as we settled ourselves for the journey I counted in my head all those coach journeys of my childhood and youth, from criss-crossing the former Yugoslavia to those school trips to the dull flatlands of northern France or the fairy-tale riverbanks of the Rhine valley. Belgian service stations and cross-channel ferries. Bus drivers trading their Nancy Sinatra for The Prodigy, under sufferance. Smuggled vodka and orange. Firecrackers and WWII watchtowers. More chocolate croissants.

The destination provoked its own memories. A journey to the coast was an escape from routine and normal life as much today as it ever was. I grew up about twenty-five kilometres from the sea, and not much further from one of England's great port cities, and yet the Irish Sea did not play a role in my everyday existence. On shopping trips to Southport it always seemed more a theory than anything else; an article of faith that it was somewhere over there, just out of sight beyond the expanse of sandy, muddy flats. In Liverpool we would go down to the Albert Dock, but the Mersey was very much a river, the sea again somewhere else, just out of sight. The coast was, instead, a place of holidays, of long summers on Anglesey or those school trips to France and their crumbling concrete watchtowers. It was package holidays to Tenerife or Corfu. First beers, first kisses and the endless possibilities of big skies and wide-open spaces. There was a potential at the seaside that seemed improbable among the cabbage and potato fields of our West Lancashire hometown. The canal bank was just not the same.

As the bus eased its way out of the ZOB and through the streets of Berlin towards the motorway, I scribbled some notes about nostalgia and the coast. It is not just me. You can find it in Pulp's dead seaside town, or Springsteen on the Jersey shore. It is old steamer timetables hanging in ice cream shops, postcards of sunsets, or the sexual frustration of caravan parks. When Katrin first took me north to the resorts of the Baltic, I was struck by how much they shared, in architecture and atmosphere, with their English counterparts.

And yet for all the nostalgia, for all that the seaside represents childhood and innocence, carefree days and endless sunshine, the discoveries of adolescence, the coast also has its dark flipside. On Anglesey we used to watch the yellow sea rescue helicopters carry out exercises on the jagged rocks battered by the swell. In the local churchyard stood a memorial stone to the members of a lifeboat team who died in their attempts to save those sinking in a storm offshore. In the north of France, beyond the watchtowers, were the war memorials and the stories of the D-Day landings.

And there is always the sea itself. Massive and powerful, with the potential to sweep you from the rocks, your body never to be found. It swallows ships whole, and doesn't return everything it takes. It is that contradiction, between the potential tragedy of the sea or the ocean and the carefree innocence of our nostalgic memories, that makes the coast such a fascinating place, and the Baltic is no different. It was another reason why I was on the bus, heading for Lübeck.

*

A couple of years ago, we were staying in a small wooden cabin on the edge of a town on the Baltic island of Usedom. Behind the cabin was a housing estate, a mix of local residences, holiday lets and second homes, but to the front was a dirt track, a beech forest and a path up to the top of the sandy cliffs and a lookout point. I was reading Jan Morris at the time and, one morning, as I ran up through the woods nursing a head rough with the whisky of the night before, a phrase that I had been reading the previous evening continued to echo. The Baltic is, she wrote, *the most ominous and eerie of Europe's waters*. A place of wars and frozen expanses, of the movement of armies and invisible submarines. A place fought over and died for. As I reached the lookout point on the cliffs, I gazed down on to a Baltic that was flat and calm, the sun low and weak in a clear sky. A couple of swans paddled between the breakwaters and cormorants dived for fish, sending ripples across the lake-like surface of the sea. In the distance I could see a tanker heading for Poland and a ferry on its way to Sweden. The

Baltic that morning was peaceful, serene, and yet I knew what Morris meant.

She wrote those words not because of anything intrinsic in the landscape, but because of what she knew of the history of those waters. It was her own knowledge, of the history of the lands and the sea they surround, that formed the Baltic of her imagination.

We don't stand alone on the mountain or the shore, Philip Hoare wrote, as he reflected on swimming at the lake in Wannsee in the south of Berlin. It is a place I know well, where villas are set among tall trees; a place of rowing clubs and beer gardens, of Sunday strolls and bike rides to islands populated by strutting peacocks and tales of Prussian royal adultery. It is also the place where, in one of those villas at the end of a leafy lane, leading members of the Nazi bureaucracy planned the Holocaust in technocratic detail before retiring for brandy and cigars in a room with bay windows looking out across the lake. Know this, and your swim in that lake takes on a whole new meaning. The ghosts of Wannsee stood with Hoare on the shore. The ghosts of the Baltic were waiting for me at the end of the autobahn.

*

Twenty kilometres from our destination and the bus driver pulled off the motorway to a service station. The smokers descended into the open air with relief. The rest of us wandered over to the restaurant and the attached shop and attempted not to spend too much money on dry rolls, boiled sausages and bars of chocolate. The driver's warning echoed across the expanse of tarmac growing damp in the drizzle that had started to fall as soon as we arrived.

No more than fifteen minutes.

Once again I was at that Belgian service station, my teacher's voice sounding more in hope than in expectation. I pulled out my phone and called Katrin. I wasn't used to travelling alone. Not any more. My reference points and flashbacks were all over a decade old, if not more. I was out of practice.

*

The bus arrived in Lübeck too early for me to check in to the guest house by the station that I had booked. As the drizzle turned to rain I hurried towards the Lübecker Altstadt, the old city centre, in an attempt to find a pub that might be showing the Liverpool match, or at least somewhere warm and dry to kill a couple of hours. I failed. Lübeck appeared to be shut down, deserted and abandoned as I moved through the streets. I retreated to the guest house, where the owner handed me the keys with no small talk or instruction, other than to watch my head on the beams in my attic room. That evening I ventured out to a Vietnamese restaurant by the station, where I ate alone in an empty room, with only the two waiters for company as the rain battered the windows. My plan for the next morning was to follow the river Trave to the coast and the old inner-German border at Priwall. The weather forecast on my phone told me to expect more of the same. I ordered another beer and drank a toast to the Baltic rain and whichever ghosts were waiting to join me on the shore.

Back at the guest house, I pulled the cotton shopping bag from my rucksack and laid out the photographs on the bed.

Two girls, playing in the sand. The sun casts strong shadows as the flags fly, stiff in the breeze, above the wicker beach chairs. The family are together, sitting on the lip of a giant hole that the children have spent the morning digging. No one looks at the camera when the shutter closes; they focus instead on their own conversations or the dolls the girls are playing with, the exertion of the morning's activities forgotten. The scene moves now, from the beach to an open-air swimming pool – the family

posing at the edge – and then a street scene, the girls dressed
neatly in jackets and pigtails, ready for church ...

As I passed my fingers over the photographs, moving
them towards me to get a better look, one in particular caught
my attention. It showed the children in the forest, with a
group of friends. The girls were wearing white dresses and
the boys lederhosen, held up by braces. The youngest boy
could not have been more than four or five, and he carried
in his hand a flagpole. With no breeze in the forest the flag, a
triangular pennant, hung limply against the pole. But there
was something I recognised. The hint of a circle. A pattern
in black.

I looked again at the image from the beach, the flags flying
proudly in the breeze. There it was. A dark background
and a white circle; at its heart, the swastika. Summer, 1934.
A year after Hitler came to power. Smiling faces on the
beach, the sun high in the sky. Holiday snaps of carefree
days and childhood games and the knowledge of what is to
come. Jan Morris looking out across the Baltic. Philip Hoare
swimming at Wannsee. The contradiction of the coast. The
contradiction of *this* coast.

Gathering together the photographs, I put them back in
the bag. The wind that had been knocking at the window
had subsided. I looked through the wet glass to the darkness

of the winter sky. I thought of the young girl who grew up to be the woman I knew at the end of her life. I remembered the first time I met her, walking through the streets of eastern Berlin, close to the zoo, in late afternoon. I thought of the meals at their apartment and the first time we took Lotte to meet them. I thought of the sunny day when we said goodbye. In those photographs were stories that were now lost to me, to all of us. As I prepared my things for the walk to the border the following morning, I thought of all the questions for that young girl in the photographs and the old woman who held my arm as we crossed the street, all the questions that I never thought to ask.

II

Dead German Writers
(Lübeck & Travemünde)

Thomas Mann returns home – Shopping trips across the Trave – Walking to the inner-German border – Off-season holiday camp – The sinking of the Cap Arcona – The Lübecker Altstadt and the Hanseatic League – The sinking of the Wilhelm Gustloff – A tale of two brothers – East Prussia and the 'Lost' Baltic – Alleyways and crow-stepped gables

In June 1953, the Nobel Prize-winning writer and son of Lübeck, Thomas Mann, returned to his hometown and, from there, made the short trip up the River Trave to Travemünde and the Baltic coast. It was an emotional return after years of exile, and he would write later in a letter to a local newspaper that, *the memory of having once more breathed the air of Travemünde, that children's paradise, 'sits smiling to my heart' as the line runs in Hamlet.*

He had been away for a long time, not only from the town of his birth, but from his country as well. Like his older brother, the fellow writer Heinrich Mann, Thomas had been in exile since 1933, leaving Germany a few months after Hitler's rise to power. The visit to Lübeck and Travemünde in 1953 was only his second to Germany since the end of WWII. By then, Heinrich had been dead for four years. He never made it back. Two years later and Thomas would be dead too, but at least he managed to return for one final visit to the place by the sea that was home to some of his happiest memories.

The brightest hours of my youth, he wrote, *were those holidays in Travemünde, and when the four weeks, which had seemed a little eternity when they began, were over and we returned to daily life, my breast was torn with tender, self-pitying pangs.*

Those summer days in the resort town were spent on the

beach or rowing across the river to Priwall, where he and his siblings would comb the sands for amber. Sometimes they would listen to the spa band playing their morning concert in the park, or wave at passing ships. But it was not just that Travemünde was an idyll, in and of itself. What made it so special for Thomas was the contrast of those summer weeks with the rest of his life upstream in Lübeck. For both brothers, Lübeck was a place of stifling conformity and dull conservatism, where the expectation was that they would follow on in the merchant business that had made the Manns one of the town's most respectable and pre-eminent bourgeois families. It was not to be. From an early age, both Heinrich and his younger brother Thomas were clear that this was a world that they wanted no part of, and were clear in their ambition to escape the confines, both mental and physical, of the old port by the river. In the meantime, the summer weeks in Travemünde would have to do.

*

I reached Travemünde by train, crossing the street from my guest house under grey skies to reach the platforms laid out beneath the high, vaulting station roof. In the summer the platforms would be thronged with people heading for the beach, but today it was just me, a couple of mountain-bikers and a group of elderly hikers leaning on their overlong walking poles. Travemünde was the end of the line and the train was fairly empty when it finally arrived. I climbed aboard and we moved off, making slow progress through the edgelands of the city as we headed towards the coast. Through the grimy window I could make out all the trappings of a true harbour town, from the cranes and the warehouses to the dry docks and the boatyards. For a time the railway hugged the riverbank, passing through a landscape of reeds and inlets, boathouses and rowing clubs. On the one side, grassy wetlands stretched away into the murky distance. From the opposite side of the carriage I could see car showrooms and big box supermarkets, parking spaces and industrial estates. One of the stations was named for a branch of IKEA, the yellows and blues of its looming, windowless walls bright against the dull sky.

The distance between the deadening experience of Thomas Mann's daily life as a young man in Lübeck and the exhilarating escape of the seaside is less than twenty kilometres downstream, and within half an hour I was stepping down from the train at the harbour station, once again greeted by a fine drizzle. It turned to rain as I walked down to the river, past small hotels and holiday rentals, cottages and a kindergarten. The ferry to Priwall was at the jetty as I crossed the car park and the waiting zone built for summer traffic, following a woman who wheeled her bicycle across the damp concrete in front of me. On board, she rearranged the shopping bags in her front basket and greeted the young man in the high-vis jacket who was there to check the tickets and make sure the cars – of which there were a couple already loaded on – were parked in the right spaces.

She looked around, smiling at one of the drivers through a fogged-up car window. She knew them all at this time of the year, the deckhands and the passengers, when there were not so many tourists making the crossing, taking the boat on that back-and-forth dance of the two ferries that passed each other every ten minutes at the centre of the river. Yes, she knew the passengers and the deckhands, but not the captains. They stayed locked away on the bridge, piloting their boats the short distance across the river to the other side. Back and forth. Back and forth. Was this what they dreamed of when they imagined being a ship's captain as young men? Was there a hierarchy at the captains' club – should such a thing exist – whereby the ferry boat captains of the Trave shared a table with the pleasure boat captains of the Berlin or Schwerin lakes, whilst those who took charge of the tankers and the cruise ships, of the ocean-going vessels, sat at the other end of the room, in smug contentment at their superiority?

The rain was falling heavier now. She adjusted her carrier bags once more, on her way back home from the daily shopping trip to Travemünde. She had been making this trip for years, since well before the changes, when Priwall was a peninsula cut off from its hinterland by the fortifications of the inner-German border. The road that now led from the ferry into the Mecklenburg-Vorpommern countryside was back then a dead-end street, closed off by concrete and wire and guarded by shadowy figures in the watchtowers, whose binoculars gave involuntary signals in the summer sun as they flashed unintelligible messages at the West German bathers down on the Priwall beach.

That was a time! How did people live like that? Surrounded, claustrophobic, making their home on a peninsula that was, to all intents and purposes, now an island; Priwall only accessible via those two ferries criss-crossing the Trave. They were the villagers' connection to shops and school, to work and with the rest of West Germany. She could remember those days well, and although the road into the old East was now open and the concrete and the wire long gone, she still took the ferry across the river to buy her groceries. Some things had changed. There were more cars of course, for now they had somewhere to go other than just the village at Priwall. A whole other country beyond the old border.

All your shopping done?

The deckhand did not check her ticket. She replied with a smile and a nod. To an outsider she looked like every tourist's middle-class fantasy of a rural village shopper and her basket of produce, purchased from local traders who knew her name, her habits and her tastes. But in reality the basket was filled with bags from Aldi or Lidl, like everyone else. Different supermarkets had their strengths. Lidl for cheese. Aldi for wine. She did still get her bread from the bakery, happier to shop there in the winter than the summer because of the lack of queues. Were there more tourists now, than there had been before? It was hard to say. At this time of year the resort was quiet, visited in the main by those no longer tied to summer holidays, and for whom the number of days they could afford was more important than the weather in which to enjoy them. They could be observed in the morning as they stared through the steamed-up windows of cafes and hotel breakfast rooms, morosely contemplating the choppy waters where the river met the bay as they mournfully stirred a cup of coffee. The sugar had long since dissolved, but still they kept stirring.

As the paper bag which contained her bread rolls changed colour, as it took on water, she turned to her fellow foot passenger and looked him up and down.

Where are you headed today?

On hearing the answer she made a half-hearted attempt to stifle a laugh.

The border! Well, there is not much to see. A lump of rock and a lot of sand.

She shook her head and pushed her bicycle slightly forward, closer to the overhang created by the bridge that offered the foot passengers a modicum of shelter. The rest of her thoughts remained unspoken but could be read in her eyes.

The border! Who comes to Priwall in the rain, in the winter, to look for something that is not even there any more?

*

It was a good question. The ferry arrived at its destination with a bump. She moved forward with her bike even as the ramp was still being lowered and she was the first ashore, weaving between the potholes and the puddles that had gathered on the uneven tarmac before the car drivers started their engines. I let them all off before following across the expanse of the quayside and on to the Mecklenburger Landstraße – the road to the old border – just beyond the ticket office. With my cycling companion out of sight, and the rear lights of the cars retreating along the lane, I was soon alone. In ten minutes there would be another small convoy, marking the arrival of the other ferry, and again ten minutes after that. In the meantime, I had Priwall to myself.

It appeared on first viewing to be a nice enough place. Detached, red-brick houses were set back from the road, giving the cumulative impression that this was a place of neat gardens and net curtains. The smell of woodsmoke drifted up and out from stoves, fed by the woodpiles covered with racing-green tarpaulins down the side of each house. To the left, low dunes separated properties from the beach and protected them from the winds whipping in off the sea. To the right, I could see down to the lagoon that made Priwall a peninsula, an inland sea fringed with reeds and sheltered from the elements.

As I reached the edge of the village I came upon a huge complex of brick buildings – ghostly and abandoned – locked away behind a low wall and a high fence. Climbing up on to the wall, I attempted to get a better look, holding on to the fencing. It had been a Luftwaffe barracks during the war and later, in those years when Priwall had been an island, a hospital. I debated hopping the fence to get a closer look but at that moment a couple of workmen emerged from one of the doors, crossing the overgrown wasteland that had once been the parade ground and later a place for patients to take the sea air, towards a gap in the wall on the other side. I saw now that the main gates were open and a portakabin had been installed on the edge of the site. Next to it stood a row of pink portaloos, resting at slight angles on the uneven ground, and a skip.

At the gate I saw that the old guardhouse by the main entrance was still in use. It housed a small nursery, with a playground fenced off from the rest of the complex to stop small children straying into the wasteland of rubble, weeds and broken glass that surrounded it. A workman passed, carrying a wooden window frame on his way to heave it into the skip. I asked him what they were building but he didn't know. He was only here to clear the place out. Find what is valuable, what can be recycled. Dump the rest.

Our job is just to make it safe.

He shrugged.

Through cracked windows I could see tags on the brickwork and other evidence of spray paint. Around the corner, close to the perimeter fence, there were the remnants of a bonfire. Stones had been arranged around the edge, with blackened beer bottles piled on ash at the scorched heart of the circle. The small children had their playground. The big kids also had theirs. I walked on.

Not long after leaving the old barracks behind, the pavement ran out. Now I walked the final kilometre to the border along a grassy and muddy verge, hoping that no camper van or car would pass through the deep puddles closest to me. It had stopped raining and the sky had lightened. Close to the border I reached a car park for the colony of holiday cabins squeezed in between the road and the dunes. Beyond the dunes the wind blew gentle waves on the lagoon. I was there. Where East Germany once met West. By the side of the road stood a granite boulder and an information board:

NEVER
AGAIN
DIVIDED
3 FEB 1990

Now the division was marked not by wire fences, watchtowers and armed guards, but by more subtle symbols. The road in the old East was in better condition, the potholed *Landstraße* I had been walking alongside giving way to smooth tarmac at the exact moment Schleswig-Holstein became Mecklenburg-Vorpommern. In the East a new, neat and separate bike path had been built, running alongside the road until the border, where it too gave way without any real warning to a patch of muddy grass. On infrastructure at least, the old East was in better condition than the old West.

From the memorial stone I followed a sandy path that led between the old border zone – now a strip of overgrown bushes and young trees, behind which lay a neatly-ploughed field – and the holiday cabins I had seen from the road. Most of them were shuttered for the winter, although there were a couple of telltale columns of smoke emerging from chimneys rising up above the rooftops. Past these the path wound its way between some dunes and then dropped down on to the beach. And there I had it: my first view of the Baltic, the Bay of Lübeck, looking moody beneath grey skies, unsettled only by a few small waves breaking with the slightest flash of white.

Down on the sands I looked for some sign of the old border but there was nothing to be found. Unlike on the road, there was no clue as to which part of the beach had once been the German Democratic Republic and which had been the Federal Republic of Germany. Here the reunification of the Priwall peninsula with its hinterland had been seamless, with all traces of division washed away from the sands. I gave up my search and walked instead down to the water's edge. Turning east to face a coastline of seemingly endless dunes, beaches and sandy cliffs, I was looking from the starting point of my journey towards my eventual destination. The Polish border lay some two hundred and twenty kilometres away as the gull flew, but the meandering nature of the coastline and its islands and peninsulas meant there were some two thousand kilometres of shoreline to explore. At that moment, on the beach, it seemed like more than enough to be getting on with.

*

The journey east began by walking west, back to the Priwall ferry for the short trip across the water to Travemünde. At first I walked the sands, aiming at the tower of the Maritim Hotel that stood on the opposite bank of the river, but after five minutes of slow progress I gave up and followed one of the boardwalked paths through the dunes to the sheltered track behind. Now I was walking through the colony of holiday cabins. They had been built close together, with tiny walkways running down either side between the walls and high fences erected to give some semblance of privacy in these cramped conditions. The track was rough and uneven, and though I walked alone I could see it on a warmer day, filled with strolling couples and bike-riding kids, legs spinning in too low a gear as they moved between their cabin, those of their friends, and the wide expanses of sand beyond the dunes. Outside a kiosk, locked and shuttered for the winter, I paused to pull a water bottle from my bag. I took a sip in the place where the cheap inflatables would be piled, next to the baskets of flyaway footballs and beach toys, a rack of old postcards never bought. I could smell the suntan lotion and the sweating tubs of penny sweets, and could hear the flip-flops slapping against the cool, tiled floor. It was the smell and the sound of a Welsh caravan park, transplanted to the Baltic.

All the businesses in the colony, like the kiosk, were closed for the off season. In the window of the pub a sign thanked us for a great summer and reminded us they would be open again for New Year's Eve. The fast food *Imbiss* was taking a break from offering deep-fried sustenance for hot days. The next-door restaurant, where the same sausages and battered fish were served, only substituting china plates for the paper trays, was deserted. A little further along the track I came to the pizzeria, where the plastic chairs and tables had been piled up in the corner of a terrace and had collected wind-blown leaves that also clogged up the decorative fountain. A plaster reproduction of Michelangelo's *David* had fallen in a storm and lost an arm. A few metres on, another kiosk. Grille down. Dust sheets on the counter. No ice cream or beers today. No emergency rations of tinned ravioli or condensed milk. No suntan lotion. No penny sweets.

There were some signs of life in the colony. At a garden near the end of the track a couple worked diligently, preparing the ground for the arrival of spring and another long summer.

We've been coming here for years.

A turned head, waiting for the nod of confirmation. It came.

Since Johannes was a boy. And now he brings his own kids. How about that? Our grandchildren enjoying this place, just like their father did … Why would you want to go anywhere else? We have everything we need …

I thought of the bicycling lady from the ferry. What did she make of the summer influx of visitors to the peninsula, swelling the population of Priwall by three, four, five times what it was now? Standing room only on the ferry. The smell of barbecues and the tinny beat of weakly amplified MP3s. Dogs had their own beach. Nudists too, where once they had bathed under the watchful eyes of East German border guards.

On a wooded headland I reached the spot where the bay met the mouth of the river, opposite the Maritim Hotel. As so often at the Baltic coast, I was conscious of the absence of salt in the air. According to the Internet you can drink these waters, the saline content of the Baltic Sea being so low that it will not dehydrate you. I decided not to test this theory. Instead I stood and looking out across the water. There was not much to see. Slight waves. A few gulls buffeted by the breeze. A solitary boat.

There was not much to see, but plenty that I knew was there.

*

On 3 May 1945, three days after Hitler blew out his brains in a Berlin bunker, and only twenty-four hours before the German generals signed the unconditional surrender to end the Thousand Year Reich after only twelve, the SS began to load ships in Neustadt Harbour, north of Lübeck. Four ships, including the *Cap Arcona*, were filled with around 40,000 prisoners from the Neuengamme concentration camp. The plan was to commit one last crime before the curtain fell: to take these ships out to sea – filled as they were with prisoners from over thirty different countries – and scuttle them. An evidence-destroying act of mass murder, to take place in the shallow waters of the Bay of Lübeck.

To RAF pilots, however, these boats looked just like the

troop transports they had been targeting for months in the waters north of Germany. And although it is strongly suspected that their commanders knew these boats were filled not with enemy soldiers but with prisoners, the instructions to the pilots were that these were transports of SS officers fleeing to Norway. And so the fleet was attacked from the air.

We used our cannon fire at the chaps in the water, RAF Pilot Allan Wyse of the No. 193 Squadron would later write. *We shot them up with 20mm cannons in the water. Horrible thing, but we were told to do it and we did it. That's war.*

Most of the SS officers who had been accompanying the prisoners managed to escape the sinking ships and were rescued by German trawlers. The prisoners themselves were left to their fate. Those who managed to get off the burning ships were shot in the water or, if they made it to land, were executed on the sands by the SS. The RAF bombing raid and what followed resulted in the death of over 4,000 concentration camp survivors, and for over three decades their remains would continue to wash ashore, to rest on beaches all along the Bay of Lübeck and further down the coast.

Standing on the promontory and looked out across the Bay of Lübeck, I tried to put together the idyll of Thomas

Mann's childhood with the desperate horror of the sinking of the *Cap Arcona*. Did knowing this story change how I saw the Baltic that morning on a Priwall headland? Of course it did. Landscape is neutral. As is the sea. It is what we know that shapes our impressions, shapes our feelings about place. The stories of the beach, of the sand and the dunes, of the towns and the cities. Thomas Mann rowed across this river to search for amber on the beach I had just walked along. When he returned in 1953, over sixty years had passed. Two world wars and the horrors of the Holocaust. As he breathed the sea air once again, lost in his own childhood memories, bodies were still being washed ashore from the *Cap Arcona*. No wonder he retreated to a more innocent time. I kicked at the sand as a church bell sounded. Half an hour until my train back to Lübeck. For the time being I left the stories on the shore, turned my back on the Baltic, and made my way to the ferry and across the river to catch the train.

*

Back in Lübeck I walked from the station to the old town, an appealing jumble of buildings surrounded by water in the middle of the River Trave. Despite being some twenty-odd kilometres upstream from the sea, Lübeck found its fortune as the leading trading port in the Hanseatic League, a collection of free cities and towns that dominated the Baltic from the fourteenth to the seventeenth centuries. It was one of the strongest trading blocks in the world, and serious competition for the Kingdoms and other European actors of that time. Ultimately it was the rise of nation states that put an end to this dominance, as the upstart collection of guilds and merchants and the red-brick Gothic cities they built were subsumed by great powers and their empires. Today, the former members of the League are still linked, through that distinctive architecture of brick warehouses, church spires and crow-stepped gables, and across the Baltic region it is possible to see traces of the Hanseatic era in Riga and Gdansk, Kaliningrad and Hamburg, Tallinn and, of course, Lübeck.

It lingers on in other ways. In Germany, former Hanseatic cities often have a H in front of their initial on car number plates: HST for Stralsund; HGW for Greifswald; HL for Lübeck. It provides the name for Rostock's football team, and two former members – Bremen and Hamburg – remain 'independent' city-states within the German federal system. By the 1800s, though, the golden era of the Hanseatic League was over, and although Lübeck continued to make money from trade and commerce after the decline of the League, it became increasingly clear that the town was never going to survive the transformation of shipping that came with steam, industrialisation and the arrival of the railways. Nevertheless, it remained a free city through the rise of Prussia and the creation of a unified Germany in 1871, finally losing its status in 1937 when the Nazis stripped it of its independence, as punishment for not allowing Hitler to deliver a speech in the city during the election campaign of 1932. Chastened, Lübeck was merged into the state of Schleswig-Holstein, where it remains to this day.

My walk through the city was an unstructured one, crisscrossing the island Altstadt at lunchtime on a working day. The main thoroughfares, often pedestrianised, were thronged with people, and so to avoid them I ducked down side streets, following lanes of red-brick, half-timbered houses, attempting to imagine the city in its Hanseatic heyday. The Second World War had not been kind to Lübeck, and much of the old town had fallen victim to Allied bombing raids. But the heritage industry got to work in the decades that followed, in the knowledge that the good old days were never coming back. Lübeck needed the tourist dollar and Deutschmark, and later the euro, and it was only going to flow through these cobblestone streets if it resurrected and maintained something of a late-Medieval charm. Buildings were restored. Gaps were filled in. Bilingual plaques were hammered into any building of interest (and some without), so the visitor could linger outside the old Seamen's Mission – that refuge for sailors who had come ashore but wished to eschew the delights of the brothel or the bar – or the Customs House, the church, or the honorary consulate of the city of Danzig.

The consulate building remains as a museum devoted to a city now called Gdansk. At the end of the Second World War the powers and empires had shifted once more, and Danzig was now part of Poland. With a long-established German-speaking community, Danzig was the home city of the writer Günter Grass, adopted son of Lübeck, having moved to the town in 1995. Perhaps he had been searching for something of Danzig's Hanseatic flair when he chose Lübeck, but regardless of his motivations, he was living just outside the town when he won 'the big one' in 1999. It was not long after the Nobel Prize for Literature was awarded that Günter Grass was claimed as one of Lübeck's own, and a museum was opened in his name.

*

On that day, as my aimless walk through the streets led me to the exhibition at the museum that bears his name, Günter

Grass was alive. Now, as I write these words, he is dead. When I came upon the museum and decided to wander the rooms of the house, exploring the exhibition devoted to his life and work, I pictured him as I had seen him in photographs: a high-backed chair and a pipe, next to a desk and bookshelves. Or standing at a doorway, looking out on to his garden. I remembered a football match on television a few years earlier, as St Pauli of Hamburg took on Bayern Munich, and Grass was there, in the raucous atmosphere of the Millerntor Stadium, picked out from among the punks and the anarchists on the terraces, pipe clamped between his teeth. As I made my way through his museum, scribbling words in my notebook, and reading again some of his work, he was still out there, in his armchair or his garden. A few months later, in a Lübeck hospital, he died at the age of eighty-seven.

We need to ask ourselves: how did it happen?

I wrote the words down from a question posed in large letters on a wall of the exhibition. It was *the* question. The key question. The one which Grass spent a career and the best part of his life asking, forcing himself and others to answer. Whether he was working at any given moment as a writer, a sculptor, an illustrator or a campaigner, it appeared to be Grass's role to act as the conscience of a nation emerging from the darkness of those twelve years of National Socialism. He refused to allow his society to let the memories of the crimes committed in their name gently slip away. He was relentless in his commitment to not forgetting, and to never stop asking the question. He spoke uncomfortable truths and was unflinching in his condemnation of those who, he felt, had not atoned for their own action or inaction in the past. All of this would, in turn, make the revelation that Grass himself made at the start of what would be his final decade all the more explosive. In the first volume of his autobiography, he let out the truth that he had long kept secret: that in the dying moments of the war he had been a member of the Waffen-SS.

Grass was a hypocrite! No matter that he was seventeen. No matter that he was drafted. No matter that those judging him did not seem to have the capacity to put themselves in that young man's shoes. Grass had kept it a secret all those long years. That was the crime. That and the fact that he himself would excoriate others on the grounds of their own wartime history or Nazi-tainted past.

We need to ask ourselves: how did it happen?

The Nobel Prize-winning former member of the Waffen-SS: these were and are the two facts that seem destined to be his shorthand biography for evermore. In the museum, in *his* museum, with Günter Grass still alive and living some fifteen kilometres away, they did not shy away from asking this question not only of the German people, as Grass had often done, but of their subject himself. After all those years of keeping the secret there was no longer any hiding place, not even in the house that bears his name.

From the main room I climbed the stairs to reach a temporary exhibition inspired by Grass's 2002 novella *Im Krebsgang (Crabwalk)*. The novella tells, in part, the story of the sinking of the *Wilhelm Gustloff* in Baltic waters during the final months of the Second World War. The exhibition of documents, photographs, images and recordings took me right back to Priwall, looking out over the Bay of Lübeck to the place where the *Cap Arcona* went down. The *Wilhelm Gustloff* was another German ship, named for a Nazi martyr, and was sunk by a Soviet submarine as it attempted to evacuate East Prussian refugees from their homeland during the Red Army advance. In happier days, the *Wilhelm Gustloff* had been a *Kraft durch Freude* (Strength through Joy) cruise ship, engaged by the Nazis' leisure organisation to take good, National Socialist workers on holiday throughout the second half of the 1930s. By the winter of 1944/5 the ship had been repainted and refitted and was in service as a floating barracks, before being transformed once again into an evacuation ship. As the Soviet troops began to win territory in East Prussia – lands which are now part of the Russian Federation and Poland – the German population began to flee. On 30 January 1945, twelve years to the day after Hitler had been appointed Chancellor in Berlin, thousands were crammed aboard the ship before it began its final journey, making slow progress through the dangerous waters. It was aiming for Kiel, a port on the Baltic coast north of Lübeck. It never made it. A Soviet torpedo was launched and was unerring in its accuracy. The *Wilhelm Gustloff* went down and some 9,500 civilians perished, lost to the icy Baltic. It remains the largest death toll from the sinking of a single ship in maritime history.

And it was a sinking that was, for a long time, barely discussed. Nearly ten thousand civilians were dead; but they were Germans, killed in the midst of a brutal war of their own making. In any case, these thousands paled into insignificance when lined up against the millions elsewhere, and so, as with the bombing of Dresden and Hamburg, this loss of civilian life was basically ignored both within and without Germany. The consequence of this wilful attempt at forgetting, at ignoring history while the traumatised survivors were still part of the society, was to surrender the tale and any lessons to be learned to the Far Right, to nationalist and neo-Nazi movements who would make firebombing of German cities and the sinking of the *Wilhelm Gustloff* central to their mythology, to their songs and parades, and their grievances shared with fellow travellers in the darker recesses of the Internet.

This surrender of the disaster to the Right is itself part of the story of *Crabwalk*, of how young nationalists in the 1990s shared information online about Germany's history, and used the belief in and anger towards crimes committed against ordinary Germans to fuel a sense of victimhood out of the events of the Second World War. Alongside this, the novella tells the story of the man Wilhelm Gustloff and the murder that made him a Nazi martyr, the history of the ship that would be given his name, and the Soviet submarine captain who would launch the torpedo from the cold depths of the Baltic. It is a slim and yet powerful book, reflecting on the impact of history and of memory and forgetting. I bought a copy in Lübeck and read it over two consecutive evenings, the wind rattling against the window of my attic room, and the imagery of the novella would haunt my explorations of the Baltic coast from thereon in. Back at the museum, as I moved through the exhibition on the top floor, I did not yet know the story, but was most struck by a series of underwater photographs taken by the Swedish artist Jonas Dahm.

Since the 1990s, Dahm had photographed hundreds of shipwrecks on the Baltic sea floor, including the *Wilhelm Gustloff*, whose ghostly hull peered out through the gloom of green-tinged waters in a photograph at the heart of the exhibition. As I looked at the pictures Dahm had brought back with him from the depths, I contemplated a question that I would later ask of *Crabwalk* itself: what were they trying to say?

What is it about these crimes (against Germans) that followed other crimes (by Germans)? By Germans or by *the* Germans? Questions begged more questions. What about the fight against forgetting, about the power of memory, regardless of the victims? And then ... what about the life of the photographer, constantly submerged in deep water, picking over and perhaps even disturbing these mass graves?

A few hours earlier I had stood on the promontory at Priwall and looked out across the Bay of Lübeck. I had looked north to where the *Cap Arcona* had gone down after an attack from the sky. I had looked east to where – many, many kilometres away – the *Wilhelm Gustloff* had been sunk from below. And now I imagined the Atlantic sucking the waters back through that narrow channel between Denmark and Sweden, the Baltic plug pulled, and the transformation of a featureless sea into a cracked and fractured landscape of sandbanks and crevices, of breathless fish and the thousands of skeletons, of ships and of people, resting on the damp sands. Skeletons that we know are there as we look towards the horizon, should we choose to think of them, even if it is only the divers among us who will ever see them.

*

I left the Günter Grass-Haus in the twilight of a winter afternoon and hurried through the streets to another literary landmark of the city, beneath disturbed flocks of crows and gulls that flew above me, silhouetted against the darkening sky. The Buddenbrook-Haus is another literary museum, devoted to the life and work of Thomas and Heinrich Mann, housed in the very building that was the model for the family home in the novel that would win Thomas the Nobel Prize. *Buddenbrooks* is an epic tale documenting the decline of a family over generations, with stories and characters pulled from the experiences of the Mann family and the people Thomas knew and observed in his home town. Although Lübeck was not explicitly named in the novel, it was clear to all who read it – and especially those from the town itself – where the inspiration came from. Not long after its publication in 1901, a handwritten key to the characters began to circulate in Lübeck society:

Family Buddenbrook = Family Mann
Thomas Buddenbrook = Senator Heinrich Mann
Tony = Elizabeth Mann ...

The town was scandalised. Here was a son of the city shitting in his own nest. The reputation of the Mann brothers – already so different to their fine, upstanding father – would get even worse four years later when Heinrich had his turn. His novel *Professor Unrat*, later filmed as *The Blue Angel* starring Marlene Dietrich, skewered Wilhelmine society, and in particular the education system, in a way that was, if anything, more brutal that Thomas's gentle satire in *Buddenbrooks*. The two brothers would become two of the most respected figures of early twentieth-century German literature, and Thomas regarded as arguably the foremost writer of the century as a whole, but Lübeck never really forgave them.

This traditional old town, Thomas would write, *is completely indifferent to the development, distinctions and success of its hardworking sons ... it appears almost as though Lübeck follows the careers of such sons not only without pride, satisfaction or pleasure, but even with a certain shamed annoyance ...*

Despite the fact that both Mann brothers had managed to incur the wrath of the city they left behind on the death of their father, their relationship was – in the early years – a strained one. Heinrich was older, a political man, acutely sensitive and aware of events and how they shaped and moved society in general. Thomas was younger, a self-confessed 'non-political man' for much of his life. He was also more successful than his older brother. It was politics, and their differences in that regard, that drove a wedge between them during the First World War, as Thomas fell enthusiastically behind the military effort and the patriotic struggle whilst Heinrich – almost alone among German intellectuals and literary figures, at least at the beginning – was both pessimistic and vocally anti-war.

My brother, Heinrich wrote scathingly in August 1914, *enjoys it, as he does everything, aesthetically.*

To Heinrich, 'non-political' was simply not an option, and at the same time, while he remained gloomy at the prospects for peace, Thomas appeared to revel in the potentially cleansing power of war. Thomas seemed smitten, by the idea of a service to a higher cause and the romanticism of strength in unity, all made easier by the fact that he himself would never have to set foot in a trench. He outlined his thinking in *Thoughts on Wartime*, an essay published in 1914. Heinrich took his time to respond, but respond he did a year later with an essay of his own. It was, on the surface, concerned with Emile Zola and the Dreyfuss affair, but really it was about Germany. Thomas was smart enough to understand what Heinrich was trying to say and read it not only as a criticism of his position on the war, but as a personal attack. It would cause a break in their relationship, and one that might have been predicted not only by those who knew the two men, but by the two brothers themselves:

The war simply brought our differences to a head.

After the First World War the Manns would be reconciled, as Thomas began the long process of recognition that, in such times – indeed, perhaps in any times – to be a 'non-political man' was not only an untenable position but even morally reprehensible. Still, as they moved closer politically, and would both – by the end of their lives – regard themselves as fundamentally socialist or social democratic in outlook, in exile after the rise of the Nazis it was once again Heinrich who would take the initial public stand while Thomas remained silent. Although a committed anti-Nazi, this silence was in large part dictated by a desire to see his books continue to be published in Germany, even as he dared not set foot in his native land. Once again he would come to realise his position was impossible and he would begin to write and speak against the Nazis, in both Europe and America, until the end of the Second World War.

It might have been thought that Lübeck – itself stripped of autonomy by the Nazis for daring to refuse to grant Hitler a platform to speak, and then destroyed by the bombs of a war he and his cronies brought upon Germany – could have finally begun to forgive its most famous son. But after the war, in part due to the fact that Thomas willingly gave speeches and allowed his books to be published in what was first the Soviet zone of occupation and later the German Democratic Republic, he remained a controversial figure in his home town. In 1955, two years after his return from exile and that visit to Travemünde, Thomas was granted the freedom of the city on the occasion of his eightieth birthday. Recognition at last! But it turned out that this acknowledgement by the city authorities, this celebration of the Nobel Prize-winning son of Lübeck, was only possible because half of the council chamber had walked out in protest before the vote. In a city like Lübeck, it seems, memories are long.

In the Buddenbrook-Haus I explored the lives of these writers and the wider family, contrasting the approach of the exhibition with the museum I had left earlier. I scribbled a note in my notebook:

Interesting. Grass – alive and scandals are up front. Mann – long dead and little mention.

Of Thomas Mann's patriotic and enthusiastic propaganda during the First World War there was barely a word. Of his silence during the early years of National Socialism, a similar hush. It felt, as I walked the rooms, as if the edges had been smoothed from the characters of both Mann brothers, whereas at the Grass exhibition it had been upfront and challenging in dealing with its subject. Later, when I learned of Grass's death, I wondered how – over time – the exhibition in his name might change once more. Memory and forgetting: a subject for the lives of writers, as well as their work.

*

I went to the pub. In a town that had once had hundreds of breweries, this was the last one standing, a gloomy cavern of dark wood and copper, old tin beer advertisements and a basement of exposed brick archways and long benches. I sat upstairs, where I could get a little light, and began to read *Crabwalk*.

East Prussia.

There it was, the unmentionable German Baltic. The 'lost

lands' to the east from which the refugees were fleeing when the *Wilhelm Gustloff* was sunk. In 1930, with the medal from Stockholm and the prize money in his bank account, Thomas Mann headed east to the town of Nidden, a German-speaking community just beyond the East Prussian border in Lithuania. He was looking for a place to write and the Baltic coast once again became a place of refuge from everyday life. Now, in adulthood, it was a bolthole; a means of escaping the fame and attention surrounding him:

We were thrilled by the indescribable and unique beauty of nature in this place, he wrote, *the fantastic world of sandy dunes mile on mile, the birch and pine groves full of elk between the Haff and the Baltic, the wild splendour of the beach.*

As with his childhood paradise of Travemünde, Mann's time in Nidden was limited. Three years after buying the property the entire family were in exile. Nidden would soon fall to the Germans and the house in the dunes was requisitioned for personal use by Hermann Göring, the morphine addict who became Hitler's right-hand man. When he wasn't commanding the Luftwaffe, Göring spent his time establishing hunting estates and lodges across the German-controlled lands, reserving acre upon acre of woodland for his own personal use. But his enjoyment of Nidden and the Baltic coast would also prove to be short-lived. Arrested for war crimes following the German defeat, the master of the hunt found himself in captivity, where he crunched down on a cyanide capsule in his cell the night before he was to be hanged at Nuremberg.

In the pub I pulled out my phone, selected the Maps function, and scrolled my fingers along the coast from where I was sitting to what was once East Prussia. Nidden, renamed Nida after becoming part of Lithuania before Mann bought his house there, was supposed to be a place of refuge for the writer and his family. But his son Klaus – who was, like his uncle, far more politically aware than his father – had known even in 1931 that there was no avoiding the reality of what was happening to their country, even if you bought a house across the border:

> In good weather we could hear the raw shouts of the commando and lustful singing of young voices drift over to us from the Fatherland. That was Nidden – primitive and picturesque – but not without a certain gloomy and melancholy appeal.

With the phone illuminated on the table I began to sketch out a rough map of the Baltic coast between Lübeck and the Polish border. From east to west, marking the places I had been and would return to, and those I was yet to visit. Places I knew from Katrin's family and places I had read about in books. But I knew that the stories on this shore would not be confined to these lines in the sand, that stories from further east would be lingering like the mist above the Baltic dunes. From Travemünde to a wooden house in Nidden. From the *Cap Arcona* to the *Wilhelm Gustloff*. From Schleswig-Holstein to East Prussia. I put down my pen and folded away my scribbled map, put the phone in my pocket and *Crabwalk* in my bag. The day was done. I ordered another beer.

*

A few hours later I stepped out into the darkness, walking from the pub towards the harbour, footsteps echoing in the narrow streets as the sound shared the otherwise quiet night air with the rattle of a trolley-bag being pulled along the pavement by a young woman ahead of me. I passed the old warehouses where the Mann family once stored their goods and which were now occupied by run-down cafes and the black-painted doors of nightclubs. I passed by those alleyways that are part of Lübeck's Hanseatic charm, depicted in all the guidebooks to the city and once home to the working people that gave them their name.

Most were gated and locked shut for the night.

Bäcker-Gang.

Branntweinbrenner-Gang.

Spinnradmacher-Gang.

Schlachter-Gang.

Garbereiter-Gang ...

The bakers and the distillers, the spinning-wheel-makers and the slaughtermen. One alleyway was still open, a tunnel through the street-side buildings to a narrow courtyard of cottages, of chairs and tables, flowerpots and barbecues. A few lights shone behind curtained windows. It felt like trespass and so I backed away, down through the tunnel and on to the street, back into town past the churches and the old Seamen's Mission once more. The mission was still in operation, run by the Lutheran Evangelical Church, 'supporting seafarer's dignity' as it has done for over a hundred years. Nowadays most who passed through its doors were from East Asia, using the mission's facilities to call home, to access the Internet and to get support during their time in the city, such as help with shopping trips. During my walks through Lübeck it sometimes felt like this was a museum city, restored after the war to reflect a long-lost past, fixed as a memory like a Florence or a Venice. But some of the links, to the sea and to the old ways, were clinging on.

The crow-stepped gables of Lübeck's Gothic architecture were overbearing in the half-light of a city at night. I stumbled down a cobbled street, past more alleyways, until I reached the other side of the old town and the remnants of the city wall into which crooked houses had been built. There were no other souls on the street now, no one walking in the sodium glow of the lamps shining down from above. On the other side of the canal a car edged slowly down a deserted street, but otherwise the scene was still.

A door opened in front of me. I had to stop, to allow a young woman wheeling a bicycle to emerge into the night. She flicked on her lights front and back and rode off, down towards the bridge that led to newer neighbourhoods on the opposite side of the canal. Beneath the street lamp I could read the stickers on the ground floor window of her house. Opposition to neo-Nazis. Against Transatlantic free trade agreements. Refugees Welcome. Another set proclaimed support for VFB Lübeck. I looked with interest at the doorbell. All day, in my explorations of the city, I had been searching for a name. A name to give to a particular story from the Baltic shore. The doorbell was illuminated by a weak bulb, the letters handwritten on to a thin strip of paper: *BARTHELS.*

As she turned the corner at the bottom of the street, to

cross the bridge out of sight behind a collection of tall, dark buildings that occupied the space where the city walls once stood, I walked away, heading for my attic room in the guest house by the station.

III

Barthels
or
The Decline of a Family
Part One

They are coming tomorrow.

Heinrich stands at the window of his living room, in the attic of the hotel that bears his family's name.

Tomorrow.

He presses his forehead to the glass, blocking the reflection of the lamps in the room behind him. Now he can see, out and down. Over the sea. A gentle winter's swell, the waves not so much breaking as nudging up against the wooden legs of the pier. Down to the dunes, where the grass is dusted with frost as it clings to the ground beneath the sands with gnarled and tight-gripping roots. Eighty-two years.

Tomorrow they are coming to take him away. But it does not matter. They can remove him from this scene, but they cannot take it away from him. He will always have it. He will always have this view.

*

The tip-off came a few days ago. The man, a customer who had built up such a bar tab in those years of hyperinflation in the twenties that he was always good for a spot of information, had worked in the town hall for years. Now he worked for the Communists, yes. And no doubt had a party card proudly tucked into his fake leather wallet. Before, he worked for the Nazis. And before that the Republic, such as it was. And before that the Kaiser, and on and on. At some point Heinrich had let part of the bar tab slide. It was the best investment of his life, as the information received from the eternally grateful bureaucrat meant he had been able to keep his nose clean with the authorities regardless of which banner they marched under. Red or brown. War or peace. Heinrich had managed to hold it all together. This hotel that is fifteen years older than he is.

Three more years and it would make the hundred, but the information has trickled in as it always has done, and Heinrich has no reason to doubt the truth of what he heard. The hotel will not make it to a hundred. Not with a Barthels in charge. This is the last night. So be it.

He can imagine the scene. A knock at the door. A suit, from Rostock or maybe even Berlin. Heavy-rimmed glasses and the appropriate piece of paper. There are some suits asleep in the hotel beneath him. Perhaps it is one of them who will come with the confiscation order, who will usher Heinrich out of the front door and down the path to a waiting car. Heinrich knows already that he will resist the hand on the shoulder. The bureaucrat will not be able to tell him where they are going, or what will happen next.

He steps back from the window. All these rooms in this apartment under the eaves. Built for a family long-since disintegrated. Too many rooms for one man alone. All those years since his son left. His daughter. His wife died. His son is also dead, lost to the war. His daughter is over there, lost to the West. Married to a small businessman. No wonder the suits are coming tomorrow morning. He is surprised it took them so long.

Crossing the carpeted living room, slow but steady on his feet, Heinrich dims the lamps and moves through to the hall. There he puts on his shoes and checks his appearance in the mirror. The final *Rundgang*. The last inspection. At this time of night he rarely meets someone in the halls. It is not that sort of hotel. But you never know. Once satisfied, he turns away from the mirror and opens the apartment door.

Quietly he descends the stairs, those hidden, spiral stairs his grandfather had tucked away in a corner of the second floor. The guests don't tend to stray to this end of the corridor – sometimes children, exploring every nook and cranny – and his grandfather had planned it well. For ninety-seven years the layout of the building ensured a level of privacy for the family, even as they lived right on top of the business. When his grandfather moved to the town from Lübeck, over a century ago, he had been a doctor. His practice in those early years was mainly treating the fisherman, the farmers and their wives. The main business of the town back then had been herring, pulled from the sea and packed in salt. A small community, and Heinrich's grandfather was the only doctor. And then came the railway, in all its fast, frightening, noisy glory. Heinrich's grandfather had spotted the opportunity. The health benefits of the seaside were already known for the upper classes. But the railway would make them available to those further down the food chain – if not all the way – and so the doctor acted. Property and a bank loan. Advertisements in the newspapers of Berlin and Hamburg. The new hotel began by offering health retreats, with consultations held in a small practice on the ground floor. Over the years the patients became guests and the demand for medical advice declined. They were looking for something else, and so the consulting rooms were turned into a library and a bar. Sometimes Heinrich still works of an evening, pouring beer and schnapps for visitors and locals alike. It is, he likes to say, his own version of his grandfather's consultations. The prescription from Heinrich is always the same. Half a litre of pils. A shot of *korn*.

The halls of the hotel are quiet. No conversations from the occupied rooms, just the occasional snort or the rhythmic undulations of a heavy breather. The night porter is also asleep on the fold-out bed in the office behind reception. Heinrich doesn't wake him. Instead he takes the master key from his own pocket and opens the bar. Through the glass double-doors he can see the breakfast room prepared for the morning. In the fireplace the last embers are glowing softly behind the metal guard. Heinrich pulls it aside and drops a log on to the fire. He listens for the familiar snap and crackle of the heat meeting the dried wood. He watches as the tiny sparks jump and then float. He pulls the guard back into place as the fire catches, the first flames licking the side of the log. Above him the guests sleep. Across the hall the night porter does likewise, as do the live-in staff, downstairs in their cellar quarters. Only Heinrich is awake, and tomorrow they are coming.

At the bar he pours himself a glass of schnapps and takes it over to the armchair by the fire. Two portraits look down on him. Two doctors. His grandfather and his father. When the bureaucrat from the local offices had warned him a few days ago, he had suggested using the time to move anything of sentimental value someplace safe. When they come, they will take it all; down to the last ashtray or poker for the fire. But where should he hide two portraits as big as these? In the woods? Beneath the gloomy pines that surround the town? In a hole dug from an ever-shifting sand dune? No. He had given a small bag to Maria, the housekeeper, and told her to look after it. As he knew she would. He knew that she would tell anyone who asked that it belonged to her. And he knew that she would not look inside. That was Maria. He hoped that she would keep her job. Likewise the night porter. The gardener. The receptionists and the cook. That was what the bureaucrat presumed to be true and Heinrich was inclined to believe him.

No, they could have the portraits and do with them what they pleased. He doubted they would stay in their positions, but then he also doubted that his father – supporter of Bismarck, loyal to the Kaiser – would have been happy to look down upon a hotel run by socialists. His grandfather on the other hand, that son of Lübeck, might have found it grimly amusing. Not his father. In the aftermath of the first war, with Germany defeated and the Kaiser spirited away to lonely exile in Holland, Heinrich's mother had said that the only mercy was that his father had not been alive to see it. She said the same on the day Heinrich hoisted the Nazi flag in the garden, again on the advice of the bureaucrat. He can remember the scarlet against the blue sky, the arms of the swastika dancing in the breeze. His mother had been almost ninety at that point, and he was glad when she passed away soon after, before they learned what they learned. She had found the flag distasteful at the time. If she had known what he knew now, she would have been ashamed.

*

It was his mother who held the business together. His father, who had left the town as soon as possible to go to Berlin to study medicine and become a member of the university duelling society, had never shown any interest in the hotel. His passion had been for politics, for the manoeuvres that would lead Prussia to war with France and eventually unify Germany. He worked for it in Berlin, a loyal acolyte, but by the time France was defeated and the Reich established, he was already back at the seaside town, his father's illness necessitating his return. Grandfather hung on for another ten years, but was unable to work. Father in turn was unable to escape. Within a couple of months, resigned to his fate, he married a local girl. Her father's farm supplied the hotel with milk and eggs. A good match, his grandfather said, thinking of potential future discounts, but Heinrich was sure that the rest of the town noticed and registered his arrival; a baby born only six or seven months after the quick engagement and wedding ceremony.

For those first eight years of Heinrich's life his grandfather and father circled each other in those rooms beneath the eaves, those rooms that seem so plentiful now but at the time seemed so cramped and restrictive. It was a relief, Heinrich can remember, when his grandfather finally succumbed to his illness. But it did not lead to an improvement in his father's mood. If anything it made it worse, as he stepped out of the shadow and into the role of the patriarch, stalking the attic rooms or walking the promenade, rarely engaging with the guests or the day-to-day running of the hotel which he had inherited. And so it was Heinrich's mother, the former farm girl, who raised the family's only child, ran the hotel, and tolerated a husband whose bitterness increased with the number of years in his body.

Was it an unhappy childhood? He doesn't think so. His father was, it is true, in a permanently bad mood, but he was rarely mean and never cruel. The hotel did well and Heinrich spent most of his childhood in material comfort. When not in school he would play with friends on the beach or in the woods, where they created their own adventures and worlds that the promenading holidaymakers that they spied on from the bushes could never have access to and would never understand. Unlike his father, Heinrich had no dreams of escape. No desire to leave the town. But his mother had other ideas, so she sent him away. To Switzerland

and Baden-Baden. London and Karlsbad. He was to learn hostelry from the bottom up, to pick up languages and make new experiences. It was an exciting time. The turn of the century. In London he met Clara, the daughter of a German diplomat. She married, as they say, beneath herself, but had no problem swapping her old life for the seaside town Heinrich had grown up in. Ten years after he had left they returned. A year later, his father died.

The doctor died of a heart attack, and it was Clara who found him, sitting in his chair in the attic living room, his newspaper scattered across his knees and the floor. With his death Heinrich's mother retired from the hotel, handing control to her son and his wife. Despite the grief, Heinrich remembers these years as the best of times. Clara gave birth to a son, then a daughter. Even the first war didn't seem to really register. Indeed, in many ways it was a surprise to discover Germany had lost. It did not feel like a defeated nation. Not in the beginning. And his son had been too young to fight, and Heinrich too old. They felt lucky.

*

He finishes the schnapps and pours another. A second glass, then a third. He is hoping it will help him sleep, but he knows that it won't. Too many memories are swirling, too many ghosts disturbed and bothered. No, he will not sleep well tonight. Not in the knowledge they are coming. His third schnapps finished, he pulls himself out of the chair.

Should he go to his daughter? Would they even let him? The borders have been closed but he is an old man now. What could they possibly want with him? He imagines taking the train. First to Rostock and then to Berlin. Crossing to the west of the city and catching a plane. Or perhaps he could even travel cross-country. A train south to Munich and then another, down through the winelands, the Alps rising on the horizon. Lake Constance. His last visit had been before the war. He had been glad then. Glad that his daughter was away from the cities. Glad for his grandchildren too. He was gladder still when it was the Americans that took their small town by the lake, instead of the Russians. The stories …

When had he last seen her? They had come a couple of times after the war. Once in 1946 and again a few years later. Then the situation hardened. The borders closed. When her letters arrive now he can tell they have been opened, sense that they have been read by strange eyes. She seems to sense this as well, as her tone has changed over the years. More factual. Only details. Both grandchildren are at university now. One in Munich, the other in Freiburg. A success story.

Yes, he could go there. Down to the south. But somehow he can't imagine it. Even if the war had turned out differently it wouldn't have been his land. It would have still been another country.

He locks up the bar and climbs the stairs to his apartment. Inside the door he pauses, looking down at the umbrella stand. Two walking sticks, inexpertly carved by teenage hands:

H

K

The letters are scored into the handles. He can picture that summer – 1919? 1920? The war was over. Klaus was fourteen or fifteen. They would take walks together, following the shoreline along the dunes or inland, through the forests. The walking sticks were Heinrich's birthday present, but it was not long before Klaus grew out of walks altogether, and he never lived long enough to grow back into them.

Berlin.

Heinrich's father had been drawn to the capital, and it had claimed his son as well. Not long after his eighteenth birthday he moved south. He was going to be a journalist. He was going to work in theatre. He was going to become a painter. All of them and any of them. That was the promise of Berlin. The letters back home were sporadic, empty of detail. He returned on a visit every six months or so, but only when things were going well. He never asked for money. Never asked for help. But there were times, in between the visits, when things were not going well. They were the times of silence. The times of absence. As the decade continued, and as the 1930s approached, the periods of silence and of absence increased.

In a small town the tentacles of gossip and rumour stretch much further than can ever be imagined; indeed, all the way to the capital. They managed to deliver snippets of (mis-) information via sons and daughters, cousins and distant relations, all drawn to Berlin and all with their own agendas when it came to reporting back to the coast. Klaus was running with the Communists. Now he was running with the Nazis. He had been arrested. He was an alcoholic. He had been seen in a 'bar for boys' (but what was the witness doing there?).

After Hitler took power, Klaus disappeared from view. The rumour mill dropped in volume to a whisper; to hints and innuendo. Once more the news came that he had been arrested, but this time he had been sent to a prison camp. No one spoke about it out loud, and yet somehow the whole town knew. Heinrich spoke to the bureaucrat but all enquires turned up blank. No one came to speak to them about Klaus. Finally, there was no news at all, official or otherwise. In the country as a whole, the Nazis tightened their grip.

Under advice from the bureaucrat, Heinrich did what he should. He flew the flag, hung the pictures and gave the salute. But he never voted for the Nazis – when you still could vote – and he was suspicious of their policies. 'Strength through Joy' was supposed to bring tourism to the masses, but what was the place of a small hotel like the Barthels' in this brave new world of mass resorts and giant cruise ships? There were more stories, the whispers of camps and of foreign labourers and political prisoners. There was one down the coast. Could Klaus have been there? They did not dare ask. And then there was the thing with the Jews. Now, people say that they did not know, that they could not have known. But Heinrich knew they were lying. Had they had their eyes closed the day that the Jewish-owned clothing store was attacked, the glass shattered across the pavement? Did they not notice that the handful of Jewish families in the town had gone? You did not need to see the camps with your eyes to know what was happening. And there were enough jokes …

He can remember the last time he saw Klaus. The war had begun, raging for two years. Success after success. The might of the German army meant that this time there was no question that they were going to win. Klaus arrived one morning in his uniform. He was on leave, he said, as he hugged his father and mother, a few weeks off before he was sent back to the front. Heinrich had sensed right then that something was not right, but Clara was sick – they were unknowingly approaching the endgame – and he was too preoccupied with her to wonder about how long his son was staying. He was just happy to see him after seven long years, to share beer and schnapps each evening after Clara had drifted off into uncomfortable, uneasy sleep. Where had he been? What had he been doing? But he never asked. Not about the Communists or the Nazis. Not about prison or boys. Instead they just drank, both aware that it was a moment that could not last.

They came for Klaus like they will come for Heinrich. A knock at the door. A man in uniform. A car waiting at the end of the path. No words were said. Not by Klaus. Not by Heinrich. Clara watched her son being taken away from the upstairs window; Heinrich, from the front step of the hotel. Two years later he received a telegram. Klaus had been killed in action on the Russian front. Something told him his son was dead long before that. Clara had died not long after Klaus was taken away, slipping gently, finally away, into silence, in the darkest hour of the night.

It was on the day of Clara's funeral that Maria had come to him in a state of agitation. He should have known but it took a while to sink in. Heinrich's granddaughter was born six months later, although only Maria and he knew that this was the truth of the situation. In the last years of war there were many absent fathers and lots of single mothers. After the Russians came through there were even more. Maria's story was that her fiancé had been killed at the front. Heinrich could have moved them up to the attic but she never asked and he never insisted. So Maria and her daughter stayed down in the staff rooms, and the situation was accepted.

*

Heinrich moves through the small kitchen to step out on to the balcony, into the cool night air. The sea is agitated now, the waves loud as they hit the beach. Tomorrow they will come for him. He thinks of Maria's daughter in her white blouse and blue neck scarf. He would have thought that after the Nazis the Germans would have had enough of uniforms, but apparently it was not to be. There is money in the bag, should Maria ever choose to look. She could have it. They both could. It will be breakfast time; Maria will be helping with the guests. He can see her quizzical look as the men in grey suits cross the floor in the direction of the office. Yes, they will not be in uniform. And one day Maria will tell her daughter who her father was. Who Heinrich was. Why hadn't he brought them up to these rooms? All these empty rooms.

No answer.

He steps back inside, looks at the clock. They will come in the morning.

No.

This is not how the story is going to end.

IV

From the City to the Sea (Heiligendamm)

Warnemünde in the rain – Scarborough, Margate and the rules of bathing – Waiting for the train – All (rail)roads lead to the coast – Merkel, Bush, Sarkozy and Blair … all sitting on a wicker beach chair – The White Town on the Sea

It was Katrin who introduced me to the Baltic, during my first summer in Germany. It was 2002, the year of the World Cup in Japan and Korea, and I was working in a backpacker hostel in Berlin-Mitte. She was on reception, one of the few genuine Berliners in an international staff, but her connection to the Baltic coast was such that she wanted to show her new friends this place that meant so much to her. By the time our small group made a journey north, I had known her for six months and was fairly convinced that I had fallen in love. It took her a little longer to reciprocate.

Our group of five rented a car from a chain hotel in the centre of Berlin for our day trip to the seaside. It was August, but the weather was terrible, the windscreen wipers working hard for the three hours it took to get us there, swishing back and forth as they fought their losing battle against the rain and the spray from the lorries heading for the Rostock ferry. My main memory of that journey is the music. The radio, its DJs hyperactively enthusiastic as they delivered their lines through forced grins before queueing up a steady stream of 1990s hits. All Saints. Shaggy. Roxette. On the outskirts of Rostock, the dual carriageway swung around the city centre to pass through the estates' concrete-slab apartment blocks, which characterise the otherwise suburban edge of many East German cities. The rain continued to fall. Spice Girls.

Bryan Adams. More Shaggy. I raced water droplets down the car window as I had done as a child, to the backdrop of a looming apartment block decorated with sunflowers, the sky gunmetal-grey beyond. Not long after, we came to Warnemünde – Rostock's resort town at the mouth of the river that links the city to the sea – and found a parking space down a side street. As the rain drummed on the car roof we sat there for a time, considering our options. Other than turning back, we had none.

We climbed out and pulled our hoods up over our heads. Made our way to the beach.

To this day, I have no idea why Katrin chose Warnemünde as the place to introduce to us to the Baltic. When I ask her now she has no real answer. There is nothing particularly wrong with the resort town, but there are certainly more beautiful places along the coast that she could have taken us to. The weather did not help, and the wide expanse of sand was empty as we followed the boardwalk down from the promenade and on to the beach. Who else would be there, leaning into the wind, faces scrunched into a fixed scowl as the spray from the sea and the rain mixed and mingled and stung our cheeks? Some of our group went swimming. Why the fuck not? The others sat on the damp sands and waited. I was one of them, and spent my time trying to work out what was wrong with this beach. With this sea. The scale was all wrong, that was the first thing. And the rain. But the main issue was that there was no evidence of tides. No seaweed on the sands, no debris left behind by retreating waters. Then I noticed another absence: there was no salt in the air. All the smells and sensations that I identified with the seaside, with the coast, were absent that day at Warnemünde. And despite the squall, the winds whipping in from Scandinavia, there were barely any waves worthy of the name. On a stormy day in late summer, the Baltic was not so much an angry sea as a disconcerted lake. And I was in love and she did not know it. And I had Roxette and Shaggy competing for space in my head.

We walked the length of the beach to an oversized hotel, where we took the lift to the top floor and drank overpriced coffee and ate dry cake, surrounded by miserable holidaymakers. We walked back into town and, for want of anything better to do, went to a bad Mexican restaurant for an approximation of a burrito. All except the driver proceeded to get drunk on beer and weak cocktails as the rain lashed against the restaurant window, a final act of resignation that this was the day and there was nothing we could do to change it. The Baltic beyond that window was not so much ominous and eerie as miserable and unimpressive. At that moment I did not feel any hint of ghosts in Warnemünde, of stories to be discovered. The weather was too bad, I was too self-absorbed, and all I could think about was why people would come here for their holidays. On the way home the radio gave us Radiohead.

I couldn't imagine what would bring people to this distinctly uninspiring stretch of coastline, or how it had captured, and continued to capture, Katrin's imagination. It would take us a little while to get together, and even more time for her to persuade me back to the Baltic. But in the meantime, hundreds upon thousands of people did, as they have done since the eighteenth century. The path from the German city to the sea is a well-trodden one.

*

In 1626 in Scarborough, Yorkshire, Elizabeth Farrer was exploring the base of the cliffs when she came upon a mineral spring. The waters, coloured by the minerals they contained and staining the rocks where they emerged from the cliffs, were soon rumoured to cure minor ailments and the Scarborough Spa was born. From that moment, visitors were drawn from across England and beyond to this town on the North Sea to take the waters. As the eighteenth century progressed they began to not only take the waters, but to take *to* the waters, delivered to the surf via elaborate rolling bathing machines that preserved the modesty of the aristocratic ladies they contained. Inside they could change into their bathing costumes, hanging their land clothes beneath the roof in order to keep them dry. Once the contraption was far enough out to ensure a certain level of privacy, the bather could descend the steps and enter the water. A bathing attendant would keep an eye on things, including holding the rope around the bather's waist should the water be particularly rough or their swimming technique not up to scratch. And as the popularity of the Scarborough resort grew – now featuring a concert hall, gardens, a promenade and shops aimed at the well-to-do guests – physicians and doctors across the country began to write of the health benefits of cold water bathing. Scarborough's influence spread and new resorts sprung up along the English coast. Margate and Brighton were particularly popular, especially with continental visitors such as Friedrich Franz I, Duke of Mecklenburg-Schwerin. It was following a visit to Margate that the duke returned home inspired, with the intention of founding his own resort town on the Baltic coast. In 1793 he did just that.

In the development of his resort, called Heiligendamm, not

far from the city of Rostock and just a few kilometres down the coast from Warnemünde, the duke was advised by his physician, Samuel Gottlieb Vogel. A Professor of Medicine at Rostock University, Vogel was as convinced as his English colleagues as to the benefits for health and general well-being of cold water bathing, and in advising the duke on the creation of what would be the first such bathing resort on the German-speaking coast, he became known as the Godfather of the German seaside. A year after the foundation stone for the *Kurhaus* was laid – the centrepiece of an ensemble of white buildings that would draw aristocratic bathers from across central Europe – Dr Vogel laid out his rules for bathing so that all would be clear as to what was, and what was not, acceptable when it came to taking to the water:

The best times for cold bathing are the morning hours – late or early – and before, or after, a light breakfast …

So began the rules, which covered everything from the practicalities of bathing to the mental state of the bather, and specific issues relating to clothing and women:

One should not bathe with negative emotions. These include frustration, anger, grief, indignation etc. …

The more serenity, cheerfulness, confidence and hope with which one submits to Neptune, the happier one will be ...

It is generally not recommended to bath in shirt, short trousers or indeed any form of costume ...

For comfortable bathing, the meal the night before should be light and fully digested, and followed by sleep that is both peaceful and resting ...

Women should not bathe during their monthly period, unless with a doctor's approval ...

One should not enter the water too timidly or slow, nor bold or with sudden movements. One should then cover the body with water up to the neck a number of times, in an up and down motion ...

Thus Vogel laid out the rules in a handy, pocket-sized book and the bathing machines, pulled by horses, were led down the beach at Heiligendamm and out into the waters. The upper classes flocked to Heiligendamm, convinced of the health effects and attracted by the exclusivity of what soon became known as 'The White Town on the Sea', where the buildings were designed to look just like the mansions and palaces they had left behind at home. This private seaside world would last, as with England, only as far as the Industrial Revolution, as the railway linked the ever-growing cities with the coast. The era of exclusivity was over, as the seaside, and society in general, was transformed in a way that the duke and his doctor, as they built Heiligendamm in the 1790s, could hardly have imagined.

*

It is the railway that linked the city to the sea, and despite the arrival of the car, the bus and the autobahn, it still does. I was travelling to Heiligendamm by train, starting my journey at Berlin's Hauptbahnhof, a steel and glass cathedral to rail travel built on the banks of the River Spree and opened just in time for the World Cup in 2006. It emerged on the riverbank like an alien presence, occupying a wasteland close to where the Berlin Wall had once divided the city, a place that has long felt like an edgeland zone; neither part of the old West Berlin city centre that had grown up around the Zoo Station, nor the historic heart of the city that stood along Unter den Linden a few hundred metres away through the Brandenburg Gate.

In some ways, the new main train station was part of the unification process, an attempt to link together the two sides of the city that had once been separated by a no man's land of barbed wire and concrete; of floodlights and secret shoot-to-kill orders. One of the first people killed attempting to escape across the border after it was closed in the summer of 1961 was Günter Litfin, shot as he swam the Humboldthafen, a small river harbour that stands in the shadow of the train station. Slowly the area around the station and the harbour is being filled in, with new tower blocks and hotels, all linked to both sides of the city by new U-Bahn and tramlines. But still, it feels windswept and unfinished as you approach the station on foot: a project incomplete. The gaps in the city, where memories linger of the dark days of the twentieth century and its victims, like Günter Litfin, have yet to be filled.

Do people think of these things as they cross the empty concrete plaza to the station, and on to the subterranean platforms where their regional express to the seaside is waiting for them? In the summer the platform would be thronged with people waiting for the train. I imagined them in their Hawaiian shirts with their buckets and spades, inflatable dinghies fully blown, waiting for the comedic moment of attempting to squeeze through the sliding doors of the train. Today, my fellow passengers wore Gore-tex jackets and woolly hats. Holdalls and trolley cases. A couple of impossibly young soldiers heading home on leave, their camouflage rucksacks catching the attention from the opposite end of the platform. Only one family looked like they were heading away for an off-season holiday, their conversation filled with references to grandma and grandpa.

Can we go swimming in the sea?

Dad shook his head with a grimace.

But there was no doubt that some of my fellow travellers would be heading to the seaside for a week or two of bracing winds and wintry walks along the promenade. The idea that the coast is a healthy place for relaxation and recuperation began with Dr Vogel and remains pervasive across Germany to this day. Health insurance companies will still finance seaside cures, especially for children with respiratory issues, and the clinics and health spas of the Baltic and North Sea coastlines are ready to receive visitors/patients all year round. So the platform was pretty busy by the time the train emerged from the tunnel and pulled up alongside the platform. It took a while, as we moved slowly through the north Berlin suburbs, for all the passengers to settle down and find a seat for the journey. The noise in the carriage dropped as we looked down on the city outside the window, down on to balconies of withered plants, sacrificed to the long winter, and the garden colonies and allotments of frozen soil. A stream of joggers breathed hard on the desire path of a dead railway. A stream of cars on the autobahn.

What about the swimming pool?

The young boy looked at his dad across the top of his comic. The sister read a book as mum swiped and stabbed at a tablet. Dad folded the newspaper across his lap.

Yes, we can go to the swimming pool.

The boy returned to his comic satisfied that even in the winter, a trip to the seaside was not going to be an entirely dry affair.

*

In the 1840s, the branch line to Blackpool opened in Lancashire, and the first working-class resort at the English seaside was born. By the end of the nineteenth century there were over a hundred resort towns on the English coast, and the transformation from aristocratic rest cure to leisure destination for the masses was complete. On the Baltic, the city of Rostock was linked to the German railway network in 1850, and within thirty years branch lines had opened up all along the coast, to the duke's model resort at Heiligendamm but also to a string of former fishing villages that were transforming, one by one, into resorts for the general population. Heiligendamm may have stayed fairly exclusive, but there were plenty of other options for the growing middle class to spend their summers and the working class to make the most of holiday weekends. The Baltic became 'Berlin's bathtub' or 'Hamburg's bathtub', as the cities swelled and grew. German unification in 1871 was achieved on the ground via the continued spread of the railway network, and visitors came from across the new country to resorts that stretched from the North Sea islands in the west to what is now the Russian Federation, back then part of East Prussia. By the end of the nineteenth century, the German love affair with the seaside had well and truly begun.

*

My train reached Rostock after a couple of hours and I headed west by road, through the countryside towards Heiligendamm. It had snowed overnight and the landscape of Mecklenburg was black and white; a countryside in greyscale. To the side of the road ran the railway line that links the resort towns along this stretch of coast, and I remembered it from my only previous visit, back in 2007 at the tail end of the G8 summit hosted by Angela Merkel in the grand hotels and villas of Heiligendamm.

That summer the arrival of the leaders of the free and not-so-free world had provoked an exodus of people to the seaside, travelling north by road and rail alongside the more traditional holidaymakers. Police patrolled train platforms and carriages, looking for people who fit the bill of protestors rather than tourists, attempting to prevent them getting even close to the summit site. Messages were passed by Internet and text message, friends warning friends of the clampdown:

They won't let you on the train. Hide your banners. No political t-shirts. Take the bus instead?

Police targeted groups of young people, especially those dressed in black. Mostly they looked for groups who gave the impression that they were on their way to a festival, which in a way they were:

Watch out on the train. The pigs will be undercover.

That was the advice, and so the young people carefully assessed the carriages they were sat on, batting away the questions of strangers. The young man with a novel and a nice smile might not just be idly curious.

Where are you heading?

To visit family. Know your answer. Be ready. *They live by the sea.*

At a certain moment, perhaps once Berlin was behind them, travelling through the landscape of green and yellow fields, lakes and tall pine trees, they could start to relax. From Brandenburg and into Mecklenburg-Vorpommern, ever closer now. Passing villages of red-brick farmhouses clustered around a church. Passing solar power installations and the remnants of GDR industrial projects. Passing graffiti wherever there was an empty patch of concrete or a bridge support, mostly proclaiming loyalty to one football team or another. And then:

Fuck the G8.

At Rostock there was an even greater police presence at the station; Robocops of bulky torsos and tiny heads, helmets at the waist. Some checked IDs or scanned the crowds. Shouts and songs. The whole world would be watching, and both sides knew it. Through the crowd they pushed, avoiding any official attention, attempting to slip through the cordon of control and into the city. Some were staying with friends, or camping in the gardens of online acquaintances. Others at an ad hoc campsite that had sprung up on the edge of town. Later, the organisers of the protest would claim that over 80,000 had attended, had made it to Rostock. The police

– the same the world over – estimated the figure was closer to 25,000. No matter. At night, tens of thousands of people were in the city of Rostock, facing down the police.

For the most part the atmosphere was peaceful, positive, joyful even. This was not the story told in the media, of course. The bulletins and newspaper columns led with a few random acts of violence; a fight captured on camera. It was always the same. In the lead-up to the summit, the business owners of Rostock had been encouraged to barricade their stores against the mob. With the constant sound of helicopter blades in the air and the massed lines of black-clad, anonymous police, it was not surprising there was tension in the air as the opening of the summit grew nearer.

Merkel. Blair. Bush. Sarkozy … The leaders had been flown in to a cordoned-off airfield and then helicoptered to Heiligendamm. But you cannot run a global political summit without supplies and ordinary staff, and so, as the day approached, the protestors moved out of Rostock and into the countryside around Heiligendamm in an attempt to blockade the land routes to what had now become a fortified compound. It was a mass exodus, a music festival on the move. Not everyone knew where they were going as they travelled back roads and forests, attempting to breach the security cordon across yellow fields of rape shining bright in the summer sun. Some followed the tracks of the tourist railway, but they were easy for the police to handle. More successful were those who moved through the wheat fields. Under that hot sun, with the police weighed down in their riot gear, a few thousand protestors traversed the waist-high fields to reach the single road leading in and out of Heiligendamm. They sat down on the hot tarmac, buoyed by the news that they had managed to delay the start of the summit. It would take water cannons and other strong-arm tactics to remove them, to reopen the road, but they had won a small victory. The whole world was watching.

The next day their story would be told. A day travelling through the fields and on to the road. The water cannon and the long march back to Rostock. A yoga protest, peacefully facing down the armed police. Friends arrested, some released. But the front page of the newspaper featured all eight prime ministers and presidents, sitting on an oversized wicker beach chair built especially for the summit and placed in the garden of the five-star hotel. Outside there were more protestors picking their way through the fields, but the summit had begun. There would be more sit-ins, more water cannons, more yoga … what else could they do?

*

We had arrived in Heiligendamm in 2007 the day after the summit had finished. Our way into the town was still blocked and so we had driven on to neighbouring Kühlungsborn. Protestors still walked the verge or were crossing the fields, as if unsure of what to do with themselves now that the objects of their protest had been flown clear in yet more helicopters. In Kühlungsborn itself, we were greeted by the sight of some of the 16,000 police who had been brought north for the summit from across the Federal Republic. Now they were off duty, still wearing their uniforms but walking the promenade with their helmets off, licking at ice cream. Others sat on the sea wall, their boots on the sand. A couple paddled in the gentle waves.

Now the road to Heiligendamm through the woods was clear. I had long wanted to see that collection of white buildings that had come to define the historic resort; an ensemble of classicist and historicist architecture that gave Heiligendamm its nickname on postcards and in the newspaper resorts from the G8 summit. Moving ever closer, through the forest, 'the White Town on the Sea' began to emerge as ghostly apparitions through the trees. Into the village – little more than a single circular road, with the resort buildings on the seaward side and a forest plus railway station in the centre – I aimed for the promenade, a public right of way between the Grand Hotel where the summit had been held and the beach. There seemed to be no way through. All the properties were fenced off, with gates and signs warning that only those with a right to be there should even think about proceeding.

Only for guests of the Grand Hotel.

I looked around. There did not seem to be any high-paying guests who might object to my presence and so I entered the grounds, walking as purposefully as I could along icy paths that snaked between the snow-covered lawns dividing the strange, white buildings. Not far from the promenade and the sea, which I could hear beyond a privet hedge, I came to a boulder commemorating Duke Friedrich Franz I and his Margate-inspired resort by the sea. Beyond the hedge was the Baltic, where the waves were breaking on frozen sands. But I was defeated by a locked gate. With no guest card in my pocket I could not access the promenade path. Through the gate I could see it, that public right of way on the other side, but with no card I was out of luck. I would have to take the long way round.

Retracing my steps through the Grand Hotel, I walked up to the train station and a map that led me to the promenade and the beach. I wondered about the guests of the Grand Hotel Heiligendamm. Even in the depths of winter, the prices were eye-wateringly expensive. And beyond the hotel, there was nothing else in the town. No shopping street or restaurants. No bars or boutiques. Everything was contained within those white buildings, and with no guest card you were not getting in; without the guest card there was very little point in even coming to Heiligendamm to have a look. The railway may have opened up the seaside to the people of the city, but in Heiligendamm, the long tradition of exclusivity remained.

At the station a signpost pointed me in the direction of the beach, along a winding forest path that went to the very edge of the village and the last of the villas. Here the buildings were yet to be renovated, and were crumbling and cream-coloured – more nicotine-stained than white. Eventually I came to a gravel car park and a path through the dunes.

From the beach, which was the orientation to which Heiligendamm had been built, the resort looked frankly preposterous. Fake castles and colonnaded ballrooms that even the wealthy gangster in his thick, towelling robe might reject as being a bit tacky. Perhaps it would look different under blue skies and above green lawns. Perhaps it would have some kind of charm, with or without the buzz of the G8 helicopters. I doubted it. It was not the cold wind or the overwhelming white against grey of the scene that made it strange and not a little distasteful. It was the unwelcoming nature of the place; a place that asked immediately of its visitors for evidence of belonging, and that forced those who did not have it to walk the long way round on a muddy path through the trees, hidden from those with their guest cards and their towelling robes. It was, I considered, as I made my way along the promenade as the wind whipped in off the Baltic and across the sands, a fitting location for Merkel's summit, even if they were not the reasons she might have chosen it.

V

The Boys and Girls of Summer (Kühlungsborn)

Breakfast with the past – From here to the Soviet Union – Peter Döbler's long swim – Along the promenade to the Villa Baltic – Holidays in East Germany – Traces of a summer camp and 99 Luftballons – Becoming Crooked Sea Needle

In the breakfast room of the hotel I waited for Katrin's parents, surrounded by the people of Kühlungsborn. They had been captured and preserved at a certain moment in their lives: on their wedding day or anniversary, during their working week or at their leisure. Their photographs occupied almost every centimetre of the walls, a hundred and more lives stacked one upon the other. They represented the history of a town that did not even exist until 1938, indeed, did not exist at the moment almost all of these photographs were taken. Kühlungsborn was founded a year before the war, through the amalgamation of two former fishing villages to create a single resort of some two thousand residents. The two villages were renamed Kühlungsborn East and Kühlungsborn West, and were linked by a tree-lined promenade of villas and hotels that cut through the forest that had once separated them. The fusing of the two villages was designed to reduce costs and to usher in a golden era of prosperity as happy tourists bathed and strolled beneath the swastika flag. It did not quite turn out that way. The Kühlungsborn that emerged from the war found itself in a country defeated and occupied, with a very different future ahead of it.

Those who lived through the war and what came next were not the people whose photographs looked down from the walls of the breakfast room. When the interior designer was faced with this space, they had opted for brass light fittings and other furniture that belonged more to a Victorian station waiting room or buffet than a seaside hotel just a few hundred metres from the beach. The nod to the coast came with a selection of barometers and ferry schedules, a model sailing ship and a captain's hat gathering dust on a shelf above the orange juice glasses and extra bread baskets. There had been a limit to the nautical knick-knacks to be sourced in the local souvenir boutiques, and the high walls needed to be filled. And when faced with the photographic archives from the town, the interior designer must have been faced with a choice. German history being what it is – and this was a *breakfast room* they were decorating, not a documentary series – the designer had taken the eminently sensible decision to stop the story somewhere in the mid-1920s. This meant everything was in black and white. There were no swastika flags flying above the town hall. No Soviet troops on the promenade. Nothing of once-private hotels confiscated and run by the state. No off-duty police officers licking ice cream after the summit down the road.

With all the potentially contentious aspects of German history avoided, I was left to share the space with images of overdressed early bathers in outlandish costumes, alongside a romanticised vision of the fishing industry that tourism would eventually usurp. Ruddy-faced and bearded sailors stood over nets as they pulled them in. A line of boats rested on the sands. The tourists arrived, skipping lightly through the surf as a family of four posed on a wicker beach chair, their backs to the dunes, facing out to sea. A swimming competition had taken place, with a line of entrants looking down on the splashes created by muscular arms and legs, the tan lines of the swimmers detectable even in black and white. Next to an old beer advert, close to the door, a couple posed on the beach in full evening dress. He wore a top hat and tails, with a well-groomed moustache. She was in a gown, wrapped in a feather boa, with a hat perched at a carefully-considered angle. They stood on the sands, the sea behind them, next to the telltale stripes of yet another beach chair.

That morning I seemed to be the only one taken by this vision of Kühlungsborn past. The rest of my fellow diners concentrated instead on their muesli and smoked salmon, the little bowls of yoghurt and the pre-sliced Dutch cheese. On the breakfast buffet there was one nod to our location: a pile of rollmop herrings, whose sour burst of fishy vinegar was bracingly washed down with bitter, black coffee to cure the most stubborn of hangovers. Good morning. Heads turned only when the cook emerged from the kitchen to deliver another huge metal tray of cooling and congealing scrambled eggs to its place above the flickering blue flame of a paraffin burner, but otherwise it was eyes down and muted conversation. Mind your own business. The guests were almost exclusively couples, of an age where there were no children to get in the way of midweek, term-time trips to the coast. As I moved through the room between my table and the buffet I caught snippets of conversation that told me I was the only non-German in the room. The reading material of choice was the local newspaper or a smartphone on the lap. Outside it was cold. It had snowed overnight. I finished my breakfast and climbed the couple of steps up from the breakfast room to the hotel lobby. There, sitting in an uncomfortable armchair, Katrin's dad was waiting for me.

*

Katrin's parents live in Berlin, but travel to the Baltic at least once a year for a week or a long weekend at some point over the winter. They've had a long connection with Kühlungsborn, and not just from holidays, so Fritz had offered to show me the town himself. That morning we walked from Kühlungsborn East to Kühlungsborn West, from one of the old villages to the other, alongside the promenade that ran behind the dunes. To reach the path we followed the street from the hotel past a strip of hotels, guest houses, restaurants and boutiques that led down to the beach and the pier. The overnight snow had been pushed to the side of the road and stood in neat piles above the gutter and the grids into which it would eventually melt. At the end of the street we paused to look down from the start of the pier on to the sands. Snow on a beach is a strange thing, an alien presence. The few wicker beach chairs that stood in the shadow of the pier's supports wore frosty crowns. Ice crystals clung to the tough grass that grew out of the dunes. Winter had arrived in Kühlungsborn and it felt eternal.

Beyond the beach the Baltic was deep grey and rolling, somewhere between calm and choppy. A flock of unidentifiable black ducks rode the waves. Fritz told me that some years the sea even froze. I had heard this before but it was only now, with the snow piled up outside ice cream stalls and souvenir stands, with cancellations on the railway and villages cut off from their neighbours, that I could start to imagine it. Kühlungsborn felt positively Siberian.

From here to the Soviet Union.

Although the ships Fritz sailed on did not leave from here they did cross the Baltic to Latvia and Lithuania, to places that lay somewhere out there, across the freezing sea. And as Fritz told me his stories and we walked, shoulders hunched against the biting wind, the presence of a watchtower looking down on the promenade did not feel at all out of place. Standing beneath it I imagined that it must seem incongruous to the summer holidaymaker, strolling from their hotel to their rented beach chair, from the ice cream shop to the *Biergarten*; a strange intrusion into their mood of escapism. Now, with the wind picking up and lifting loose snow from the beach in order to whip it across the path and into our exposed cheeks, it seemed like the most natural installation in the world. It took us back to the time of Fritz's early adulthood, of Katrin's childhood, when this stretch of coast was not only a place of leisure but also a border zone, part of that Iron Curtain that divided Europe. All coastlines are borders of sorts, but in the German Democratic Republic it meant something else. And it also meant that, during those years, imagining the seaside as a place of escape had a very different meaning than it did before, or has done since.

*

It meant something different to Peter Döbler. In the newspaper photograph, captured many years after the event, he sits among porcelain lamps, paintings of rural landscapes and brass candlesticks, looking directly at the reader from behind his large glasses. Together with his neatly cropped hair, full face and open-necked shirt, it all gives the impression of a man who is exactly what he appears to be: a retired doctor, living surrounded by the belongings he has accumulated during a long, fairly distinguished and more-than-fairly remunerated career.

In 1971, that same man walked into the water at Kühlungsborn until it was deep enough to submerge most of his body and then floated towards a sandbar a little way out to sea. Beneath the waterline he held a small bundle. For the next few hours, as the afternoon wore on, he swam. Back and forth. Back and forth. He had been doing such swims for years, mammoth physical efforts out by the sandbar within sight of the beach. Time passed, as it always had done, and slowly the beach began to empty as the afternoon gave way to evening and the air cooled. On the beach and the promenade there were patrols, but they ignored the swimmer. Perhaps they had seen him before. Back and forth. Back and forth. For hours at a time. What a crank! And so Peter Döbler swam in peace until the beach was fully empty. No more patrols. No more tourists.

And then he began to swim again, really swim; only

stopping some twenty-five hours later in the coastal waters of another country.

As a teenage boy, Peter Döbler's favourite book had been *The Old Man and the Sea*, and the young Hemingway fan long nurtured the ambition that he too would one day catch a blue marlin like his literary hero. At school he was a diligent student, his grades suggesting a bright future. There was a problem, however, and that was his father. A self-employed accountant – which in some countries might have worked in Peter's favour, but to the GDR authorities his father was viewed through suspicious eyes. For Peter, as the son of a capitalist, this meant that his path to higher education was blocked. He wanted to become a doctor but was told in bureaucratic language, that was nevertheless clear in its meaning, that there was no university place for him. He applied anyway, and during the enrolment period became the beneficiary of a cruel twist of fate. His father very suddenly became sick, with an illness that would cost him his life. With his death, Peter was no longer the son of a capitalist. His way was now free. He was allowed to study medicine.

Unsurprisingly, Peter Döbler was upset with a system that judged sons for the so-called 'sins' of the father and played with their futures in such a way, and things soon got worse. In 1968 he refused to sign a petition protesting the American involvement in Vietnam. It was not that he was particularly in favour of American overseas interventions; it was just that he felt it would be hypocritical for the GDR to protest such an act at the very moment Soviet tanks were patrolling the streets of Prague. Of all the satellite states of the Soviet Union, the GDR was nothing if not loyal, and once again Peter found himself under scrutiny from the authorities because of his oppositional gestures. By this point he had qualified as a doctor and was married, but he found his career path blocked. He was unable to secure an apartment. Among other factors, this would eventually cost him his marriage, and he was no closer to catching that blue marlin.

By 1969 he'd had enough. He began to make plans, preparations to leave. Telling no one but his mother, he got to work on a strategy that was based around three pillars: Physical, Practical, Emotional.

Physical: He was a good swimmer, and the sea seemed a more porous border than the fortifications that had been erected between the two Germanys or through the heart of Berlin. His research took him along the Baltic coast – a boat from Poland? – to the Aegean Sea and the idea to swim from Bulgaria to Greece. Eventually he arrived at Kühlungsborn.

From the resort, it was fifty kilometres to the West German island of Fehmarn, north of Lübeck. A long swim. And so he began to train. Ten, fifteen hours at a time, building the strength he would need to escape East German waters.

Practical: He researched maps and committed them to memory. He taught himself to navigate by the stars. He read up on the potential physiological effects of such an undertaking and how to counteract them. The water, he determined, needed to be at least eighteen degrees Celsius to lessen the risk of hypothermia. And then there were the patrols. Spending a night close to the border control watchtower, he looked out to sea through his own binoculars. What could these guards make out, in the darkness? Not much, he decided. But he came away suspecting he would need to keep his arms beneath the water. Breaststroke it was, then.

Emotional: Aside from his mother, who in any case knew what he was planning, he let his friendships cool off and wither away. It is surprising – or perhaps it shouldn't be – how easy this can be. Decline a couple of invitations for drinks and eventually you won't be asked any more. Avoid social situations, small talk in the workplace. Friends become acquaintances and then, slowly but surely, not even that. He was leaving them behind long before he even set foot in the water.

The bundle that Peter Döbler rested on the sandbank on that July afternoon in 1971, two years after he began his preparations, contained a diving suit, weights, an inflatable swimming ring, chocolate and tablets. Some reports would later state that these were appetite suppressants. Others that they were amphetamines. Either way, the intention was the same; to keep him calm in the water and provoke a state of mild euphoria, allowing him to deal with the mental difficulty of swimming for over twenty-four hours. A well-trained doctor who knew his capabilities and limits, Peter Döbler was not worried about his body holding out. He was worried about his mind.

As the afternoon turned to dusk he changed into his diving suit on the sandbar and made his first strokes towards the open sea. In the darkness he read his compass by moonlight, nibbling on chocolate and taking a pill every hour. As it grew light he caught sight of a West German ferry and, stopping the relentless breaststroke that had brought him this far, called and waved his arms. Despite his frenzied movements and shouting he failed to catch anyone's attention. More to the point, he realised he would not have the strength to do it again. If he wanted to keep swimming, that was all he could do. Stroke by stroke. Ever closer.

The morning progressed. Clouds rolled in above the sea. Lightning flashes were followed by thunder at ever-decreasing intervals, as a summer storm raged for an hour or more. By the time the weather eased he was over twenty hours in. He kept swimming. And then, finally, after over a day in the water, he saw land. Fehmarn. Boats. A sailing dinghy pulled alongside and the skipper asked him what he was up to. Through the slight chop of the waves, the spray flashing in his face and against the hull of the dinghy, the swimmer explained himself.

The captain looked down at the floating figure and then back along to the coast, towards the storm that was still raging and the East German beaches beyond. He looked back down at Peter Döbler and then, after a moment's pause, lowered the ladder. Within sight of the shore, there was no longer any need to keep swimming.

*

As we explored the exhibition beneath the watchtower a light snow began to fall. From the founding of the German Democratic Republic in 1949, the coastal border had been an issue, but it was the building of the Berlin Wall in 1961 that brought matters to a head. The number of regulations relating to the zone along the Baltic shore increased, as did the number of new policies designed to keep the water border secure. First came a regulation that all fishing and sports boats had to be registered with the authorities. By 1970, hotel managers were required by law to inform all guests of the border regulations. Two years later, perhaps in response to Peter Döbler's successful escape attempt, civil border surveillance units were created, made up of volunteers patrolling the coastal zones. More often than not, they were couples disguised as normal walkers or holidaymakers. By 1974, hotel staff were legally responsible for reporting any guests who arrived with kayaks, rubber dinghies or any other sea-going vessels. And such guests could expect a short interruption to their holiday as they were interviewed by officers of the border patrol.

The exhibition told the stories of the escapees, of the border guards, and of the civilian volunteers to the coastal patrol. As so often with the history of the GDR, it was the last group that was the most ambiguous. The question comes, as it does with the Ministry for State Security – the Stasi – and its numerous informants, down to what motivates such individuals to work for such a regime? In a world where we like things to be simple, for it to be a binary choice between good and evil, the truth is almost always more complicated than that.

Later that night, as I sat with Katrin's parents in a steakhouse, I asked them about a television programme I had heard about. Unusually for a German television show, it had been critically acclaimed beyond the country's borders and was set in East Berlin during the years of division.

Those type of things don't interest me, Fritz said. *I have my memories. I know how things were. I don't need a television show to tell me what life was like ...*

As we walked away from the watchtower, the path slippery with the light dusting of snow, I was thinking about memory and about how describing the past is never as clear-cut as we would like it to be. The stories we hear, the ones we respond to and linger on, the ones that inspire a new page of the notebook, are the ones that grab the attention. Peter Döbler's story would be interesting even without his epic swim because it tells us *something* about what life was like in the GDR. Falling foul of the regime because of his father's status and his own political conscience, he found his way to university and his later career was blocked. No apartment. A failed marriage. Escape was, for Peter Döbler, the rational choice.

For Katrin's parents, things were a little different. Fritz was the son of committed Communists who joined the navy but never the Party. Gabi was – and still is – a teacher. They fell in love, brought up three kids, went on holiday and enjoyed friendships. They were never overly supportive of the system that they lived under, nor were they victims of oppression. It was a life, filled with the things – love, family, friendship – that make for a good one. I once met a member of the East German opposition, a poet-dissident who had been locked up in the infamous Hohenschönhausen prison by the Stasi for his activities. He had a theory when it came to totalitarian regimes.

Ten per cent do very well, he said. *Ten per cent fall foul of the authorities, either through no fault of their own or because, like me, they agitate for change. Eighty per cent just do their best to get by. Do their best for their family. To live the best way they can. Like everyone else around the world …*

He was in the ten per cent who fall foul of the system, eventually 'sold' to West Germany in the 1980s in exchange for hard currency. People were interested in him, he said, because he was one of the two extremes. They wanted to hear his story. Likewise those of the bosses, living in their fortified compound in the woods. Or the Stasi agents. Or the celebrities who became informants. What drives such people? Ideology? Power? Fear? Why does someone agree to work for the Stasi? To become a civilian border volunteer? Why does someone else choose to rebel? To fight back?

These are the questions that fascinate us, but they do not apply to the majority. No one asks them *their* story.

I do not know what provoked the poet-dissident to say this. I do not know if his numbers add up. But despite having been arrested, imprisoned and sold, he still wanted to encourage us to consider life for people living beyond the extremes. To encourage a wider understanding of the past. As we walked along the promenade his words came back to me, and I asked Fritz questions. About whether he had looked at his own Stasi files. About why he hadn't. About his brush with the authorities when his sister moved to Austria and he was no longer allowed to go to sea and was transferred to the sporting department of the navy. Their life had been okay. Better now, of course, but okay then. There was nothing to be explained. Nothing to be discovered.

We fell into silence. I wondered if I was annoying him with these questions, even though he and Gabi had invited me to Kühlungsborn, that these were stories they wanted to share.

There was not much life on the beach between Kühlungsborn East and Kühlungsborn West. A couple of dog walkers and photographers making the most of the limited and eerie half-light. Foolhardy runners dodged icy puddles, and the sole kiosk open along its length did a healthy business in hot fries and mulled wine. The small crowd that had gathered around it picked at paper plates piled high with thin chips and *Currywurst*, the ketchup an explosion of colour in an otherwise bleached scene.

In Kühlungsborn West the buildings were grander, the upper-class brother to the lower-class sibling back down the shore. Here the buildings were larger, decorated with turrets and colonnades, porches and balconies. Many had been renovated, spruced up in an attempt to attract the deeper pockets more normally found further down the coast in Heiligendamm. But perhaps the finest of all the buildings stood abandoned, looking out across a wide concrete plaza to the beach and the sea beyond.

BALTIC.

The letters were moulded into the dirty-cream facade, on the curve of the entranceway above the sweep of steps leading down from the double front doors to the high wire fence that blocked access to the site. The neo-Baroque villa was still standing, although it was well on its way to ruin, despite the weather-beaten placard that promised a wondrous architectural imagining of what might one day be.

This was Goebbels' villa, Fritz said as we approached.

Another big house expropriated by another big Nazi. The Villa Baltic was built by a Jewish lawyer called Wilhelm

Hausmann, and would later be the resting place for both Hausmann and his wife when they died only a few years after moving in. By 1931 it had become a holiday retreat for Jewish academics and their families, but this would only last until 1935 – by which time the two villages that would become Kühlungsborn had been declared 'Judenfrei'. The Goebbels Foundation took over the house, removing the graves of Wilhelm and Mathilde as they did so. Within a decade the villa would be looted by the Red Army, as Goebbels arranged the deaths of his children before crunching down on cyanide capsules in a Berlin bunker. Throughout all of this the lights of the Villa Baltic would have burned brightly, just as they did on that July evening as darkness fell and Peter Döbler made his underwater strokes in the direction of Fehmarn, dreaming of the blue marlin he would one day catch as the captain of his own boat in the Cape Verde Islands. As we stood in the shadow of the ruin, no lights to be seen, that all seemed a long way away.

*

From 1949 and the creation of the German Democratic Republic in what had been the Soviet zone of occupied Germany, to the heady days of 1989 and the protests that began outside a Leipzig church and would bring down both the Berlin Wall and the regime that built it, the Socialist Unity Party did its best to involve itself in nearly every aspect of people's lives. One of the tools it used was the Free German Trade Union Federation (FDGB), an umbrella workers' organisation that was responsible for ideological control in the workplace and, less ominously, numerous social services for workers and their families. This included holidays. The reach of the FDGB was remarkable. At its peak in 1986, some 9.6 million citizens of the GDR were members of the federation, more than half of the country's total population of 16 million.

Eighty per cent just do their best to get by. Do their best for their family. To live the best way they can. Like everyone else around the world ...

And go on holiday. The words of the dissident-poet reflected the trade-off that maintained an unsteady peace within the German Democratic Republic. A reasonably high standard of living – by the standards of their fellow Warsaw Pact members – was the exchange for control of everyday life and the anti-democratic nature of the system the Socialist Unity Party implemented. People may have been forbidden to travel to the West, their way blocked by the barbed wire and concrete of the border zones, but everyone still dreams of escape from the everyday, whether they are Thomas Mann in the stifling atmosphere of a bourgeois household in nineteenth-century Lübeck or a young woman in East Berlin working in a factory making sewing machines for export (and much-needed hard currency). Everyone dreams of escape and everyone wants to go on holiday. The Party recognised as much, and in the GDR, the state-controlled FDGB was the biggest travel agent of them all.

From the early 1950s, in towns like Kühlungsborn, the FDGB began to take over properties such as the Villa Baltic, as well as numerous hotels, pensions, guest houses and campgrounds. In this they were aided by the *Aktion Rose* of 1953, when properties not only by the coast but situated alongside lakes, in the forests or in the mountains were nationalised and put under the control of the federation. Some of them had been family businesses dating back centuries, and in many cases their owners were members of that suspicious lower-middle class that had been the bedrock of Nazi support in the 1930s. During the process a number of former property owners were arrested and imprisoned, sometimes on the grounds of contact with the West, for perceived criticism of the GDR, or for a history – whether real or imagined – of Nazi sympathies or pre-war fascist activities. *Aktion Rose* resulted in the imprisonment of over four hundred business owners, mostly for violations of laws relating to the protection of public property. From that moment until the fall of the Berlin Wall, access to trips to the Baltic Sea for citizens of the GDR was almost entirely controlled by the organisations of the state.

*

From the Villa Baltic, Fritz and I continued to walk. We had not yet reached our destination, a small residential complex on the very edge of town. It was a place I had visited many years before: a complex of holiday apartments with their own private access down to the beach. During the GDR it had been a holiday camp and, like the Villa Baltic, in the hands of a state institution. In this case, the camp was not run by the FDGB, but by the East German Navy. The armed forces in the GDR had a number of roles in society beyond the defence of the state and, theoretically, its people. They ran sporting institutions, not only at the highest, elite level, but also for their staff and families. They also ran holiday camps, such as this one on the edge of Kühlungsborn, to be used by the children of the navy to have a couple of weeks by the sea each summer.

Following his sister's emigration to Austria and his

redeployment within the navy, Fritz had spent a couple of summers working at the summer camp before eventually moving to become the manager of the naval football team in Stralsund. For most of his time at Stralsund the team played in the second tier of East Germany's Oberliga, the highest level of football in the country, and a competition dominated through much of the 1980s by a team from Berlin. Dynamo were the record champions in the GDR, a fact they still proclaim proudly on their website. They were also the team of the Ministry for State Security, otherwise known as the Stasi.

As we walked through the maze of streets between the Villa Baltic and the former holiday camp, past a small cinema and a campground covered in snow, where a few hardy caravaners were enjoying a winter holiday beneath the pine trees, we talked about football as well as how holidays worked in the GDR. Some families had access to a dacha, a small cabin in the woods or part of a garden colony that allowed people, especially apartment dwellers, to escape the city for weekends or summer vacations. But if you had no dacha or no family or friends who could get you access to one, and if you were not a member of the FDGB or other state institution that controlled the vast majority of hotels, holiday camps and campgrounds, then it could prove very difficult to arrange that escape from everyday life, especially during the school holidays.

After the fall of the Berlin Wall, reunification, and the vast sweep of economic reforms and rationalisations across the former territory of the German Democratic Republic, the hotels and campgrounds and holiday camps were either returned to the families from which they had been confiscated during *Aktion Rose* or otherwise privatised. On the lane out of town now, we passed the red-brick, thatched house that had been the residence of the camp director. Fritz had been invited there for a barbecue at the end of one of the long summers working at the camp. Now the house was a holiday cottage, with a small sign by the front gate offering a website address, Skype, email and telephone number for anyone interested in making a booking.

Not far beyond the campground and the director's old house we reached the former holiday camp. This was the very edge of town. The camp, on the beach side of the lane, was now holiday apartments. Across the street stood a small estate of concrete-slab apartment blocks, built as navy accommodation back in the GDR and which now provided homes for people who actually lived and worked in Kühlungsborn. As his father shovelled snow from the communal front door to the pavement, a bucket of grit standing on the step, a little boy in full ski suit made unsteady process across an untouched expanse of white leading to the next building along. We turned to enter the grounds of the old summer camp, where Fritz had once worked and where Katrin and her sister had come in later years as the daughters of a naval officer for summer holidays of their own. It was Katrin who first brought me here, about ten years before, on a hot summer's day not long after the birth of our daughter. As then, a sign on the gate warned Fritz and I that this was private property, only to be entered with permission. Fritz ignored it, pushing instead at the gate and – finding it unlocked – holding it open for me so that I could enter.

The complex was built around a central landscaped garden. Two sides were made up of apartment buildings, four storeys high with steel balconies bolted on to the outside. At the end of the garden, a wooded area separated the complex from the dunes and the beach. The final side was occupied by a low-slung building with a corrugated roof, almost entirely hidden by bushes, young trees and ivy climbing its crumbling walls. This was not a fancy place. The apartments seemed to be very much mid-range, perhaps owned by Berliners and Hamburgers who used a letting agency to rent them out when they were not using them.

On a late winter's afternoon there were a few lights burning in the windows looking down on the garden, but otherwise the complex was empty. Most of the parking spaces by the main gate were unoccupied. There were no tracks through the snow covering the garden path down to the woods.

Standing there, in the half-light of the afternoon, it was hard to imagine this as a socialist holiday camp. Apart from the strange, half-hidden building on the other side of the garden, it looked for all the world like a reasonably modern apartment complex, built in the past couple of decades. One which you could find not only on the Baltic coast of reunified Germany, but in a resort on either side of the English Channel, on the edge of a new development in Spain or elsewhere on the Mediterranean. But as we made first tracks through the snow, Fritz pointed out the clues that hinted to what had been here before. The apartments had been topped with new red-slate roofs and clad with balconies, but look closely and they were the same concrete-slab blocks as could be found in the estate across the street. These had been the dormitories for the kids and – outside of school holidays – where athletes had roomed when using the facility for training camps. It was in one of these buildings that Katrin would have slept, in a dorm with a number of other girls.

Between the two apartment buildings was the former

sanitation block, for showers and toilets, which now housed communal utility rooms and places to store bicycles. And the crumbling building across the garden, covered in ivy, was the former cafeteria, now abandoned to the elements with broken windows and loose guttering that hung down to mingle with the tangle of bushes at the base of the slowly rotting walls.

In the garden, Fritz pointed at a ship's mast and lookout point that was standing on the edge of a playground by the trees.

That was there then, but the rest of it ... the rest of this, it all used to be clear.

With a sweep of his arm he encompassed the whole of the garden. What was now a collection of winding paths and flower beds, with an ornamental pond and a stream crossed by a small wooden bridge, had been the roll-call square. From the ship's mast flew the flag of the GDR or the navy and, at the most important moments of her three weeks each summer, Katrin would have stood here, listening for her name on arrival or for the final official farewell before it was time to go home. I wondered aloud how many of the residents or visitors to these apartments even knew of the history of this place, how there came to be a ship's mast standing in their shared garden, to be clambered upon by kids today as it had been then, imagining adventure on the high seas. Fritz shrugged and moved off, towards the corner of the garden, looking for a path between the trees.

Over here, he said, pulling aside a bramble bush not far from the wall of the old cafeteria.

I followed him and we were swallowed by the canopy. The weak light was weaker still beneath the trees, and what made it through reflected on the snow that was at our feet and clinging to the branches all around us to create an unreal, dreamlike space. We stopped, startled by a couple of deer who jumped as quickly from the path and into the undergrowth as they had landed in front of us. We gave them a head start and then pushed on, searching for more traces of the past life of this place.

Somewhere in there, Fritz pointed in the direction that the deer had gone, but which was too overgrown for us to follow, *there was an open-air theatre. For plays and performances the children used to put on. But I can't work out how to reach it. Maybe the path has overgrown. Maybe …* He looked around. *Maybe I'm mistaken. I don't think so …*

We passed a collapsed rabbit hutch: a pile of splintered wood and twisted chicken wire. We reached a locked fence, through which we could see the beach and the Baltic beyond. Next to it was another wooden structure, larger than the rabbit hutch, that had collapsed in on itself and which was slowly returning to the earth, vandalised and half-swallowed by weeds and bushes.

That was the lifeguard post. We used to sit and monitor the beach. Make sure no one was getting into any trouble.

We stood for a while at the fence, Fritz once more looking out across those familiar sands in what was now another country. Another Baltic view. Another locked gate. Another collection of memories. As we gazed out to sea I saw the *Cap Arcona* floating on the still-cold spring waters. I saw Peter Döbler making steady progress with his breaststroke, only his head visible above the waves. Fritz told me stories of his own: of supervising the kids and the sports days of the naval base; of the training camps for the elite cyclists of the GDR; of the time he was put in charge of the music at the end of camp disco and got himself into trouble.

What did you play?

'99 Luftballons', he replied with a laugh.

Nena's anti-war classic. The kids danced, but one of the functionaries was less than impressed at the mix of Western music and impressionable minds. The fact that the song had been released on the GDR's own Amiga record label, and that it had been bought in a normal East Berlin record shop, did not appear to be a legitimate argument in its favour.

Fritz's memories of the camp were happy ones. As we turned to walk back through the woods, across the garden and through the gate, down the lane and back into town, I wondered how many people there were, all adults now, who had memories of this place and the summers spent here. Many hundreds. Thousands probably. I wondered how many of them remembered the path through the woods and the rabbit hutch, the roll-call square and the communal showers. Lights out in the dormitories and the sound of Nena and her balloons, crackling out from the speakers in the camp cafeteria.

*

I don't remember how old I was, the first time I went, Katrin said, as we sat in our kitchen in Berlin. It was a few days after my return from Kühlungsborn, driven back from the coast in Fritz's Mercedes through the cold and icy flatlands of northern Germany.

I guess I must have been about six. Maybe seven. And I don't remember the journey from Stralsund at all, although I must have sat with my sister as I did not know anyone else who was going. So my first real memory was probably standing out on the square in front of the accommodation blocks, waiting for our names to be called out by the camp director. They put us into groups of ten, each accompanied by an adult who was the group leader. They were all students, so were probably only nineteen or twenty, but they seemed old to us. My group leader that first year was called Ute. I remember her name very clearly although I cannot tell you which other children were in my group. A few years ago I found the group photographs from every year we went to camp, four in total, and of all the children on those photographs I could only name one. And that was because she became a sort of pen pal for two or three letters after we returned home at the end of the summer. But that fizzled out. And although we were all navy kids, it felt like there were different kids every year, so the friendships only ever lasted for three weeks and that was it.

But anyway, that first day. I can see the moment very clearly. My name was called and I walked over to stand by Ute and then I waited patiently to hear my sister's name follow because it hadn't – it did not – occur to me that there was any possibility that we would not be in the same group. And then it dawned on me, very slowly, that Ute wanted to lead us away and the camp director had moved on to another group, and Bine was not with me and I was expected to go off with this woman and these children I did not know into this dorm room all on my own. I must have looked sad, because Ute told me not to worry, but I burst into tears anyway.

Ute kneeled down and told me that at the camp there was a rule. Everyone has to give everything a try. But if after three days I still could not stand to be without my sister, then I could move into her dorm and be with her. I think about an hour later I had made friends with my roommates and then that was it. I didn't care about being on my own any more.

When I think about the camp now, what I remember is simply playing in the grounds with the other kids. There were of course official, planned activities. Perhaps one or two a day. We would visit a navy boat or walk into town. Once or twice during the three weeks of camp we would have a day trip in the bus. But in general, what I remember was that it was pretty free and relaxed. Of course, we had certain jobs to do – washing up, cleaning and things like that – and once a week there would be a flag ceremony. The jobs were an important part of it for me actually, the feeling of independence that the camp gave me. Up to that point I had always felt like I was in Bine's shadow, as she was less than a year older than me. Up to then I was always 'Bine's sister'. The camp gave me confidence.

We would get letters from home. I have very vivid memories of these moments, of the times the post arrived. If there was a parcel you could hope there were sweets inside. Chocolate, or something similar. We would save them up for special snack parties, after lights out and when the group leader had already told us to go to sleep. One time I received a parcel from my grandparents. It had chocolate in it. Bine wanted me to share, but I refused. Even at that age I was sure that there was no way our grandparents would have sent me a parcel and not Bine. She would get her own chocolate, so she had no need to have any of mine. That was my thinking. But her parcel must have got lost in the post, and she never got any chocolate. We told this story about twenty years later to our grandmother, who was of course mortified … a few days later, Bine got a parcel through the post.

But yes … confidence. That is what I got most from those camps by the sea. There was a special ceremony each year, a kind of 'seaman's baptism' in which Neptune would emerge from the water and choose one child – already agreed by the group leaders – from each group to be thrown into the sea. They would come back with a new name and would be paraded through the camp and into town to the bandstand. For the first couple of years I hadn't worked out that they would only pick kids who they knew would want to do it, and I was terribly afraid that I would get chosen even though I later realised there was no chance it could happen. By the third year I was sure I wanted to do it. I don't remember her name, but I dropped hints to the group leader from almost the first day that I quite fancied being picked and it worked. I was chosen by Neptune, tossed in the water. I came out as Crooked Sea Needle and got my parade and a certificate presented to me at the bandstand.

*Look, I have the picture. That's my group. One of my certificates.
It's funny to look at, with all those symbols of a country that no
longer exists, even though you were just there, at the camp ...*

Katrin paused, looked out of the window and into the
darkness of the courtyard that falls away beyond our fifth-
floor balcony.

We should go back there again one day.

VI

Half an Island (Fischland-Darß-Zingst)

The Bodden – Svantevit and the Professor – A bungalow by the sea (and what it contains) – Zeesboote and the captains of the inland sea – Paul-Müller-Kaempff and the artists of the shore – Ahrenshoop to Born – Dead men of the village – A view to the city

From Kühlungsborn I headed to Rostock and then on by train to Ribnitz-Dammgarten, a sorry-looking town on the line between Rostock and Stralsund. Ribnitz-Dammgarten stands on the banks of a lagoon known as the Bodden, an expanse of brackish water that separates the mainland from the Fischland-Darß-Zingst peninsula, itself an unwieldy name that speaks to a long and fractured history. All three were once islands, divided from the mainland by channels that linked the Bodden with the Baltic. The last to join was Zingst, after a storm in 1872 that filled in the narrow gap to complete the peninsula.

The lagoons of Mecklenburg-Vorpommern – the many Boddens that stand between spits of land, islands and half-islands – are a fundamental part of the Baltic landscape. The tourists may head for the long stretches of beach between Travemünde and the Polish border, but for thousands of years the focus of life has been the sheltered waterways, teeming with fish. The Bodden has a hold over the local imagination in a way that the open waters of the sea do not, and there is a certain poetic and melancholy appeal to the reeded banks that hide shy birds from all but the most patient of watchers: in the inlets and coves and sandbanks; in the fields of sheep and cows that run down to the water; and in the thatched villages and their small harbours that face not the Baltic but the Bodden. As I caught the bus from Ribnitz-Dammgarten it followed the single road that led on to the peninsula from the west. The Bodden approached and retreated when viewed through the right-hand side windows of the bus, across ploughed fields and wide expanses of marshland through which drainage channels had been cut in dead straight, unnatural lines.

Out to my left was the Baltic, but as we made slow progress via villages and off-season campgrounds there was no sign of it, hidden as it was behind a high dyke and the dunes. Fischland-Darß was formed at the end of the Ice Age and the wind and waves have been shaping it ever since, eating into the sandy cliffs to cause erosion in some places – up to 60cm a year – and deposition in others, to form new landscapes where once there was only water. The dykes are a semi-successful attempt to control the process, to fix the peninsula where possible in what was surely, ultimately, a losing battle. Just before the town of Wustrow we reached the narrowest point of the peninsula, the waters of the Bodden lapping close to the road that ran in the shadow of the dyke; the beaches and the sea just a few metres away on the other side. Wustrow was the end of Fischland. Just beyond the town limits was the border with the Darß. I was nearing the end of my journey.

Outside, the fields and verges were dulled, a combination of browns and greys that were waiting for the first colours of spring and the brightness of early summer. We normally come to the peninsula in May or June, to stay in our friend's dacha, a cabin that stands between poplar trees on the border between Fischland and Darß and which has been in the family since the days of the GDR. The group of friends have been coming since their schooldays and, as partners join and kids arrive, the group grows ever larger. The bungalow doesn't get any bigger, but still we come to welcome in the summer.

As I looked out of the bus window I tried to conjure the vivid Baltic colours of those visits. The light green of the young wheat fields, the bright yellow of the rape. The blue of the sky and the white clouds racing across it. The red and the blue paint slapped on to walls beneath the thatched roofs of the old fishermen's houses that are now, for the most part, holiday cottages. The houses were still there as the bus entered Wustrow, but the colours too had been subdued by the greyest of late winter skies.

I climbed down from the bus and walked through the town, seemingly alone. During the three May bank holiday weekends the season will start. The first cyclists will arrive at Ribnitz-Dammgarten and begin to ride the paved path along the top of the dyke, unnecessary maps strapped to their handlebars. Queues will form at the ice cream stalls and the stands where they sell fish rolls and Rostocker beers, and every guest house and holiday rental will have a sign saying *BELEGT*. No room at the inn, and there hasn't been since our regulars booked the week after they left a year ago. At the souvenir stands kids will hassle their parents for kites and plastic footballs, both soon to be lost to a gust of Baltic wind, and their parents will wonder if those they have left back home will be happy with an ashtray, a beer glass or a snow globe, all emblazoned with the words *FISCHLAND-DARSS-ZINGST*. Beside the counter are piles of tea towels and yet more cycling maps. Postcards and tankards. In a factory in Bangladesh they are sorted by destination. Fischland and Darß. Cornwall and Brittany. Gotland and Bornholm. Don't forget the captain's hats.

Do you remember when …?

Of course I do. We go there every year.

I followed Wustrow's main road down from the bus stop towards the pier, past the imaginary crowds of later in the year and the line of bank holiday motorbikes. Where the pier will be lined in summer with people there was only a line of gulls standing on the wooden handrail, joined by a solitary cormorant about halfway down. I almost had Wustrow pier to myself, but there was someone else already sitting there, on a bench by the statue of Svantevit. He looked like a teacher (retired) or a professor (Emeritus) and was scribbling notes or drawing in a little book. I walked out along the pier to the very end, to feel the breeze and marvel once more at the absence of salt in the air, and when I returned he was still there. He did not acknowledge my presence, but continued to write or draw, his focus on his book or the concrete statue in front of him. I sat down on the opposite bench and looked out to sea. I had a long walk planned, from Wustrow to Ahrenshoop and then on to Born, but for now I was happy to sit a while and watch the surf.

*

Svantevit. That's what it said at the base of the statue. Did the Professor known that already when he flipped his notebook open? Almost certainly. In Wustrow they called it *Swantewit* and had even named a restaurant for it, for that four-headed Slavic god that had been worshipped here back when Wustrow was a Slavic settlement on what was then still an island. That was where the name of the town came from. Wustrow – *The Town on the Island.* For much of the Middle Ages the majority of the population along this stretch of the

Baltic coast was Slavic, and it was their gods who held sway. Things change, of course. The tallest building on Fischland is Wustrow's parish church. And Fischland was now part of a peninsula. A *Halbinsel*. Half an island.

Svantevit was a deity of war and vengeance worshipped across the Slavic lands from the Baltic to the Balkans. His temple was at Kap Arkona on the island of Rügen, maintained by the Rani tribe who held sway along the coastline between the island and Fischland from the ninth to the thirteenth centuries. Across the water from Wustrow, Svantevit would ride out from his temple on a white horse, and any great undertaking required a sacrifice in front of his statue and his horn filled with fresh mead. In the twelfth century, the sacrifices proved insufficient, as the Rani were defeated by the Danes and Christianity was forced upon the tribe. Monasteries and churches were built and wooden temples and statues were destroyed. Over the following centuries the settlement of Danes and Germanic peoples along the Baltic shore led to the gradual assimilation of the Slavic population. Germanisation left little trace of the Rani along the coast, except for place names and a handful of legends that continued to be passed down by families living along the shore.

As I sat in front of Svantevit a kindergarten class arrived, all barely able to walk in their winter suits as their teachers led them up the ramp towards the pier. As soon as they saw the statue they began to climb upon it, and the Professor closed his notebook with a flourish. One of the teachers sat down next to him on the bench but they exchanged no words. The scene, previously soundtracked by only the waves and the gulls, was now filled with the noise of excited and excitable children. I didn't mind. It was evidence that this was still a place where people lived, where they worked and brought up their kids. A place not completely surrendered to the tourists. As the kids played, the Professor got up, brushed some imaginary crumbs from his trousers, and wheeled his bike out from behind the bench where it had been leaning against the fence. With a nod in the direction of the teacher, who now sat alone in front of the statue, he climbed on and rode off, away down the dyke in the direction of the tall line of poplar trees and the colony of dachas where my friend has her cabin.

It was there, I felt, he would have got his nickname, not because of his job but because of how he looked; to the children who came to the colony with their parents or to visit grandparents, who would see this man with his beard, this man who gave off an aura of calm strictness and who was there on the lane or in his garden throughout their long summer holidays by the sea. An ever-present. A contract for the lease signed in the GDR. Fifty years or death, whichever came first. Both must have seemed a long time away. Both were getting closer now, but the bungalow was still standing. If he signed the lease almost half a century ago he would be a child of the war, perhaps even sent off to fight as a callow teenager, in those last desperate years when it was known all was lost and the sense of waste and futility was all the greater. But what was the option? He would be one of that generation who had gone off to fight an unjust war. Where was the heroism in that? If someone asks for stories it is better to change the subject.

You couldn't understand it. Even if I was smart enough to tell it.

A handful of survivors from a class of twenty-five, all sent east to fight at the age of seventeen. Guilt at the relief you felt when you were not one of them. Guilt at the knowledge, at the boasts heard but never quite believed, boasts of those who had chosen other units with other ... responsibilities. Years fighting. Longer years in Soviet prisoner-of-war camps. Returned to a country defeated and transformed. Still barely twenty years old. A generation traumatised and without even victory or a sense of being on the right side to make it all feel worthwhile. A new flag on the flagpole. A new orthodoxy. A new appeal to solidarity. No wonder a bungalow in the woods seemed like a good idea. A bolthole by the sea. A small wooden bungalow in the shadow of the poplar trees. A place to drink beer, protected from the outside world by a tall, bushy hedge. Fifty years or death. They had been good odds at the time. Especially compared to those who had been left behind.

*

I followed the Professor down the dyke, along the cliff-top path above the beach to my left with a dune landscape, undulating and grassy, stretching out to my right. We would be coming here again in spring but this time we would not be staying at our friend's dacha. The old GDR contract her grandfather had signed before he built the cabin on the land had run out. Notice had been served. He had built the cabin over the course of one summer in the 1960s, a simple construction of thin walls and single-glazed windows that meant it was only inhabitable during the warmer months of the year. Inside, a central living room led to a tiny bathroom, small kitchen and two bedrooms. Over decades the cabin collected many things. They were piled in cupboards, in the shed at the bottom of the garden, and in the memories of all those people, family and friends, who spent time at this small patch of land. At some point in the 1990s the land was transferred into private hands and it was soon clear that, for those on old GDR contracts, there would be no chance of an extension unless people were willing to pay the new market rates. Across the colony old bungalows were torn down and replaced by new, flat-pack Scandinavian-inspired structures that could be used – and more importantly rented out – all year round.

And so the time had come. Time to clear out the cabin and the shed, the decades of accumulated *stuff* that had migrated north from Berlin. Plates, blankets, cups and bed sheets. Dinner sets and three-piece suites. Blankets and badminton racquets, egg cups and a cuckoo clock. There were guidebooks and maps, some still priced in Deutschmarks and yet others that had been printed in the GDR. There were artefacts of family holidays: the mosquito spray and sun cream; buckets and spades and plastic sunglasses; board games missing pieces and dice and packs of cards. There were books that no one could remember bringing and that straw hat that many, caught out by unseasonable weather, had reached out to wear and was now immortalised in countless family photographs. It would be time to clear all that out and the pile of blankets in the corner, there for cold evenings outside or when the rain drummed down on the corrugated iron roof.

It would be time to take down the pictures and the

postcards and the laminated information that tells guests how to use the temperamental toilet. The light switch in the bathroom that, if pressed at the wrong moment, turned on the lights in the neighbouring bedroom, would now never be fixed. And once everything had been salvaged that was still wanted, and the rest loaded into a skip or taken by the carload to the local tip, the digger would arrive and remove the house itself. A summer's worth of work and half a century of memories dispatched in an afternoon. A new house built. And, fifty years from now, a new collection of mismatched bed sheets and dishes, guidebooks priced in euros (remember that?) and a new collection of board games, some of which will be missing their dice.

I walked through the colony but there was no sign of the Professor. My friend's bungalow stood empty, but otherwise unchanged. The gate was open, so I walked down the side of the house, to peer in through the window. It was gutted, save for a couple of final bin bags by the door and the outline on the walls where the pictures of the village and the beach once hung. The time had not yet come, not quite, but soon. On my next visit to the peninsula it would be gone, I was fairly sure.

I moved on, following the concrete slabs of the track to the main road and the footpath down past Lidl and back into

Wustrow. The town was still quiet, although the bakery on the corner by the church was open and a handful of customers sat at tables by the window with their coffee and cake, watching the occasional car pass by. I stopped for a coffee and picked up a regional newspaper. In the local section the newspaper trumpeted the fact that Fischland-Darß-Zingst had more millionaires per capita than anywhere else in Germany, most of them in Wustrow and neighbouring Ahrenshoop. Not bad for the poorest state in the country. I looked out of the window at the modest, empty town I had grown to know over the past decade of springtime visits. How was this even possible?

But the clues were there. In this bakery where I now sat. In the boutiques that lined the street down to the pier. In the new hotels that had opened in Ahrenshoop and the large houses behind the dunes and single-lane tracks down by the Bodden. In our friend's dacha colony where, one by one, the GDR-era bungalows were being replaced by something altogether more modern and upmarket. It was a process I had seen before, not least in the Berlin neighbourhood of Prenzlauer Berg. This formerly working-class district of nineteenth-century tenement blocks had been one of my first homes in Berlin, in the early 2000s, following two decades when it had been transformed from the home of East Berlin counterculture in the 1980s to an anarchic, artistic mix in the 1990s to, by the time I got there, a district of trendy cafes and organic supermarkets, art galleries and vegetarian kindergartens. The bars that had made its name and its popularity were forced out by high rents and noise complaints. A neighbourhood that was, until the fall of the Berlin Wall, still bomb-damaged from the Second World War and made up of buildings that were for the most part still coal-heated, became a neighbourhood with some of the highest real estate prices in the city.

It seemed as if this transformation I had witnessed in Berlin was now happening a few hundred kilometres to the north, and I was suddenly reminded of a conversation with someone who had once spent a lot of time in Wustrow and Ahrenshoop, but no longer.

Ahrenshoop? she said, when I told her where we were going for a May bank holiday weekend. *You know what we call Ahrenshoop? Prenzlauer-Berg-on-Sea.*

I finished my coffee and folded the newspaper over, leaving it for the next person to read. The skies were closing in and it was time to walk to Ahrenshoop.

*

I made my way down a narrow, cobbled street, down past yet more thatched houses towards the harbour. On the half island, the harbours of the towns and villages tend not to face the open water of the Baltic and are instead located on the muddy shore of the Bodden. The harbour was quiet at this time of year, although smoke was rising from behind the kiosk where the herring and mackerel hung from hooks as they were prepared, ready to be sold by the kilo or sliced and stuffed in bread rolls with a slice of lettuce. Beyond the smoke hut, reeds marked the edge of the Bodden, and beyond them dark, wooden boathouses stood on stilts above gentle breeze-blown waves. In the summer the quayside would be busy with people, strollers and cyclists, walking out to the end of the jetty for views across the water to the mainland and the colony of wind farms turning steadily on the horizon, waiting for a trip on one of the brown-sailed *Zeesboote* that were once the main fishing vessels of the region, but which are now almost exclusively used to ferry tourists out across the Bodden and along its shore. The *Zeesboote* were there now, sails tied to the masts, but no one was waiting for a trip.

The *Zeesboote* are named for the nets they used to drag behind them, collecting the fish of the inland sea, but they have not been used for commercial fishing since the 1980s. The captains still look the part though, making their catch on shore as they hustle for business in competition with the smokehouses and beer gardens that surround the harbours of the peninsula. Once out on the water, the brown sails filled with whatever wind is blowing on the given day, and as the boats round the headland, the captains will play their role, recounting stories and legends of events on the water, of the biggest storms and the biggest catches, and tales of sea monsters lurking in the shallow depths. From a small box beneath the tiller they will produce a bottle of rum, supposedly distilled in the shed at the bottom of the captain's garden and the perfect medicine against the cold sea breeze blowing. Whether the rum was actually distilled in a garden shed in Ahrenshoop, Wustrow or Born, or whether Lidl own-brand has been funnelled from one bottle to the next, is a debatable point, but the captain's promise is the captain's promise, and no one on board will be willing to challenge it.

The harbour at Wustrow is in an inlet of the Bodden at one of the narrowest points of the peninsula, and for my walk to Ahrenshoop I had two options – the dyke path I had been on earlier that led past the bungalow colony, or a longer route that followed not the straight line of the cliff-top path, where the sand martins buzz in and out of holes in the sandy walls, but following the contours of the Bodden shoreline. Here, in springtime, the swallows and swifts dart and dive above the fields, picking off insects that hover above the young wheat or rapeseed flowers waving in the breeze. But now the fields were barren; ploughed and waiting. A solitary birdwatcher stood out on the headland, searching for passing colonies of geese or cranes. Further along the shoreline path two horses trotted, ridden gracefully by riders in thick jackets and helmets. From where I stood it was impossible to tell if they were male or female. I walked on down the path after them.

The path, running at just above sea level, felt exposed; the reeds and the lagoon on one side, marshy fields drained by deep channels and ditches on the other. It was one of those places that give the impression they could be reclaimed by the water with ease, through another of those big storms that turned islands into peninsulas and created legends for the *Zeesboote* captains. Subconsciously I began to walk a little quicker, increasing my pace and my stride length, estimating the distance to the houses of Wustrow that stood on a rise across the marshy fields, wondering how quickly I could cover the ground. And then, beyond a plantation of tall pines and a collection of farm buildings, the sandy track gave way to tarmac and I had reached the first of the small settlements that linked Wustrow and Ahrenshoop, right where the old border between Mecklenburg and Pomerania once stood, the dividing line between Fischland and the Darß.

As with elsewhere on the half island, and indeed all along the Baltic shore, these houses that had once been home to the fishermen and farmers who eked out a living from the sea and the land were now, in the main, holiday homes or the permanent residences of those who had retired to the coast. A handful of artists had also set up shop, their homes doubling as studio and gallery spaces, with hand-painted invitations on weather-beaten boards to come inside and inspect the paintings, the pottery or the sculptures. There was not much passing trade on this day, and on previous walks I had also seen honey, fresh eggs and jam laid out along the path. Help yourself and leave money in the tin. But not today. The wind blew stronger, whistling through the reeds that were so tall by now that even from my vantage point on the raised dyke path that protected the cottages from the lagoon, I could not see the icy grey waters of the Bodden. Sometimes a path had been forced through the reeds, leading down to a jetty or landing stage, but these were all cordoned off with a rope or a chain-link fence, signs stating baldly that this was *PRIVAT* land hammered into the marshy ground.

Soon I had reached another harbour. More *Zeesboote*. Another smokehouse. Another beer garden. As with Wustrow, it was deserted, save for a couple of mallards waddling across the grass in the direction of a play area, the swings rocking gently in the breeze. I followed the path up towards the main road, where the village of Ahrenshoop was strung out and stretched along its length.

*

That first glimpse of Ahrenshoop ... Even at the end of his life, eighty years old and living alone on the Motzstraße in Berlin – the city at war – Paul Müller-Kaempff could remember the day in 1889 when he discovered the village. He was hiking the coast with his friend, the fellow artist Oskar Frenzel, and in those days Ahrenshoop was little more than a single row of thatched cottages laid out along the road that led between Wustrow and Born, sheltered from the sea winds by the dunes and with a narrow creek leading down to the Bodden that allowed the fishermen to pull their boats inland, to relative shelter, regardless of the weather conditions. By this point tourism had begun its transformation of the Baltic coast as the railways shuttled the city dwellers north to the resorts springing up along the shore, but it hadn't yet reached the Darß. For Paul Müller-Kaempff, it was exactly what he had been looking for.

The epiphany had come to him on a visit to Lake Garda.

Or better yet, it had been on his return to Berlin from Italy, where he could unfavourably compare and contrast the noise and the smoke and the bustle of life in the industrial city with the peace and clean mountain air he had left behind. He allowed himself to be persuaded that what he needed was a retreat, a place of escape that would give him the space and inspiration he needed to do his work. As he stood on the cliff top between Wustrow and Ahrenshoop, looking down on the thatched roofs of the village houses, he was sure that he had found it.

Many years later, in the aftermath of the first war, as hyperinflation wiped out his savings and added to the gut-wrenching feeling that he had nothing to show for a long and distinguished career, he knew that it had not only been a mistake to turn his back on Ahrenshoop once he had found it – selling the property that he had bought there – but that the years around the turn of the century that he had spent moving between the Baltic coast and Berlin had been among his most happy and productive ones. In the beginning he had spent his summers in the village, lodging with Frau Schumacher or at the Pension Charlottenhof. Not long after, others began to follow him north. He thought of them all, meeting for drinks at the Hotel Bogislaw. Hans and Otto. Friedrich and Fritz. They ran up such a tab in the smoky back room that their only way out of the debt was for Müller-Kaempff and Friedrich Wachenshausen to paint the murals in the ballroom, of some of their favourite local scenery.

A year after that, in 1892, Müller-Kaempff moved to Ahrenshoop permanently, building a house in the grounds of Frau Schumacher's residence. Now they all began to come. He ticked them off, one by one, in his mind. Anna. Elisabeth. Fritz. Hugo. Carl Friedrich. Heinrich. The anonymous fishing village of that most narrow of Baltic peninsulas, sandwiched between the Bodden and the sea, had become the most famous artists' colony in the German-speaking lands. Life wasn't perfect. Even when his popularity was at its greatest, Paul Müller-Kaempff could not live from his paintings alone. And that was before the tidal wave of expressionism washed across the cultural scene and left him stranded on his Baltic sandbank, out of time and out of fashion. So he built a painting school in Ahrenshoop, with lodging rooms in which artists and would-be artists could sleep. He made enough money to become that thing that no self-respecting artist should ever aspire to: a respected member of the community, elected to the local council in 1895. And the school delivered him something else. A bonus. The former student called Else who would become his wife.

So what changed? Was it simply fashion? The rise of

expressionism? A matter of taste? No. It was war of course. The storm clouds that gathered throughout that fateful year of 1913 broke first in Sarajevo, and then unleashed a downpour that engulfed an entire continent. Up to that point things had been moving ever forward. New exhibition spaces in Ahrenshoop. Invitations from across the country and beyond. There were visits from royalty, awards and the occasional big sale of his work. But the war changed everything. After the trenches, after the defeat; after the millions of miserable, pointless deaths in the mud-churned no man's land there was little call for his soft, naturalistic landscape paintings any more. The Germany that emerged from those trenches was traumatised and damaged, in a way that would become ever more apparent as the Weimar Republic stumbled towards its eventual collapse and the catastrophe that was to follow.

For Paul Müller-Kaempff it meant that his work no longer resonated. He found no way to bridge the gap between his instincts and the popular mood of this changed society. One by one the old guard abandoned Ahrenshoop, even before the war had ended. In 1919, Müller-Kaempff sold his school to a pair of hairdressers. They maintained the lodging rooms but turned the old teaching space into a salon. Three years later and Müller-Kaempff also sold his house. He no longer had property, just a pile of money sitting in the bank. It would not be long before the money was worthless, as zeros were added to exchange rates by the hour and people paid their rent in cash, delivered in wheelbarrows.

There were still some years to go, scraping by with the sale of the odd painting, but the market for his work had evaporated. In Berlin he witnessed the turmoil of the Weimar years, watched the rise of the Nazis, the fracturing of society and the ever-increasing strength of the Brownshirts. It all seemed a long way from his half island in the north. If only they had kept the house, between the green fields and the yellow sands, perhaps things might have been different ...

Else struggled more than he did, and she turned, for solace, to Christian Science. In 1940, with the second war well underway and Germany stepping triumphantly over neighbouring lands, she fell sick. She refused medical treatment, instead preferring to leave her healing (or not) to divine intervention. None came, of course. Outside war was raging and Germany was winning, but none of it mattered to Paul Müller-Kaempff any more. On 5 December 1941, the Red Army of the Soviet Union counter-attacked against the German troops, five months into Hitler's Operation Barbarossa. The eastern front had opened up and, although none knew it yet, the tide had turned. On the day the counter-attack began, the day that momentum in the war shifted, Paul Müller-Kaempff – founder of the Ahrenshoop artists' colony – died in his apartment in Berlin.

*

Ghosts stalk the Baltic shore. Some are forgotten, left to die alone in a dingy Berlin apartment building – but then are eventually, belatedly remembered. Paul Müller-Kaempff has a street named for him, close to the beach, and his legacy is visible throughout Ahrenshoop. The former painting school that became a hair salon once again welcomes artists on residencies from across the Baltic region, and the village's status as one of the original artists' colonies continues to attract numerous visitors, who come to explore the studios, galleries, museums and other exhibition spaces.

Even after the original colony died away during the First World War, the town continued to attract artists throughout the Weimar Republic, the Nazi era and beyond. Perhaps because of its isolated location on a narrow spit of land on the very edge of the country, the thing that attracted Paul Müller-Kaempff from the beginning, it would become a refuge for those artists who – for one reason or another –

had fallen foul of the regime. One such internal exile was Gerhard Marcks, who moved north in 1933 after the Nazis had dismissed him from his post as the director of a school of applied arts near Halle. Four years later, and Marcks's work would be included in the infamous exhibition created by the Nazis of 'degenerate art'. Being included in this exhibition could have caused Marcks to fear for his liberty and even his life, but if it did, he did not allow it to move him and he chose to keep his exile to the edge of Germany, waiting out the remainder of the Third Reich and the entirety of the Second World War on the Baltic coast.

After, during the German Democratic Republic, an official artists' retreat was created by the authorities, to be used by those whose work found favour with the regime. But despite this stamp of approval, Ahrenshoop remained popular with those writers and artists who were searching for the isolation they needed to allow them to work and think beyond the orthodoxy of the mainstream socialist society. As for Thomas Mann in Travemünde, or those GDR citizens who retreated to their thin-walled bungalows behind thick hedges and beneath the poplar trees, Ahrenshoop became a place to escape the strictures of everyday life. As so often, the Baltic coast became a place of escape.

Prenzlauer-Berg-on-Sea.

I thought of this again as I walked up from the harbour to the village stretched out along the main road. As in Wustrow, there was the usual collection of thatched houses, complemented by more modern hotels, boutiques and so-called 'wellness' spa clinics. More so than in Wustrow, I could imagine the millionaires I had read about making themselves at home. A lot of places were shut for the winter season, but just off the main road I stepped into the lobby of a five-star hotel, all wicker chairs and pastel walls decorated with tasteful, insipid landscape paintings. A place where you can dress down as long as it involves deck shoes and a jumper slung across your shoulders. Socks optional. I pretended to be interested in the breakfast buffet but it cost as much as my train ticket back to Berlin and so I beat a retreat, escaping on to the chilly street outside with the tang of freshly squeezed orange and grapefruit still tickling my nostrils.

Just down the road I came across the Bunte Stube, a bookshop built in 1929 by the Bauhaus architect Walter Butzek. Inside I found the typical seaside collection of local history, crime novels set in the region, commercial fiction and some kids' books. But it was the building itself that was the draw, speaking once more to the origins of Ahrenshoop as a place for creative minds and built at the moment the

Nazis were building their support, soon to take power. The Bauhaus's days were numbered, and the artists, architects, designers and thinkers behind the movement would be scattered. Some to exile, some to worse. I crossed the street and made my way through a collection of houses down to the fields and a path that led me back to the Bodden, and more private property signs warning me off, which, added to the price of the breakfast buffet, left me feeling that Ahrenshoop was not really the place for me. I pressed on, following the lagoon shore towards the village of Born.

*

The peninsula had thickened, the sea retreating as the land made space to accommodate the dense and dark primeval Darßerwald forest. A bird of prey hovered above a ploughed field. The wind had picked up, blowing white-topped waves that skidded across the surface of the Bodden. The wind turbines on the horizon rotated with increasing urgency. With the forest getting closer and the distance to the beach and the Baltic ever greater, the lagoon was starting to dominate the landscape and I began to understand how, before the arrival of the tourists, it was the Bodden that had commanded the attention and captured the imagination.

The lagoon was a deep shade of grey, mirroring the sky. There was nothing out on the water. The bird of prey had disappeared. I was conscious of being alone in this scene, the only movement other than my footsteps generated by the wind. Trees, windmills and waves. The coffee from earlier had worked its way through me but there was nowhere to hide to take a piss and, despite my solitude beneath these big grey skies, I felt exposed. I quickened my step again as a light rain began to fall. No shelter here. No hiding place. At sea level, I was experiencing something I had only previously felt on moorland tops or windswept mountainsides.

Born came, then, as both a relief and a surprise. I had read that the village, standing on the Bodden and a good way from the sea, had managed the transformation from fishing and farming village to holiday destination better than most, and that its collection of thatched red-brick houses maintained a certain atmosphere, but the first thing I came to after skirting a wooded and empty campground was a modern housing estate and a huge agro-industrial complex behind a high wire fence. Fears that the enormous sheds housed battery hens and unhappy pigs were unfounded, as a sign at the entrance told me that the complex belonged to one of Germany's largest and most successful organic farming companies, the products of which could be bought from a farm shop on the other side of the car park, next to a cafe that served fair trade coffee.

This place symbolised yet another contradiction of the coast. Mecklenburg-Vorpommern is at once the largest producer of organic meat in Germany and its smallest consumer. The reasons are simple and stark. In a state which, in 2015, had an unemployment rate of 14% – almost double the national average – and which is one of the poorest of the sixteen *Bundesländer* that make up the Federal Republic of Germany, organic meat is quite simply too expensive. The economic crisis that engulfed the region following the rationalisations of state industries that came with the fall of the Berlin Wall, reunification and liberal-democratic capitalism, has continued in parts of Mecklenburg-Vorpommern ever since. Such are the dire economic prospects, especially for young people in many parts of the state, some 300,000 people have left Mecklenburg-Vorpommern in the quarter of a century since reunification. This is about 15% of the total population. If you only ever visit the coast, or the picturesque towns of the lake district in the south, it would be hard to imagine. There, tourism has brought money and investment, but much of the interior of Mecklenburg-Vorpommern has still not recovered from the upheaval of the 1990s. And even on the coast, things have not necessarily changed for the better. In 1990 there were forty commercial fishermen in the town of Zingst. By 2015 there were only three. The fish rolls in Wustrow harbour? In Kühlungsborn? In Heiligendamm? Almost certainly the produce of seas far beyond the Baltic, caught and frozen and then shipped to Germany.

Leaving the organic superfarm behind, I made my way into the older section of the village. The Darßerwald was encroaching now, the trees spreading through the gardens like sand dunes swallowing an abandoned desert settlement. The forest was the source of another small yet important segment of local industry – hunting – and the game from the dark, primeval woods did in fact find its way on to the tables of the region, for those who could afford it. The tracks through the forest and the spoils it contains have long captured the imagination of hunters and other explorers, including questionable characters such as Hermann Göring, who used his position as the Supreme Master of the Hunt in Nazi Germany to declare much of the Darßerwald off-limits to the locals, claiming the deer and the wild boar that foraged beneath the trees for his cronies and himself.

As I walked through Born, I felt something that was missing in both Wustrow and Ahrenshoop: namely, the twentieth century. In the other two places you are given the feeling that progress tripped neatly from the thatched cottages that attracted Paul Müller-Kaempff, to the modern health spas and hotels that have sprung up since reunification. In Born, however, the last century felt much more apparent. The cobblestoned street was interwar in origin. The street lights distinctly East German. At the heart of the village, among cottages offering rooms to rent, a memorial remembered the men lost in the battles of the First World War. Forty men, but only a handful of names:

LANGE …
SCHULTZE …
JUNGE …

I wrote their names down in my notebook and reflected on stories of soldiers and of families torn asunder. Brothers, husbands, cousins and friends. There were too many names, too many of the same names, for such a small place. I walked on, past a local shop offering basic supplies and a kindergarten playground. Born was quiet, a little ramshackle in places. Weeds grew between the cobblestones and the concrete slabs of the pavement. But it was the first time on the peninsula that I felt I was walking through a real community, one which had maintained a contact with the past, where there were signs of everyday life. Yes, many of the buildings were holiday cottages or advertising rooms for rent, but there were also many local number plates on the cars parked in driveways, and the village noticeboard advertised events and services not specifically aimed at tourists. Perhaps it was an illusion, born out of the time of year I was walking through the village and a certain wish fulfilment after the parade of seaside resorts and their celebration of the transient and the temporary, but for the first time I felt I was walking through a place that was real.

Down by the water I looked at a map of the peninsula and marvelled at how far east it stretched. From Ribnitz-Dammgarten at the base of Fischland to almost touching the island of Rügen at the tip of Zingst. And there, at the bottom of the map, were the suburbs of Stralsund. It was in this old Hanseatic city that Katrin had spent much of the first decade of her life, before her return to Berlin. As I looked at the map a weak sun broke through the clouds, turning the Bodden a murky shade of racing green. The stories of the shore up till now had portrayed the Baltic as a place of escape; of retreat. But it was also a place where people lived. I looked at the neat grid of streets in the corner of the map, shaded grey to symbolise buildings. I knew what was there: the concrete-slab *Plattenbau* apartment blocks of the GDR, of Katrin's childhood. It was time to head for the city.

VII

Pigtails and Sunflowers (Stralsund & Rostock)

Sonnenhof, childhood memories and election posters – Hej, Pippi Långstrump – The Altstadt of Stralsund – MVGIDA march on Grünhufe – Never will it end – Rostock and the Sunflower House – We are young, we are strong … Rostock Lichtenhagen, August 1992 – Why the old East? – At the waterfront

We had come to Stralsund in search of childhood. We walked the narrow streets of the Altstadt – the old centre of the city – almost completely surrounded by water, as in its Hanseatic big brother Lübeck. There were some stories here – a theatre, a bakery, a museum – but this was not the Stralsund that Katrin grew up in through the 1980s. Not entirely. Parts of her Stralsund was here, among the red-brick buildings with their crow-stepped gables, but the rest of her city was elsewhere, out on the edge, where the streets meet the fields, where the concrete meets the soil.

We drove out and away, the old city skyline retreating through the back window of the car. The dual carriageway wound its way through an edgeland zone of open spaces around car showrooms, petrol stations and lock-up garages. The western edge of Stralsund is reminiscent of the suburbs of so many towns and cities in the former German Democratic Republic, a place of wide streets and neatly planted trees equidistant from the neat rows of street lamps. And rising above it all, looking in one direction to the city and in the other to the surrounding countryside, a collection of the boxy, concrete-slab housing blocks of the old East.

From the dual carriageway we turned off into a new town streetscape of roundabouts, windswept shopping plazas and neatly mown grass verges. The streets were laid out in a grid, each junction a crossroads. Paved pedestrian walkways linked the residential blocks with the schools and shopping halls built to make the estate self-contained and self-containing. But despite the planning, people always find a way of personalising even the most impersonal of spaces, and desire paths offered shortcuts as they criss-crossed the grasslands. We will not be told which way we should walk.

The car crawled along the street until we reached the edge of the estate at the edge of the city. A street named Sonnenhof. Yet another block, standing back from the pavement.

That's the one.

We got out of the car and stood looking up at the apartment block. It was indistinguishable from the thousands I had seen in the east of Berlin, in Leipzig or in Dresden. But Katrin pointed up to a row of windows and one particular apartment in particular. That's the one. That was their apartment.

We walked up to the front door and looked for any surnames, all those years after the family had moved to Berlin, that Katrin recognised. There were a couple, a few people who had lived through the changes of 1989-90 when the estate, the city and the country changed beyond recognition with reunification and all that it meant.

We were the first people to move in after they built the estate.

The shipyard in Stralsund, currently employing some 4,000 workers on the banks of the Strelasund – the straits between the mainland and the island of Rügen – employed at its GDR peak closer to 52,000 people. At the same time, the East German Navy had a major base in the city. With two thirds of Stralsund's housing stock destroyed in one single American air raid on 6 October 1944, which also claimed some 800 lives, one of the major challenges for the local authorities in the decades that followed was building apartments for people to live in. Altogether, between 1950 and 1987, around 17,000 new apartments were built in the city in new, planned estates on the western edge. One of the last developments was Grünhufe, on the Rostock road. The first buildings were erected in 1980 and over the following seven years it would become a district of some 2,300 dwellings. Katrin and her family moved to Sonnenhof as soon as the building was ready to be lived in. Family photographs depict a walk through an estate of brand-new buildings, wide-open spaces, and not much else.

We left the car and began to wander around Grünhufe. Some things, such as the shopping centre, were clearly products of the arrival of post-reunification capitalism to this corner of the city. But aside from the odd new building and the growth of the trees, there did not seem to be all that much difference from the photographs. Certainly the wind was continuing to blow, unimpeded, across the surrounding flatlands and fields and down the streets.

It was a walk through the small details of family memory. The washing lines that stood in full view of hundreds of living room windows, beneath which two sisters played. The slope that became a toboggan run during a snowy winter. The place where a brother broke his arm. The walk to school. The bus stop for the city. When I talk to Katrin about her childhood in Stralsund, about this estate and life in the GDR in general, she is rarely anything but positive.

I had the best of it. Primary school, the young pioneers. Summer camps and the youth newspaper. By the time I started to get old enough to understand the full situation, to understand the limitations of life in East Germany, well we were already in Berlin. The wall was down. But I was happy here ... it was a good childhood. No one can tell me otherwise.

A few years after that first visit we returned to Grünhufe, to show my parents where Katrin had grown up. It was another sunny day. The wind was once more blowing in along the grid of concrete slab streets. Sonnenhof was still there. The apartment building was still there. At least a couple of the names on the doorbells were still there. But something was different.

It was the run-up to a Federal election. Across Germany every lamppost had been commandeered by one political party or another. An alphabet soup of acronyms. SPD. CDU. FDP. MLPD. In Grünhufe three letters dominated: NPD. *Nationaldemokratische Partei Deutschlands*. The democracy in the party's name as much of a misnomer as the socialist in *Nationalsozialistiche*. In many parts of the country the right-wing NPD, who have been described as a neo-Nazi political party, find their posters defaced or removed almost as soon as they can hang them. In Grünhufe, it seemed, they were at the very least tolerated.

It is amazing what a few posters can do, what three letters can suggest about a place and the people that live there. It does not matter that Grünhufe would eventually vote overwhelmingly for parties other than the Nationalists. It was the confidence of the campaign on the estate, at a time when you could walk the entire city centre of Stralsund and not see another of their posters, that shaped our impression of the neighbourhood. Katrin was subdued. It was a violation of her old neighbourhood. Of her memories. Of her childhood. As we drove away, back to the dual carriageway and the road along which she once took the bus to the city centre, we talked about the posters, about what they said about the place she once called home.

It makes me sad, she said, as Grünhufe retreated through the back windscreen of the car.

*

The train arrives and departs Stralsund on the other side of the ponds which separate the old city from the various layers of 'new city' that developed first around the railway with the coming of industrialisation in the second half of the nineteenth century and then, later, further out with the new housing estates built during the GDR. Unlike Grünhufe, the walk from the station to the path that leads between the ponds to the old city moves through the Tribseer Vorstadt, a reasonably prosperous neighbourhood of Wilhelmine apartment blocks, within which it is easy to imagine high-ceilinged living rooms lined with bookshelves beneath ornate mouldings. Grand doorways house rows of doorbells as well as brass plates advertising the services of lawyers, accountants and physiotherapists. Whether true or not, the area feels solidly and stolidly middle-class, home to the Stralsund bourgeoisie.

On a clear day I walked back into town from the station, having dropped Katrin off for a train back to Berlin. We had rented an apartment in the heart of the Altstadt, a short walk to both the main square and the harbour. Leaving the Tribseer Vorstadt behind, I followed a narrow path with water on either side until I was swallowed once more by the narrow streets of the old city as it leads down to the harbour and the Strelasund with its view across to the island of Rügen. Like Lübeck, it is the harbour that has shaped Stralsund for centuries, through the Hanseatic League and the many and varied links with the outside world. Unlike Lübeck, however, Stralsund's history took a different turn following the decline of the League, after the devastation of the Thirty Years War and the Peace of Westphalia that followed. For almost two hundred years, Stralsund found itself under the control of the Swedish King.

Swedish rule on the southern shore of the Baltic did not begin auspiciously. The Thirty Years War had laid waste to whole regions of Europe, not least present-day Mecklenburg-Vorpommern, where it is estimated 40% of the population lost their lives, sometimes on the battlefield but more often due to the disease and famine that plagued the region following the cessation of formal hostilities; a time when property was also plundered by marauding gangs of decommissioned soldiers. At first Swedish rule brought some stability, but in many ways it made things worse as the need to quarter and feed the Swedish troops added to the desperate situation for many of the local people. During the eighteenth century Sweden's wars would also cost Stralsund some 4,000 residents, and within a century the population halved to about 10,000 residents. If Swedish rule did leave the city with an architectural legacy – baroque gabled houses, administrative buildings and the first factories of the young Industrial Revolution – the eighteenth century is now remembered as a time of smallpox and plague, of witch hunts and trials and of numerous sieges made all the worse by outbreaks of typhoid, thanks to the fact that much of the city's drinking water came from those ponds on the edge of the Altstadt.

In 1984, the Swedish Prime Minister Olof Palme came to Stralsund as part of a state visit to the GDR.

It is possible, he said, by way of apology or explanation for events a couple of hundred years before, *that this yearning for Europe has sometimes got out of hand and led us to overdo things … in that period Pomerania became more important for Sweden that Sweden for Pomerania …*

But nowadays it seems that Stralsund is fairly at ease with its Swedish history, as memories of plague and typhoid and witch hunts have retreated into folklore. As I had walked the streets of the town during the previous few days there had been plenty of blue and yellow flags on display. In any case, when you consider what was to follow the end of Swedish rule – Prussian militarism, the First World War, the weakness of the Weimar Republic, the rise of the Nazis, the devastation of the Second World War, Soviet occupation and the grey hibernation of the GDR – it is not surprising that more recent memories dominate. And if, in the 1980s, Sweden had come to be seen as the model of social democracy, of some kind of balance between the excesses of both capitalism and communism – the country of Olof Palme and *Pippi Longstocking* – then it is perhaps no wonder that connections between the city and the country on the opposite shore of the Baltic have been reinforced ever since Palme's visit in 1984. Two years after his trip to the GDR, the Swedish Prime Minister was murdered. In his memory, the square in front of Stralsund's theatre was renamed, and it remains Olof-Palme-Platz to this day.

Around that time, Katrin was spending one evening a week waiting for her older sister to complete special rehearsals in the theatre following their normal choir practice. In a neat coincidence with the wider political events of the day, Katrin's sister had been selected for a performance of Astrid Lindgren's *Pippi Longstocking,* and as Katrin was not allowed to travel back to Grünhufe alone, she had to wait. Gradually, week by week, she moved forward in the auditorium, learning all the songs with the rest of the choir, until eventually she found herself on stage with her sister and the rest of them. Whether or not the choir leader noticed, or if he had indeed forgotten which children he had actually selected, Katrin found herself part of the group, going on tour throughout the GDR and earning the first money of her young life.

After rehearsals the two sisters would go for rolls or cake from a small bakery close to the city gate not far from the theatre. As I walked down from Olof-Palme-Platz towards the Alter Markt – Stralsund's main square – the bakery was still doing good business, with a number of people sat on tables outside in the unseasonal warmth. I tried to imagine Katrin and Bine sitting on the steps of the next house along, pulling at warm bread rolls and surrounded by an old city very different to the one I was experiencing, waiting to catch the bus back home with the songs from the Swedish countryside reverberating around their heads.

Through the square I walked, past the striking red-brick town hall gable, the sky shining blue behind, and followed the winding streets down towards the harbour. There, among the old brick warehouses and the beautiful *Gorsch Fock* training ship, the futuristic OZEANUM museum of the sea was attempting to Guggenheim Stralsund by offering a striking architectural focal point for visitors. But despite this statement of intent, and the new cafes and restaurants that have sprung up in recent years, there remained a melancholy edge to Stralsund's harbour front as I stood on the well-worn flagstones down by the quayside and looked across the Strelasund to Rügen. This was a place, like Lübeck, that was still struggling to find its function centuries after its heyday. I turned from the water and hurried across to one of the harbour bars to order a Störtebeker – a local beer named for the legendary pirate of the Baltic, executed in Hamburg in 1401 and long mythologised in this part of the world. As I drank I began to feel a little more positive about the city and its future. It had plenty to recommend it, beyond hoppy beer and a maritime museum. I could see tourist buses disgorging passengers on to the quayside in summer. I could see the old town being a draw, for tourists and residents alike, with the attractions of Rügen just across the bridge. I sipped my beer and looked out of the window, following the path of a gull as it flew from one side of the harbour to the other. One thing was sure: it felt a long way from the concrete streets of Grünhufe, just a few kilometres to the west.

*

When inscribing the medieval centres of Stralsund and Wismar on to the World Heritage List in 2002, UNESCO made the point that it was the preservation and authenticity of these old cities that was the reason for them making the cut. Industry had been kept to the suburbs. Railway lines and other signs of modernity barely touched the core. Although the continued use of the city centres as the heart of urban life, and the continued operation of the harbours throughout the centuries, are cited under the heading 'authenticity', there is no mention of the October 1944 bombing raids and the two-thirds destruction of the city. With it being cheaper to build the new estates on the city limits, Stralsund's Altstadt was left to crumble throughout the years of the German Democratic Republic. When Katrin and her sister sat on the step to eat their bread rolls the paint was peeling, the plaster was coming off in chunks and the roof tiles threatened the heads of passers-by on the pavement below.

In December 1989, barely a month after the fall of the Berlin Wall and as the two Germanys scrambled to maintain control over events that would lead, ten months later, to the eventual reunification of the country, one of the first acts by the newly thriving citizens' initiatives in Stralsund was the founding of a committee to 'Save Stralsund's Old Town'. Unfortunately, delays in the return of nationalised property to the pre-GDR owners or their families added to the problems, as the ancient houses – in many cases still bearing scars of the war – threatened to collapse into the narrow, cobbled streets. On my first visit to Stralsund in 2004 much of the Altstadt was still in desperate condition, even if the first fifteen years of the new Germany had brought renovations to the harbour areas, the market squares and main shopping streets, and had indeed caught UNESCO's attention. A little more than ten years on from that first visit and it was clear that improvements had continued apace. The medieval core, as per UNESCO regulations, was looking authentically ancient, even if more recent history – once told in the very fabric of the buildings – had slowly but surely been erased.

I took to the water. A tourist boat out across the straits of the Strelasund to Altefähr on the island of Rügen and back again. I like to think that the best way to view any harbour town is from the water, imagining the sailor returning home after months or years at sea, or Störtebeker and his crew, ready to land the spoils of more Baltic nautical robbery. Aside from the white salt shaker of the OZEANUM on the harbour and the giant construction hall of the shipyard, built in the 1990s in an attempt to compete in the new globalised marketplace, the past couple of centuries retreated from the skyscape the further we travelled from shore. We were left with a view of red-brick warehouses and the towers of the Nikolaikirche, where the first town council was inaugurated in the thirteenth century and the first 'laws' of the town – the *Burspraken* were dictated to the residents living within the walls.

Stralsund seen from Rügen is a beautiful sight with its high Gothic towers, marvellously built town hall and many pointed gables with pierced brickwork. The s offshore and the busy movement of the beach give it a still greater repute.

It was 1796 when Wilhelm von Humboldt wrote those words, and from my hard plastic seat on the open top deck of the pleasure cruiser over two hundred years later it was too easy to imagine what the philosopher and founder of Berlin's university had seen. My fellow tourists clambered to the side of the boat with the best view back to the skyline, in order to take their photographs as the boat rocked gently on the swell. The commentary over the tannoy told us the greatest hits of Stralsund's history that, like most of the recent renovations of the Altstadt, appeared to pretend that the majority of the twentieth century hadn't actually happened around these parts, as we jumped from the end of Swedish rule to the first unification of Germany and then the second, in the time it took to ride just a couple of rolling waves.

*

As he leant on the balcony, cigarette in his hand, smoke curling from the corner of his mouth, it was impossible to read his thoughts. Distaste? Disinterest? At least he was not down there with them, across the street where they were gathering in front of the shopping centre. Despite heavy coats and hats pulled down over their heads, their neighbours would be sure to recognise them, those who were from Grünhufe. From the supermarket queue or the doctor's office. Outside the school gates. In the pub.

The leaflets had been pushed through letter boxes a few days before. A walk around the estate. A demonstration. A march. MVGIDA. Mecklenburg-Vorpommern against the Islamisation of the Occident. An offshoot of PEGIDA, down in Dresden. In Leipzig they had LEGIDA. With their flags and their banners. *Wir sind das Volk!* Borrowing the slogans from 1989. The last time, many of them grumbled to microphones shoved in their faces, that anyone paid us any attention.

Police vans lined up alongside the pavement, the cops in full protective gear but their helmets down by their sides. There would be no trouble. Not from a few hundred walking around the estate, and there was no sign of a counter-demo. So they would walk for an hour or so, the megaphone message garbled by the Baltic breeze, and then everyone would go home. It probably wouldn't even make the evening news. Not for a turnout like this one.

At the appointed time the small crowd that had gathered outside the shopping centre moved out on to the street and split, either side of a car with a speaker strapped to the roof. The police took up positions at the front and on either side, the vans pulling out from the kerb to drive, two abreast, at the back of the slow-moving procession. People from the neighbourhood hung out of the window to watch, or paused on the pavement. A few took out their phones, to record the scene, for Facebook or YouTube. To show partners when they got in from work.

At the front a sign professed solidarity with Russia, in both German and Russian, while flags of Stralsund, of Mecklenburg-Vorpommern and Germany fluttered in the breeze. As they walked a stream of consciousness spewed out from the speaker atop the pale blue Ford Fiesta.

And what can we expect from a Chancellor … who says – Of course I don't always do what the people want. How can I, when I know better? And what are we left with? Why do we have the euro? Why do we have the television license? Why do we have sanctions against Russia? It's a disgrace!

Half-hearted applause from the back of the procession. For those at the front, the wind had blown away the message before it could reach them. So many messages, so few people. Asylum seekers and refugees. Muslims and Syrians. Fundamentalists. Russia. We are the People. Words and labels. Everyone needs someone else to blame. Frau Merkel or some poor sod trapped in the back of a fruit lorry. We all need someone to blame.

Once around the block and they reached the shopping centre once more. The crowd gathered again, rolling up their flags. Some were smoking, others just stood there, as if unsure what to do next. It was not the same without a counter-demo to shout at, with just a handful of afternoon shoppers and the bored-looking police. As the street lights came on they began to disperse, some back into the estate, others away towards the city centre, where the vast majority of residents were ignorant or indifferent of the protest march on the fringes.

Wir sind das Volk? Doubtful.

*

Throughout the year of journeys, back and forth to the Baltic from Berlin, there was a clear sense of tension rising in the country. The sudden rise of PEGIDA – Patriotic Germans against the Islamisation of the Occident – in Dresden had appeared to fizzle out amid leadership infighting and ill-judged Hitler impressions. But Chancellor Merkel's commitment to take some 800,000 refugees, mainly from conflict zones in Syria and Afghanistan, saw the country begin to split along familiar fault lines. Many backed the Chancellor's move, responding with time, money and support. Others railed against what they saw as an influx destined to change Germany, and German society, for ever. For every gang of young Germans volunteering their time and the spare rooms in their apartments, there was another holding the spray can or the petrol bomb. The attacks on hundreds of women on New Year's Eve in Cologne at the hands of what were described as a thousand men of 'Arab or North African appearance' – an event it took the media and civil society an irresponsible amount of time to talk about, let alone tackle – heightened the tension further.

All the while the influence and support for the various groupings, the PEGIDAs, LEGIDAs, MVGIDAs and the AfD continued to grow. The latter, the political party Alternative für Deutschland, had begun as a Eurosceptic party, targeting its ire at Greece, Portugal and the supposedly profligate south. By the time events unfolded in Cologne it had changed course, aiming to become a party of the populist

Right similar to those gaining strength throughout Europe, but which had long been taboo in Germany. As the evening bulletins, chat shows, newspapers and my social media feed were filled with debate and discussion around the refugee crisis, anti-foreigner violence and the response of the state and civil society, I picked up my copy of *Crabwalk* once more. I read again the story of the sinking of the *Wilhelm Gustloff* and its impact on three generations of a German family. Of the rise of neo-Nazism, particularly in the former-GDR as the 1990s wore on. In a book of powerful images it was the final line that haunted my thoughts:

It doesn't end. Never will it end.

Günter Grass was dead, and I couldn't help but wonder what he would make of it all.

*

We went to Rostock to find the Sunflower House. Not long before we left I spoke to someone about our trip and she told me a story, about what those sunflowers on the side of the building represented to her.

It meant we were nearly there, she said, talking of her summer holidays to visit her grandparents in Warnemünde, the place that Katrin had dragged me to in the rain, that place that would always remind me of bad burritos and cocktails, soundtracked by Roxette. After hours crammed in the car with her family and a multitude of possessions, as her father told them yet again the stories of Rostock's shipyard, of the oldest university in northern Germany or the ferry to Sweden, and as the motorway gave way to the dual carriageway, that was the point that they began to look out of the left side of the car, waiting for the first of the *Plattenbau* to appear, counting them down until what felt like almost the very last one.

SUNFLOWER HOUSE!

Whoever saw it first, won. Not that there was anything to win, but it was part of the ritual. Like the first walk down to the beach, the first pause for ice cream or the first argument between parents and grandparents, when the uneasy family peace was broken over a misplaced plate in the dishwasher or the choice of snack for the kids. No, it didn't really matter who won, or that your chances of winning depended on where in the car you were sitting. What mattered was the fact that from the Sunflower House it was only three kilometres until the little yellow sign announced their arrival in Warnemünde. Soon the huge Neptun Hotel would appear through the front windscreen, the sculptured gardens of the Kurpark and the grassy dunes beyond which lay, they all knew, the wide expanse of golden sands and, beyond, the Baltic Sea itself. Usually her dad would pull up the car before they had reached their grandparents' house and they would clamber out, following the wooden walkway to the beach for the first glimpse of the water, the hundreds of wicker beach chairs, and their first breath of Baltic air. And it all began with those sunflowers on the side of a GDR apartment block. It was the sign that they had made it. A sign of summer. A sign that the holidays were about to begin.

*

From the bus stop by the dual carriageway that links the city of Rostock with Warnemünde, where the river meets the sea, I looked across the car park of a DIY store and a small patch of grass to the eleven-storey Sunflower House and the shopping arcade that stood in its shadow. It was a drizzly Sunday – *dreich* as it would be described in Scotland – and the shops were closed. There were few souls about in this corner of Rostock-Lichtenhagen, an estate of some 14,000 people built in the 1970s and comprised mainly of those GDR *Plattenbau* like that in which Katrin spent her childhood in Stralsund. Even by the standards of East Germany, the *Sonnenblumenhaus* was an oversized example of the tradition, stretching away from the dual carriageway for the entire length of the city block.

In the car park a couple argued over the state of their dog, and whether it would be better to get him inside or let him have a run in the rain that pattered gently against the roofs of the few vehicles that had been left overnight. A man in a black leather jacket stood in the shelter of the DIY store doorway, smoking a cigarette while staring up at the grey, overcast sky. His attention was caught by a slow-moving Audi and the sound of a car horn. We all looked. But it had been aimed at someone else and as the black car moved away we all returned to our own business.

I followed a path from the bus stop through a tangle of bushes and young trees until I was standing on a concrete pavement directly beneath the sunflowers. They were made out of a mosaic of huge tiles, like pixels on a computer screen. Further away, across the expanse of grass on the opposite side of the building from the shopping precinct, I could see a pair of enormous butterflies decorating another, smaller housing block. When people look at these suburbs of pre-fabricated, concrete-slab buildings on the edge of every East German town and city they wonder, if they do not live there themselves, why anyone would consciously choose to make a home in these boxy apartments divided by thin walls. But they forget, even the East Germans among them, what a revelation this housing was in the late 1960s and 1970s. For a society still emerging from the rubble and ruin of the Second World War, where the majority of city dwellings were still heated by coal ovens with toilets down the hall, central heating and your own bathroom was a big selling point. As was the open space for kids to play and the streets kept clear of traffic, by a combination of the fact that there were no through roads and the seven-year waiting list for cars. Plus, their uniform design meant that when you visited your friend's house you never had to ask where the toilet was; it was the same as at home.

On the steps of the nearest entrance, a young couple hugged and kissed before she retreated back into the building. He took the two steps backwards, still looking at where she had been standing until he reached the pavement where he walked away, bandy-legged and with hands thrust deep in his jacket pockets. The Sunflower House loomed over him like a huge wall from which hundreds of his girlfriend's neighbours could look down from hundreds of small windows. After a moment's pause I followed him down the pavement between the entrances to the different stairwells and the car park of the housing block. I was getting wet, and beginning to ask myself for the first time what it was that I was expecting to find. I walked the length of the building, rounded the corner, and walked back down the other side, this time hemmed in by the balcony side of the Sunflower House and the back of the shopping precinct. Some of the balconies had flower boxes, getting a good watering from the sky. From others flew miniature German flags, faded in the sun since the last major football tournament but still fluttering in anticipation of the next. The ground floor of the apartment block, I could see now, was occupied by a series of small businesses and organisations. Sheltered housing offices and an insurance broker's. A dental practice and a physiotherapist's. Across the way, the shopping precinct housed a Lidl and a SKY supermarket. The row of shops that linked the two was occupied by a drugstore, an estate agent's, a florist's and a hairdresser's.

It was all so very ordinary. The city centre was about half an hour in one direction. The Baltic and the beach about ten minutes in the other. Beyond the estate, open fields led to patches of woodland and a nature reserve. The buildings appeared to be in good condition, the roads well-maintained and the space between it all well-kept and neat. Despite the rain and the somewhat oppressive Sunday silence that is still a weekly feature across Germany, it was clear that there are many, many worse places to live than Rostock-

Lichtenhagen. The most threatening element on show was a piece of scrawled graffiti on the side of an electricity substation:

HANSA HOOLS.

It was either a territory marker – not that local heroes Hansa Rostock football club have much in the way of local rivals – or teenage bravado in ten letters. I thought of the boy kissing his girlfriend on the steps of the Sunflower House, only this time with a spray can in hand. As I scribbled a reminder to myself in my notebook the pages began to get wet. My trousers had begun to cling to my legs. There was no sign of let-up from above and anyway, it was clear that my search would be fruitless. Not that I really knew what it was I was looking for. Just a clue, perhaps. A sign from the past. But surrounded by thousands of lives hidden behind square windows and balcony doors, guarded by net curtains, there was nothing to find. Once more I thought of those words of Philip Hoare as he swam the waters of Wannsee in the south of Berlin. About how our knowledge of what happened *then* shapes our impression of a place *now*. I thought of what I knew about the Sunflower House and what most Germans from elsewhere in the country think of Rostock-Lichtenhagen when they hear the name, if they think anything at all. And I tried to picture the flying stones and petrol bombs, the baying mob and the police in retreat, but all I had were movie images. If there were ghosts in Lichtenhagen, in the stairwells of the Sunflower House, they were – like the vast majority of the suburb's residents – hidden indoors, out of the rain.

A few months earlier, I sat in a tiny cinema in Berlin-Mitte as the lights dimmed and the opening scene of *Wir sind Jung. Wir sind Stark (We are Young. We are Strong)* appeared on the screen. A burning Trabant and a group of riot police. The date appeared – 24th August 1992 – and then a group of young people sitting in a beaten-up camper van surrounded by the debris of two nights of rioting.

We shouldn't even be here.

A young man in the front seat laments the loss of work at the shipyards, that of his father and his brother, of himself.

But what'll I do tomorrow?

Outside the van an aggressive, hyper-tense twenty-something in black boots and a bomber jacket describes gypsies as vermin and claims that Rostock will be free of foreigners in twenty-four hours. The rest of the young people look bored as they swig their beer. The film continues to tell the story of their day, alongside that of members of the Vietnamese community who call Rostock's Sunflower House their home.

The film was released in 2015 and tells the story of the pogrom of 1992, when a group of neo-Nazis backed by others attacked – over the course of three days – two sections of Rostock-Lichtenhagen's Sunflower House, one of which housed members of the city's Vietnamese community, the other known as the ZAST – the asylum seekers' residence. Coming less than two years after reunification, these xenophobic and racist attacks were part of an outbreak of extreme right-wing activity that took place across Germany, but in particular in the 'new federal states' that had once been part of the GDR. Events in Rostock made the national and international news. For many outside Germany it became the only thing they knew about the Baltic port city. For many inside Germany as well. It would shape perception of Rostock and its people for many years to come.

And as the film was released in cinemas some thirteen years later, a new generation of asylum seekers and refugees was finding itself under attack. What began as a couple of arson attacks in January and February reached double figures by the summer months. As the end of year came around, the final figure for 2015 was 222 arson attacks across the country. Along the Baltic coast alone there were attacks on both sides of the former inner-German border. Lübeck. Wismar. Greifswald. Altogether, across the whole country and from over two hundred attacks, the authorities managed to secure a grand total of four convictions. We sat down in the cinema to watch a dramatisation of events in a particular place at a particular time in Germany's history. By the end of the summer, it felt like we had been watching a premonition.

Back in 1992, the reception centre for refugees in Rostock had been overwhelmed, predominantly by Sinti and Roma asylum seekers from Romania. With not enough space to house them, an informal encampment had developed on the grass and beneath the balconies of the Sunflower House. Residents complained of people pissing and shitting in doorways whilst the authorities seemed slow to solve either the problem of numbers camping in the open air or the concerns of locals. It would not take long to get the attention of members of the right-wing and neo-Nazi scenes, both in Rostock and beyond.

Keep Rostock German!

The first leaflets were distributed in early August, before the anonymous phone calls began. They were made to newspaper offices in the city, issuing threats:

The Romanian Roma will be chucked out on their arses.

Meanwhile, members of the Vietnamese community – most of whom had moved to Rostock as part of the solidarity between communist nations in the years of the GDR – found themselves caught in the middle. From the moment things started to unravel on Saturday, 22 August, Vietnamese residents began filming from inside the house to record and document what would happen.

It started with stone throwing, and whatever local residents would later claim, those attacking the building at the beginning came from the estate or elsewhere in the city. The police soon arrived, along with the acting mayor, who tried to calm things down. In the background, shouted voices could be heard.

They are not people. They are shit.

As darkness fell on Lichtenhagen the first neo-Nazi skinheads arrived. The police were overwhelmed. Over the following day, as news of the first attacks was broadcast on the television and radio, more neo-Nazis and other right-wing radicals arrived from across the country. Locals would later report seeing number plates on cars from all over Germany. During this period many asylum seekers were evacuated from the Sunflower House to the shameful applause of local residents. But the worst was to come on Monday 24th.

After a period of calm in the afternoon, things got completely out of hand as the evening progressed. For the best part of three days the authorities had sat on their hands, but the moment of complete abdication of responsibility took place around eight in the evening when the police withdrew from the scene. For the remaining asylum seekers in the ZAST and the Vietnamese families looking down on the baying mob from their windows, it was clear that they had been abandoned. As a crowd of some 3,000 people – most of whom lived in neighbouring buildings – cheered and shouted, the thugs attacked the defenceless Sunflower House with bricks and Molotov cocktails. Soon the lower floors were on fire and through the smoke the residents attempted to escape, up eleven flights of stairs and out across the roof. Later it would be claimed that the vast majority of attackers came from elsewhere, that they had used Rostock-Lichtenhagen as an opportunity, as a stage-set for their xenophobic hate. But anyone who watches the news footage from that evening can also see something else. A few thousand people, the majority of which were local, clapping their hands and chanting, *Foreigners Out! Foreigners Out! Foreigners Out!*

*

In 2015, as in 1992, there was an immediate hand-wringing debate about xenophobic violence and the attacks on foreigners and asylum seeker residences. And although, like in 1992, the attacks were taking place all across Germany, a greater proportion were happening in the former East. What was it about the former-GDR, with its tiny proportion of immigrants compared to the former-West, that made it so susceptible not only to such attacks but also the likes of PEGIDA or the nationalist/right populist political parties? It had been going on since the Wall came down. Günter Grass had explored the themes at the turn of the century in *Crabwalk*. What was the issue?

Back in 1992, the explanation for Rostock-Lichtenhagen centred on two main elements. The first was the neo-Nazi opportunists, those who had travelled across the country to have their very own *Kristallnacht* on the streets of the estate. But that did not explain the rest, the young people from the city who certainly did join in and the thousands of onlookers who cheered and chanted. The second element, it was felt, came from a group of people who were reeling from the pace of change after reunification, who were suffering unemployment that was unknown until a few years previously, and who had the perception they were being treated as second-class citizens in the new Germany that was being built after the end of the division. The young characters in *Wir sind Jung. Wir sind Stark* explain it throughout the film. They are not filled with hate, not all of them. They are too nihilistic to really hate. When one starts singing a neo-Nazi anthem lamenting the loss of Hitler's Germany, another responds with the *Internationale*. As they are all children of the GDR they all know the words. Their violence comes out of boredom and a fear that, in their mid- to late-teens, their lives are already defined and will amount to nothing. This does not excuse, and the filmmaker is not trying to. Indeed, the sense of violation and fear felt by those trapped in the building is shown in harrowing scenes that are some of the most powerful of the film. But the filmmaker recognises something else: if communism has failed, and capitalism is failing them, where are people going to turn next?

When people look for explanations over twenty years later for the rise of PEGIDA or xenophobic attacks in the former East, they still reach for the same explanations. There is a reason why those NPD posters hung unmolested in the estate of Katrin's childhood. That's where the 'losers' of the new Germany lived. And more than twenty-five years after reunification, the economic gap may have closed a little but it still remains. Unemployment is 50% higher in the former East. If you live in the old GDR you are 25% more likely to slip into poverty. It is in these groups of people that the

Right gain their traction. But what seemed to be different in the second decade of the twenty-first century was that despite the disproportionate number of incidences and support for the new populist right-wing movements in the old East, they were – especially after events in Cologne – building support in the West. And here was the difference. The new leadership of the Right was made up of lawyers and academics, and they did not just appeal using dog-whistle racism at people desperate for scapegoats, but they played on people's anger at the welfare reforms of the early 2000s, of the bank bailouts and the corporate scandals, the profligate Greeks and others from the south who needed propping up by hard-working German taxpayers, and then – finally – Frau Merkel's refugees. And all the while, a mix of age-old prejudices and stereotypes was being fuelled by conspiracy theories propagated by the extremely modern means of social media.

*

From Lichtenhagen to the city centre. The rain had stopped as I walked through the streets of the old town, past the same parade of shops I would find on high streets and in shopping malls across Germany. The red-brick architecture of gabled houses, mixed with more modern constructions supposed to alleviate the wartime damage and that done by East German urban planners, was not dissimilar to Stralsund. Down by the harbour it was possible to make out the cranes of the more modern port, where you can catch ferries across the Baltic, whilst standing beside old goods carriages good for nothing more than decoration, beside warehouses transformed into clubs and bars serving the student population of northern Europe's oldest university.

As I walked alongside the city walls, an attractive green strip of pathways and flower beds between old city gates and with a view across the jumble of rooftops, I even found myself vaguely wondering what it would be like to live in the city. But I couldn't completely shake those perceptions I had previously held about Rostock, most of which had been formed long before I lived in Germany, when I heard and read about the events of 1992 in Lichtenhagen. Perhaps I would have to live there, to build a new layer of personal, positive experiences atop those that had come second- or third-hand. Or perhaps the problem was wider. Perhaps the early 1990s seemed closer now because of more recent events, those that had created an atmosphere of tension in the country that was apparent every time you

read a headline outside a newsagent's shop, and that had
not existed only a handful of months earlier when I had
started these journeys north to the Baltic from Berlin.

VIII

Eyewitness History Talk

Or
The Decline of a Family, Part Two

My story begins, as all lives do, with my birth. I was born within sight of the Baltic Sea on 15 January 1942. This date is important for two reasons: one which would directly impact me and my life, and another that – whilst influential in a more abstract way – is slightly more removed.

The first is that my birthday of 15 January is the same date as that on which Karl Liebknecht and Rosa Luxemburg were murdered in 1919, some twenty-three years earlier. Despite the fact that I was born into Nazi Germany, and a Nazi Germany at war with the Soviet Union, my mother knew of the anniversary when labour started that morning and she resolved to name me for one of the revolutionaries. And so, when I emerged sometime around the middle of the afternoon (*Kaffee und Kuchen Zeit*, my Mama always said), she told the midwife that I was to be called Rosa and a few days later my birth was registered. Rosa Krausneck was recognised with an official document that featured a scribbled signature and which was stamped with an eagle clutching a swastika.

The second reason the date is important is that on that very day, hundreds of kilometres to the south-east, the first Jews were being deported from the Łódź ghetto to the Chelmno Concentration Camp, one of the first camps to experiment with gassing as a means of eliminating inmates deemed no longer fit for work. Five days after I was born, leading Nazi officials met on the banks of the beautiful Lake Wannsee in Berlin in order to discuss and plan what they called the 'Final Solution to the Jewish Problem in Europe'. That was, as is, well known, the moment the murder of Jews became industrial slaughter. Became genocide. This is important to my story only insofar as it is important to bear in mind, when you consider what would happen on German soil in the years that would follow and the choices that many Germans made in that time, that these events and these decisions were made in the shadow of the Holocaust and the crimes committed by us Germans against the Jews, the gays, the gypsies and, of course, the communists. Although my mother, who was living and working in a hotel at the Baltic shore, would tell me that the war did not really impact on life until later – indeed, until after it was officially over – this was the Germany I was born into. And I am thankful that I am of a generation too young to be held accountable for what was done in our name, although as a child of that despicable regime such things were certainly and explicitly done in mine.

Like most people my early memories are a mix of flashbacks, of specific scenes that of course I am no longer sure are real memories or simply imagined moments based on things my mother told me. I lived in that hotel, in the staff quarters, from birth until 1953. My first proper memories come in the year or so before I started school, in 1948. Before that I can only picture those fractured, individual moments. Russian soldiers moving from house to house. Mr Barthels, the owner of the hotel, shooing me from the garden as guests wanted to sunbathe in peace. The beach, with my mother, on her afternoon off.

My mother was twenty-two when I was born, and she had been barely a teenager when Hitler came to power. But her father – a farm labourer from a village near to where I first grew up on the coast – had been a card-carrying member of the Communist Party. And although he kept his mouth shut and most probably burned that membership card when the Nazis took over, he remained extremely anti-Hitler in the privacy of his home. Sadly I never knew that grandfather, as he was called up late in the war and died somewhere out to the east. My father also died fighting, or as a prisoner-of-war, or through some other miserable fate shared by so many millions at that time, and so I never knew him either. In any case, my mother was still influenced by her father when she named me and again when the Soviets arrived in 1945. I have heard a lot about what happened then, especially to women, but my mother always insisted that nothing happened to her.

Mr Barthels protected us. He gave the soldiers gifts to go away ...

That was all she would ever say on the matter. In any case, it did not seem to influence her political beliefs one bit and she welcomed the arrival of the German Democratic Republic, born in 1949 some seven years after me, as a chance to build socialism on German soil once and for all. I don't think her boss Mr Barthels was particularly enamoured with the situation, and Mama often told me – later, once we were in Leipzig – about the good-natured arguments they would have.

Things will change now, she would tell him. *Maybe one day I'll be in charge of this hotel. Maybe you'll be working for me.*

It didn't quite work out like that, although it turns out she wasn't that far off with her jokes. In 1953 the hotel was confiscated by the state, now property of the people, although Mama never worked there again and certainly did not become the boss, and Mr Barthels was also gone, having died around about the same time. The day it happened provide me with some of my strongest memories of my childhood. Eleven years old, I had gone to school and then to the Young Pioneers, so I was still in my uniform when I got back home to the hotel. Mama was clearly upset, although she was very careful to explain to me the importance of the fact that the hotel now belonged to the people, to all of us in fact, rather than just Mr Barthels.

But what will happen to him?

I can remember asking the question because, despite the fact he was my mother's boss and could be a bit scary when the mood took him, he always treated me very gently and seemed genuinely fond of me. My mother just shook her head and burst into tears.

The next morning she told me we were leaving. Mr Barthels had died, perhaps with the shock of the hotel being taken from him, and she did not feel right continuing to work there in his absence, even if it was of course better now that the hotel belonged to everyone and not to just one man. We were to go and live in Leipzig, where a family friend had found Mama a job in one of the new chemical works that had opened in the city. Thinking of it now it seems awfully quick, and maybe my mind plays some tricks on me. I cannot be sure. In any case, not long after the hotel was nationalised we caught the train south, first to Berlin and then onwards to Leipzig.

*

You will of course have noticed something in the story thus far. I was born as Rosa Krausneck, and yet you will have seen on the posters for this talk, or perhaps on the Internet, that my name is now Rosa Barthels, the same as the man who once owned the hotel and was my mother's boss. That is because, as I only learned once he was dead and we were in Leipzig and a long way from my beloved Baltic shore, Mr Barthels was in fact my grandfather and my father – who had died in the war – was his son Klaus. And although Klaus Barthels was not named on my birth certificate – there was a blank space just above the eagle and the swastika – my mother had a signed letter from my grandfather testifying to that effect. That letter is very interesting to me, for its importance and value would change over the years, which I will come to later. In the beginning at least, as we tried to build this workers' and peasants' republic on German soil, it was not particularly useful to have a small businessman as a paternal grandfather. There was more benefit to me at that time to be the granddaughter of a farm labourer who had been a member of the party since the time my namesake had still been alive.

*

In any event, in Leipzig my mother went to work and I went to school and the Young Pioneers and eventually the FDJ - the Free German Youth organisation. I was selected for the Extended Secondary School which would mean I could take the Abitur, which in turn gave me the chance of attending university. Academic achievement was not everything, though. My mother told me from a young age that not only did I have to be good at school, but it was also important that I was politically correct, and that I should be enthusiastic and committed to my FDJ activities, which of course I was. I would later discover that family background was also important in winning a university place. The signed letter remained hidden away at the back of a drawer.

In 1960 I headed back to the coast to the city of Greifswald, where I was to study languages; namely English and Russian. For my part I was most happy about returning to the coast and tried to persuade my mother to join me in the journey north. She refused. She told me it was time for me to make my own way in life, and that she was happy in Saxony. Maybe she was, but continuing to work at that factory is what made her sick. But that comes later ...

No, we shall go back to Greifswald. Oh, it was such a wonderful time, especially that first year. I enjoyed my studies and the world of possibility languages seemed to offer, not just in the fact that I might be able to use my skills to travel but in the books I could read. Around the time I was there, there was something of a kerfuffle over the removal of certain foreign books from the library, but there was enough to be going on with and I spent most of my time when I was not with my friends with my head buried in some book or other. I also tried to arrange a holiday with my mother for the summer to Hiddensee, an island off an island in the Baltic. Mama had spent childhood summers there and had always promised to take me, but with the changes it hadn't been possible. I heard that a professor in my department had a small cottage on the island, and perhaps he would be able to invite me. We became close, the professor and I, but the invitation was not forthcoming.

So that first summer we went to Thuringia, to a holiday camp in the mountains organised by Mama's workplace, and when I returned to Greifswald things had changed. Over the summer the Berlin Wall had been built, although we did not call it that. Officially, in the GDR, it was known as the 'Anti-Fascist Protective Wall', although even the most committed of us knew what it was really for. Not that we minded. Perhaps if it would stop those determined to destabilise our country, those who were determined to stop us realising our goals of a better and more equal society … well, if that took a wall, then so be it!

The other thing that changed was that I was visited one day by a man who came to my student dormitory and asked for a private conversation. He took me down the hall to an empty room where he sat me down at a table, took a notebook in his hand, and began to talk. He was from the Ministry for State Security, he said, and he wanted to talk to me about some things that had come to their attention. At this moment he paused, and I remember this very clearly, he looked over the top of his glasses and then down at his notebook. *Flick, flick, flick.* He riffled through the pages until he was happy.

Ah yes, he said. *It concerns your relations with a certain Professor X.*

I remember being startled. Shocked even. I don't really want to talk too much about my relationship with the professor. He was older than me, and married. And in any case it is as much nobody's business now as it was then. But I could see that, far from any trip to Hiddensee, this situation could be extremely problematic for me. As the man with the notebook began to tell me. As he talked I can remember losing my train of thought as panic took over. I only heard certain words ... Inappropriate ... Expulsion ... Disciplinary ... Resignation ... None of them sounded particularly good. And then he offered me a way out.

If, perhaps, you could help me. Then maybe I can find a way to help you ...

*

I am sorry. I have had to pause because this is a difficult part of my talk and I want to be open and honest with you all. That is what these talks are all about, is it not? But I also know what people think when they hear that I 'helped' this man and that I spoke to the MfS. And as time has gone on, I have also begun to understand that it truly was not acceptable, that I should have refused his offer, come what may. But I didn't, and all I can offer is a little context and hope you will not judge me too harshly.

Firstly, I was scared. I was twenty years old and it was made very clear to me that my entire future was in this man's hands and that they could make life difficult for me. Secondly, I did not have any major problem with what he asked me to do. There was a list of three professors. Two in the English department and one in the Russian department. Someone at the Ministry was suspicious of what they were up to, especially as they were involved in teaching young and impressionable minds. It was vital to the survival of the GDR, for this brave new world we were building, that subversive elements were stopped before they could do any real damage. Did I not agree? And all I had to do was write a brief report following each lecture or seminar, about the contents of the classes and, especially, any opinions the professors offered up to us as their own.

After all, the man with the notebook said, *if we are wrong, and they are behaving perfectly appropriately, then they have nothing to worry about …*

I have to admit that I found this argument persuasive. But just in case I didn't, there was a third reason for my agreeing to help: my mother.

It did not do, he said, *for a family to get a reputation.*

He did not say much more than that, and by this point, he did not need to.

*

That was how it started, and although for many people it seems to be the most important aspect of my life, I can honestly say it was not much more than this. Throughout my university years I wrote these weekly reports. Once I left I became an academic at the university myself, and they no longer asked me for reports on my colleagues or my friends. In any case, I would never have done that! No, sometimes they would come to me and ask if they could use my apartment. For an hour here or an hour there. I always said yes. What harm was there in it? Later, my husband agreed. In the beginning, at least. We all had our part to play, and the enemy was a strong one.

Ah yes, my husband and my first name change. I became Rosa Reimann in 1966, married to Stefan in his home town of Neubrandenburg before our honeymoon in Czechoslovakia. I met Stefan at university. He was also studying languages but his great passion was literature, poetry and especially the theatre. In 1963 he had gone to Berlin, where his first two plays had been performed to great success. Greifswald offered him the position of artistic director. He was incredibly young and it was an incredible privilege, but he was not sure if he wanted to take it as it would mean leaving Berlin. In the end it was the fact that I was staying in Greifswald that swayed him. He accepted the position and came back north to join me.

That was a time! Yes, there were irritations. Sometimes I wasn't able to travel for international conferences or even the opportunity to practise my languages, which would have been useful. There was still the issue of books in the library, resources that were available for research, and the fact that we spent two thirds of our time on bureaucracy rather than actual academic work ... but I hear things are not much different in universities today, whether here or elsewhere. And Stefan sometimes had his issues too, especially when he was 'requested' not to use a certain actor that he would otherwise have cast for a role ... but in general we built our own scene, around a basement bar not far from the Old Market where we would meet for drinks and conversation. Quite risqué sometimes! Making jokes, satirical swipes you know ... that kind of thing. No, it wasn't Berlin of course. But it was ours.

In 1970 our son Michael was born, and it seemed at first that our successes – in academia and in the theatre – would ensure a certain standard of opportunity for him, especially when it came to education. And things were good. I was given the chance to go to conferences, in Moscow but also in Oxford, where I could bring back certain goodies. These journeys did make me look at my home with fresh eyes, of course. Greifswald itself was a bit run-down. When I think of the city as it was then, I can still taste the smoke from the coal-dust briquettes we used to burn in our apartment and the cheap cigarettes in the basement bar, but at least we were only a few kilometres from the sea. In 1975 we finally made it to Hiddensee, staying at a guest house of the Academy of Arts. Unfortunately I wasn't able to take my Mama.

Ah yes, Mama. All this while she had been living and working in Leipzig, coming up to Greifswald to visit on the train, especially after Michael was born. She had little time for the theatre, which made things strained with Stefan at points, but otherwise it was OK. And yet I could see with every visit that her health was failing her. She blamed the cigarettes and promised to quit but I knew it was that factory. What she breathed in all day. But it was her life. Her work life, but also her social life. She went out with those women. Went on holiday with them. Many of them lived in the same apartment block and she babysat the children of her younger colleagues.

If I leave, what shall I do? What shall I have?

I had no answer. And then came 1976. The year Michael started school. The year everything changed.

*

Another pause if you please. Have I been talking too long? I can see some of you are getting restless. Very well, let us try and hurry this along. In 1976, the GDR expelled the singer Wolf Biermann. You may have heard of him. Stefan and I were great fans, even if he sometimes fell afoul of the authorities. Both of us were of the opinion that any system needed its escape valve, its means of letting off steam. We were generally supportive of what the government was trying to do but we also felt that if you were too heavy-handed, if you did not give people a centimetre of space ... if you did not let them laugh at you, even a little. Well ...

So Biermann was invited to play in West Germany, to all those hippies and 1968ers who hung off his every word, and the government didn't let him back in. A pretty good joke, you have to admit! But many people were upset by this, including Stefan. He even signed the protest letter with all those other actors and singers and writers. I begged him not to. I asked him to think of Michael. He held firm, and I admire him for it now. Not long after, another man came to visit, at a time when he knew Stefan would be at the theatre. I sent him away. I had had enough by this point, but it made me worried again. The number of meetings they wanted to use our apartment for increased and now Stefan didn't want me to agree, but I did not know how I could stop it. And then, a few months later, my mother died. A heart attack in the snow, walking home from work. The doctors blamed a congenital condition, but I knew it was that factory. I went down to Leipzig to sort out her things. I cried a little at the paucity of the artefacts of a life. I returned to Greifswald with a small suitcase. In it was the letter from my grandfather.

Throughout the 1980s, as Michael went to school and studied hard, my relationship with Stefan began to fall apart. We got a cottage of our own in the Mecklenburg Lake District, and in the warmer months I began to spend every weekend there. More often than not, Stefan stayed in the city, working at the theatre. I don't like to dwell on that time, except to say that Michael did extremely well at school and whatever was going on between his father and I, well, it did not seem to impact on him at all. In 1989, in fact, he was top of his class, and was all set to go to Moscow on a scholarship. Even his father signing that damned letter hadn't held him back.

And then the Wall came down.

In 1990, about a week after Germany was reunified, my divorce from Stefan was finalised. As part of the same process I took my mother's letter to a lawyer and had Klaus Barthels officially recognised as my father. When the divorce came through I took his name. A new start with a new name. Michael was not best pleased, but at this point he was going through difficult times of his own. With the collapse of the GDR came the collapse of his scholarship to Moscow. Nobody was interested in a political scientist of a discredited political system. He went away, to Berlin, in the early 1990s and I only saw him sporadically. It is sad when a mother has to let go of her child, but sometimes it is what needs to be done. Nowadays we see each other at Christmas, maybe once more in the year. He still loves me, I can see it in his eyes. He lets me know how Stefan is doing. I haven't spoken to *him* in over twenty years.

It is funny how life turns out. It is a cliché but perhaps one that exists because, to a greater or lesser extent, it rings true for many people. I left my teaching position not long after reunification in objection to the process they were making academics go through to justify their role in the story of the GDR. It was immoral and degrading and I wanted nothing to do with it. It was as if we were Nazis! And the West Germans were the British and Americans! But I was able to leave because of a stroke of good fortune. The hotel on the Baltic Sea, the one in which I spent those first years of my life, was to be returned to the living heirs of Mr Barthels, from whom it had been confiscated. I was the only Barthels left. I knew nothing about running a hotel but I was sure I could learn. In 1994, at the age of fifty-two, I moved home.

I could talk more about my life since, about being persuaded into politics and becoming mayor of this town of ours. I felt it important, at the time, but now I think it was a mistake. This new media we have now could teach the Stasi a thing or two about digging up people's past to use it against them. And so Rosa Barthels was condemned by the misdemeanours of Rosa Krausneck as a young student, and Rosa Reimann who did nothing more than let her flat be used once or twice a year so that men could talk. No mention is made of my five years working hard for the town, creating the new tourism bureau, winning European funding and the start of the theatre festival. The fact that the town won awards for hospitality and saw an increase in tourism numbers every year. No, people don't want to know about that. They don't ask me to talk about that. All they care about is two simple letters.

I. M.

Sometimes I think I should get them tattooed on my forehead and be done with it.

*

I am sorry. You have to forgive me. I just get upset when I think how I am now defined. *Inoffizielle Mitarbeiter.*

I. M.

An informant. A collaborator. I don't think I should be ashamed. I am named for Rosa Luxemburg, and if I have become something of a businesswoman in the latter years of my life it does not mean that I did not believe we were building a better and more equal world back then. Nobody went to jail because of me. Nobody was hurt by me. Remember how I started this talk. Think about the Germany I was born into. Think about what we were emerging from. Yes, we made mistakes, but with the best of intentions. But I have taken up enough of your time. Thank you for listening. It is always important, before you condemn, that at first you listen.

IX

Down to the River
(Greifswald)

The city at night – Portrait of the new Werther as a young man – A university city – Man of Straw – The life and times of Rudolf Ditzen – Along the river to the sea – The meaning of Casper David Friedrich – Eldena and the aesthetics of ruins – The pub and the fisherman

We came to Greifswald in the dark, driving north through the evening along an empty autobahn before following the tree-lined overland road that links the university city on the banks of the Ryck river with the rest of the world. The city seemed quiet as Katrin manoeuvred the car around the roundabout by the train station. To our left, the Gothic buildings of the Altstadt loomed above the ring road as we followed it round the route of the former city walls, until we met the river – the circle almost completed – and we found a parking space close to the harbour. At this point a road bridge crossed the Ryck, the furthest navigable point upstream from where it empties out into a Baltic bay south of the island of Rügen. The mouth lay some kilometres downstream, out there in the darkness. We climbed out of the car to stretch our legs by the harbour, a collection of wooden sailing boats tied to squat bollards on the quayside. Masts rattled in the cold wind. Wood creaked. Across the river, lights burned in apartment buildings that stood above the rough cobblestones and heavy metal wagon tracks of the harbour. Behind us, gabled red-brick buildings stood tall against the night sky. A loose sail, or perhaps it was a flag, flapped heavy against itself, the sound of a damp canvas tent door in the wind. We pushed our hands deep into our pockets, crossed the deserted street, and proceeded into town on foot.

If there was life in this city on a cold Tuesday evening it was to be found in the bars and cafes of the Altstadt. This was yet another cityscape – like Lübeck, Stralsund and Rostock before it – of red bricks and crow-stepped gables, more remnants of the Hanseatic League; of trade and merchants, warehouses and guilds. On the main square a couple crossed the cobblestones in front of us, but mostly people were indoors, out of the cold. A small group waited, huddled together by a bus stop. Otherwise the ghosts of Greifswald had free rein. Was a candle burning in the staircase window? A silhouette of movement behind the stained glass? Footsteps sounding across the paving stones, shimmering under the street lights; the telltale sign of an earlier shower. Who did they belong to?

The city at night is a different place. In the west of Berlin, the street-scene – lit by neon signs and naked mannequins in boutique windows – is the city of the 1970s, of Bowie and the kids skulking outside Zoo Station. In the Stralsund suburbs, the orange glow of the street lights above concrete-slab pavements, and below the straight lines of the *Plattenbau*, is a return to the GDR. In Greifswald it is as if the modern world has retreated into the shadows; a journey back, further back, to when the medieval streets were under Swedish control, or beyond, to when the university was riven by the theological debates that opened up the great schism of Europe and three decades of war and a landscape ravaged. A time when the masts that rattled in the harbour belonged not to well-preserved museum ships, to be admired from the quayside by coach parties on day trips, but the trading vessels that linked the cities of the Baltic, resting awhile as their crews sought refreshment in a nearby basement bar.

EVERYTHING MUST GO.

The sign, written in English, was pinned to the inside window of a clothes store on the main shopping street. In the side streets the ghosts may have been playing, but elsewhere in the city the twenty-first century refused to remain hidden for long. As we walked we began to get a sense of the disjointed nature of Greifswald's Altstadt, that had at first – and in the dark – appeared to be a medieval core almost completely intact. Now we could see where the gaps had been filled, gaps created during the devastation of the past century. We could see where, in the GDR, concrete-slab approximations of the old Hanseatic style had been built, as well as newer buildings, erected to fill the empty spaces of the Second World War half a century after the fact. Now, feeling our way into the city, we began to see the joins.

The city shifted shape once more. A group of students emerged from a cafe on the corner and moved on down the street, their voices echoing against the medieval brick and the communist concrete. At a corner *Imbiss* men with missing teeth supped from brown beer bottles at stand-up tables, eating an approximation of Chinese food dug out from cardboard boxes as they watched a football match being played on the other side of the world. On the first floor of a building that housed a bank at ground level, a figure stood at the window, backlit from a room lined with bookshelves. He wore a shirt, sleeves rolled up to his elbows, and held a glass of wine in his hand, looking down on the scene. Looking down on us.

We were by the university's main administration building as a cyclist passed by, shattering the silence of his approach with a short, sharp ring of the bell. It continued to sound as he rattled along the uneven street and Katrin lifted her camera to capture his passing; a blur of activity, legs and pedals whirring as he hunched forward on his handlebars, backpack merged with the rest of his body.

JURISTENHAUS.

He was passing the building of laws and lawyers. A reminder of the importance of this seat of learning. Which legal system? Down by the university we had slipped once more into the past. Sweden. Prussia. The German Empire. Weimar Republic. Nazi Germany. GDR. The Federal

Republic. All those years, all those laws. Gaps emerged, gaps were filled in. Greifswald was still standing.

Back at the harbour the masts continued to rattle. The new apartment buildings on the opposite bank aped the brick warehouses they faced across the water. More views into more living rooms; the voyeuristic pleasure of the night walker. A blue flickering light of a television. An IKEA lampshade, identified from a hundred paces. A couple eating their dinner across from each other in apparent silence. Marital bliss or edgy tension? Through the glass it was hard to tell. The boats continued to creak, uneasy on their moorings. A shout echoed down a narrow back lane. An unseen car door slammed. I felt the sudden wave of unease that washes over the most confident of night wanderers at some point in their explorations. As we walked to our guest house, I was glad I was not wandering alone.

*

Rattle, rattle. Ring, ring. And so it goes on, as somewhere in the city the cyclist continued on his journey, moving through the Altstadt towards a student residence or a one-room apartment just beyond the old city walls. I saw him in those few minutes before he passed us on the street, leaving his friends behind at a bar where smoke still clung to the bare brick walls beneath speakers shaking with the volume of the music that blasted out from them. The streets must have felt deathly quiet in comparison, as he rocked over the cobblestones, dodging the potholes and the drain covers, heading for home.

He loved the city at night as it transformed into the place of his romantic imagination. He loved the city in winter for the same reason. When the snows fell and muffled modernity in their white blanket. When the condensation rolled down his attic bedroom window with its view across to the dark spires of the Altstadt. People wore heavy jackets, heavy boots. The girls, in their winter dress, were as timeless as the city streets. It was all a game, of course. The city was as much about new university buildings with A+ environmental ratings as it was the dreamings of a new Young Werther, and as he rode he could feel the vibration of a message on his phone, sent via Wi-Fi and 3G, a message from the bar he had left behind. But as he chased shadows through the dark streets and thought of the words he would later scribble down about this night and the girl he had left back there at the candlelit table, he was the hero on this stage set of his own making.

It wasn't real. It was all a game. But let him play it just a little longer …

The next morning we walked through a city transformed by daylight, following a road-cleaning machine as it sprayed and brushed and scrubbed the main shopping street, as the store owners unlocked their doors and pulled out their display cases and racks on to the pavement. The tempting inducements of the free market lined up in Greifswald's Altstadt. Outside the bookshop, I stopped to look at a collection of black and white photographs on one side of a spinning postcard stand that otherwise contained multi-coloured montages of red-brick city sights. I pulled the photographs from the rack one by one and then flicked through them in my hands. They showed a city that appeared to be literally crumbling before the photographer's lens. The first was of a street where nearly every house was barely standing upright as a woman walked the pavement towards an open patch of rubble-strewn wasteland. The next featured another empty space, this time a scruffy expanse occupied by a parked car, a grocer's van and a wheel-less, abandoned wreck. The third, half-timbered houses, bricks like soft chalk, beneath the city's iconic church spires. At first glance I presumed these were of Greifswald in the immediate aftermath of the Second World War, that these were images of 1950s rubble-strewn bombsites like those that could have been found in Liverpool or the East End of London. Then I turned the pile over in my hands, to read the photographer's credit and other bits and pieces of information typed in small script on the back of each card.

1987.

These were images of Greifswald over forty years after the end of the war, of Greifswald only two years before the fall of the Berlin Wall, before reunification. It was something of a shock.

Perhaps I shouldn't have been surprised. Like so many places in the GDR, the historic centre of Greifswald was pretty much abandoned by the authorities during the 1960s and 1970s as resources were directed to building the new satellite estates of concrete-slab apartment blocks. By the time the photographs were taken, just before the GDR began its slow-but-accelerating collapse into extinction, there was a very real danger that years of neglect had condemned the Hanseatic buildings of Greifswald and that there would be nothing left to save, even if the will was there to save them. In actual fact, by the end of the 1980s the city authorities had begun to recognise the potential value of tourism to the city, which explained some of the *Plattenbau* facsimiles of old Hanseatic structures that had filled in some of the gaps, and which we had spotted the night before. But it is fair to say that whatever changes the collapse of the GDR and reunification may have brought, positive and negative, it is almost certain that they saved Greifswald's Altstadt from terminal ruin.

Walking the streets in the daylight it was easier to see the joins between the pre-war, communist and post-reunification buildings in the cityscape. We were walking from the harbour, south through the Altstadt towards the new town that had been built with the coming of industrialisation in the nineteenth century and the ever-expanding campus of the university. During the GDR, as part of the planned economy that transformed villages on the Polish border into factory towns dominated by steelworks, paper mills and oil refineries, a nuclear power station was built close to Greifswald and new housing estates sprung up along the river to house the families of the workers. But despite these twentieth-century developments, since the collapse of the Hanseatic League and through the centuries of shifting powers, changing political systems and the rise and decline of industries, it had been the university that remained the most important economic driver for the city. Greifswald had long been, and remains, a college town, and in the past couple of decades since reunification the university had developed an impressive new collection of libraries and lecture halls, laboratories and research institutes, student dorms and sports facilities.

Before we reached the campus we crossed from the medieval old town into the nineteenth-century new town, past the path of the city walls and the ring road, and passed by a villa of dark and dirty windows, half-hidden by overgrown trees and bushes. There was a small, wooden sign nailed to the door.

Fraternity, Katrin said, nodding at it. *Student corps.*

I looked at the sign and then searched the villa for further clues, but none were forthcoming. We had a friend in Berlin whose old flatmate had once been a member of a student corps, one of those secretive student organisations that are often fairly conservative, sometimes nationalist and – he hinted – on occasion even rumoured to be neo-Nazi. The flatmate still had the scars on his cheeks from the ritualistic duelling that was once a mark of respectability and membership to a very special club, a Masonic handshake visible for all the world to see. Now, in the eyes of many, the student corps were seen as something of a throwback; a world away from the modern, air-conditioned libraries and international student societies, a throwback beyond the GDR and even the Nazis or the Weimar Republic, back to the nineteenth century and the first German unification of 1871. The villa was run-down. The sign was nailed to a shabby door. But the Prussian past echoed.

*

We understand places through our knowledge of them, of what came before. In Greifswald I was re-reading *Man of Straw*, a novel by Heinrich Mann – son of the Baltic and brother of Thomas – that Katrin had found for me in a second-hand bookstore back when we first got together. It was one of the first works of German literature she bought me, albeit in translation, and as she handed it to me she told me that she had always preferred Heinrich to his more famous brother.

Heinrich Mann published *Der Untertan* (meaning 'the Subject' – other translated titles alongside *Man of Straw* have included 'The Loyal Subject' and 'The Patrioteer') in 1918, just as the First World War was coming to an end. In it he tells the story of Diederich Hessling, a provincial, small-minded patriot who is mediocre in just about every way but who, thanks to a strong sense of self-preservation with which he can justify almost any decision or behaviour, manages to rise through the ranks. Odious and morally weak, Mann created in Hessling a biting satire of the ultra-patriotism and new German nationalism that would eventually lead the young nation state, built upon an old culture, into the muddy, desperate trenches of the First World War and cataclysmic defeat. As I had discovered in Lübeck, unlike his brother Thomas, Heinrich Mann had been against the war from the beginning and had understood the dangers of the rise of nationalism in Wilhelmine Germany much earlier. He had begun plans for the book in 1906 and started to write in earnest by 1912. It would take the millions lost and the devastation of defeat before the rest of his country caught up with him and were ready for the *Man of Straw*.

In an early scene in the book, not long after Hessling has moved to Berlin, the central character is persuaded to attend a student corps meeting:

> Around him was the ring of open mouths, all singing the same songs and drinking the same drinks, and the smell of beer and human bodies, from which the heat drew the beer again in the form of perspiration. He had sunk his personality entirely in the students' corps, whose will and brain were his. And he was a real man, who could respect himself and who had honour, because he belonged to it.

Heinrich Mann had begun *Man of Straw* as a warning of what the destruction of German Liberalism in exchange for the new nationalism might lead to. The book is funny, but scary too, and Mann took no satisfaction in being proven correct. And as you read Hessling, as he attaches himself to men and causes that give his banal existence worth, you also realise you are reading a further premonition, and that Mann is creating, in Hessling, a character who is the prototype for the mediocre men who would rise to power under the Nazis, forcing the Mann family into exile and Germany, once more, into disaster.

The gate of the fraternity house was hanging from its upper hinge, the bottom one detached and swinging loose beside a chalky hole in the concrete. There were no signs of obvious life. I tried to imagine what went on behind that door. Leather and metal protectors for the eyes and nose, strapped to the head like steampunk driving goggles above bare, exposed cheeks waiting to be slashed open in the name of brotherhood and honour. Beer, sweat and vomit. Fraternal loyalty. As we walked away from the villa it seemed somewhat unfair on the city that it was this that was occupying my thoughts, thanks to the book resting beside my bed and a wooden sign that I might just as easily have missed.

*

The literature house named for Rudolf Ditzen was closed. It was the wrong day of the week. We peered in through the locked door and walked around to the car park at the back of the building. Perhaps someone would come out, ask us what we were interested in. But no one came out and there was nothing to see. There was another house we could visit, an hour or so to the south, with an exhibition about the man's life and his work, but it seemed a shame that here, in the city of his birth, there was nothing for us to discover.

Born in Greifswald in 1893, Ditzen was the son of a judge who worked in the County Court for six years before he was moved on towards his final goal of Leipzig, and the highest court in the land. Rudolf left Greifswald in the year he started school, and yet the Baltic coast would remain important to him for the rest of his life, and not only because of the place name on his birth certificate. As a child, his family would return most summers and Rudolf would remember – like Thomas Mann before him – the joy of those months by the sea. The anticipation of the packing. The excitement of the train. The carefree days exploring the dunes, playing Cowboys and Indians as the rough grass scratched at his legs, the berry-picking in the woods …

The question that many ask, those who consider the life of Rudolf Ditzen and what he became, is this: whatever happened to that carefree boy? Some lay the blame at the dinner table, where his father told stories of his work at the courthouse, of the endless parade of tales, of arson and rape, assault and infanticide, stories his father would report on soberly and which Rudolf absorbed, developing a fascination with the so-called darker corners of society into which he would eventually drift. The product of his experiences, there was one in particular that seemed to shape the future of a young man growing up in the early decades of the twentieth century. At the age of seventeen, he travelled to the coast – the North Sea this time – on a youth trip to Holland. There Rudolf contracted typhoid, and there seems to be no question that the illness changed him. He began to smoke, began to drink to excess. He nurtured a newly discovered dislike of his parents. He began to write. And he tried to commit suicide.

This was not particularly uncommon. In the run-up to the First World War, Germany was plagued by an outbreak of suicides among its young men, including three of Rudolf's classmates. A year after the Holland trip and the first failed attempt, Rudolf tried again. Making a suicide pact with a friend, but with a desire to die with honour, the two young men staged a duel. The friend died. Rudolf survived. Arrested, he was committed to a sanatorium where he continued to write. Slowly, and with everything that was going on around him, he was developing the talent that would see him published under the name Hans Fallada. But if success under this new identity would follow, the path of his life would not be a smooth one. Here are the headlines:

Contracts typhoid.

Kills friend in a duel (suicide pact).

Committed to an asylum.

Morphine addiction.

Prison.

Troubled marriage.

Bestselling debut novel.

Jailed for anti-Nazi activities.

Declared an undesirable author.

Alcoholism (and violence).

Divorce.

Appointed mayor by Soviet occupiers.

Returned to the asylum.

Alone in Berlin written in twenty-four days.

Dead at fifty-three, in 1947.

As always, the headlines only tell part of the story.

In fifty-three years of a precarious existence, Ditzen/

Fallada combined literary success with spells in institutions of one form or another, always needing to take manual work to eke out a living. It was in one such job that he was accused of selling grain on the black market and ended up in Greifswald, the city of his birth, to serve out a prison sentence. For Fallada it was as if a circle had been closed. As a child he had heard stories of the men who ended up in this very place, and now he was sharing a cell with their descendants. In any case, as a disciple of Oscar Wilde, he saw no reason to worry. It was a literary rite of passage:

I have never been treated so decently in any sanatorium or mental hospital as I am here. As long as I do my work, no one bothers me. I am in my cell, I can read, sleep, write, sing, walk up and down: no one interferes.

What the headlines do tell of is a complex man. Although Fallada's books were condemned, and in some cases burned and banned, it was also true that Goebbels was a fan of *Wolf Among Wolves* and that, in 1934, as a means of getting his book *Once a Jailbird* published in Germany, Fallada agreed to a new foreword that praised the changes that the Nazis had brought to Germany. Thomas Mann, in his Swiss exile, as well as many of the other writers who had fled, criticised such accommodations with the regime.

Not that it helped Fallada all that much. Despite the foreword, the book was attacked by the Nazi press and later in the year his novel *Little Man, What Now?* was removed from public libraries. Retreating to a cottage by a lake that was literally at the end of a road, Fallada pulled himself into a kind of inner emigration, writing children's books or other works that would not fall foul of the censor. This opposition, such as it was, was internal and not particularly effective. But still he could not bring himself to leave, and the financial pressures he was under even led him to write a story under the direction of the Minister for Propaganda, Goebbels, so taken with his novel, for the film project *Iron Gustav*. These concessions would fatally compromise Fallada in the eyes of many, especially those who suffered under the regime and who are, perhaps, better placed to judge than those of us who have never been put in the position to make such choices.

In his cottage close to the Mecklenburg-Brandenburg border Fallada lived out the war, surviving the Nazis and living long enough to see the beginnings of his rehabilitation as a writer. It was helped by one final burst of energy near the end of his life, writing a book in less than a month that adapted a true story of resistance to the Nazis, and gave the Germany(s) emerging from the ashes of war and the Holocaust a tale of ordinary people who did indeed fight back against the regime. But what the book also managed to do was convey the sense of paranoia and helplessness, and the ultimate futility of the actions taken by those who did resist. In the English-speaking world it would be published as *Alone in Berlin*, and a reissue would become a surprise bestseller in the early years of the twenty-first century, over fifty years after it was written. In German, the book was titled *Jeder stirbt für sich allein*.

Every man dies alone.

Not long after completing the book that took him barely four weeks to write, Fallada died, having left behind this final rebuke, perhaps, to those who said that people like him could have and should have done more.

*

We walked through the university campus and back towards the city. I tried to imagine the six-year-old Rudolf skipping along these streets, his father sending the thieves and the rapists of the city to the same prison that would one day house his son. And I thought again of the door to the fraternity house and what goes on behind those walls.

I stood in the swanky new library building and tried to imagine the cold brick of Ditzen's prison cell. But the more we walked, the more my perspective shifted, from the city of then to the city of now. We passed student cafes and searched the faces for telltale scars, but saw only posters for left-wing causes. We passed a former squat that was now a communal housing project, holding an open day, with information leaflets in all the languages represented at the university. A cosy-looking bar. The bookshop once again. I told Katrin how I could imagine living here in this city.

What we know. What we read. But also what we discover.

We followed the lanes back through the Altstadt to the harbour, down to the river. We had been in Greifswald for nearly twenty-four hours and had yet to set eyes on the Baltic. The path along the Ryck would take us there. In weak sunshine there were more people strolling on the quayside than the night before, looking down at the old sailing boats, reading the information boards that told them all about the places of origin and the lengths of the masts, the size of the sails and the master builder who first launched them down a ramp and on to the water. The air was alive with the sound of the rattling masts, as well as gulls and hooded crows. There is a lot of bird-life along the German Baltic coast, whether residents or just passing through, but it often felt

– and especially in the red-brick cities by the sea – that the skies were dominated by these two types of birds circling, these crying flashes of black and white.

Our aim was the Greifswalder Bodden, the bay south of the island of Rügen into which the Ryck emptied. The old towpath along the river had been turned into a walking and cycling route, linking the city with the sea, and it was clearly popular with hikers and cyclists as well as the numerous fishermen on the embankment. They remained hidden from the passing stream of people on foot and on wheels by large umbrellas or shell-like tents, transistor radios and cool-boxes by their side, their rods extending out over the calm waters of the river. Once we left the city behind us there was little sign of human life on the opposite bank. At first we looked across at the apartment developments and boathouses, the corrugated sheds of yacht-builders and a few surviving brick warehouses, but they soon gave way to a marsh landscape of rough grass and tall reeds. A sparrowhawk duelled with a larger, unidentifiable bird. Two cranes took long, high steps across a waterlogged field. A grey heron flew upstream with lazy beats of the wing. On our side of the river we passed the university boathouse and a football pitch, where an ancient roller had been left just off to the side, by the corner flag. There was the usual collection of allotment gardens, beloved of the green-fingered apartment dweller and collector of garish gnomes. Flags proclaimed their support for football teams and city pride, flying above neat bungalows and barbecue terraces. Somewhere, in the heart of the colony, a bonfire of leaves crackled, sending smoke signals up above the neighbouring gardens and across to the river. And as so often in East German towns and cities, the point where the allotment gardens – most of which were established over a hundred years ago – would normally give way to the fields and woodland of the surrounding countryside, we came across yet another estate of concrete-slab apartment blocks.

Leaving the river behind, we followed a path between a fence and a tangle of bushes on to the estate. As in Stralsund and Rostock we walked along wide, open concrete streets that ran in straight lines between the houses. Washing hung on communal lines above the grass that separated the buildings. Another mural on another electric substation. More old men in vests leaning on flower-framed balconies, oblivious to the cool breeze blowing in from the Baltic. More clean cars and polished motorbikes parked in neat rows, within sight of the balconies and their view to the spires of the Altstadt in one direction and the waters of the Greifswalder Bodden in the other. Many of these estates had been bought in recent years by British and Irish real estate investors, although aside from the Audis and Volkswagens parked on the street, the scene looked unchanged from before the Berlin Wall came down. A couple of kids rode undersized bikes down the middle of the street, dodging a teenager on his way home from football practice, his socks rolled down beneath muddied knees, kitbag weighing heavy on his shoulder.

Once through the estate we looked for a route back to the Ryck, but despite the carefully maintained path running alongside the river there seemed to be no officially sanctioned route to cover the handful of metres between it and the estate. At the very corner, over a grassy hillock that hid some kind of sewage or other water treatment installation, the locals had taken matters into their own hands, forging a desire path of compressed black dirt that we followed back down to the water's edge. As the morning had moved into the afternoon, the number of people using the path between the city and the village of Wieck that stands at the mouth of the river had increased. Dog-walkers and rollerbladers. Cyclists and strollers. More fishermen. Birdwatchers with binoculars and telescopes strapped to their backs. Families and couples. I marvelled at the towpath as a community space, the positive impact of the riverbank or the canal on quality of life, and I wondered why no one had thought to link it to the estate. The right to roam applies not only to mountain tops and high fells.

There was not much countryside between the last of the GDR apartments and the first buildings of Wieck, just a couple of ploughed fields before we caught glimpse of detached houses, a historic windmill and a cluster of thatched roofs around an imposing brick church on the opposite side of the river. Not far from where the river empties into the bay we crossed a rickety wooden bridge into the village proper, by another riverside harbour, only this time the boats that were tied up were working vessels: low-slung fishing boats piled with nets and collections of pointed sticks topped with red flags, to be speared down into the bay in order to remember where you had dropped the crab and lobster pots that stood in ramshackle piles between and beside the corrugated iron huts that lined the quayside.

It was clear that despite this remnant of a working fishing industry, Wieck was for the most part aimed at tourists, with numerous ZIMMER FREI or ZIMMER BELEGT signs on cottage windows, a row of restaurants by the harbour, and posters offering boat trips across the bay. As we moved towards the mouth of the river and the breakwater that protrudes out into the Greifswalder Bodden, we looked across to the blocky, utilitarian building that once housed the GDR's marine training school, and was now a residence used for school and youth group trips to the coast. Tied up in front was a beautiful ship, its name – *GREIF* – painted in neat letters on the side, beneath its twin masts. In the GDR this boat had sailed under a different name, back when it was a rite of passage for all young recruits into the navy. Then it was named for Wilhelm Pieck, a Communist hero who had been arrested alongside Rosa Luxemburg and Karl Liebknecht in 1919. As the nationalist paramilitaries known as the *Freikorps* murdered his comrades, Pieck managed to escape. He spent the years of Nazi rule and war in Moscow, returning to become the first president of the German Democratic Republic. His office was in a former Jewish department store in East Berlin that has, in recent years, become a private members' club. A mate of Stalin's, it was always unlikely that his name would survive on street signs or schools following reunification, let alone boats. So the *WILHELM PIECK* became the *GREIF*, while the bar that occupies his old office in Berlin was named *POLITBÜRO*; a past not so much erased as slyly hinted at.

Passing a new flood defence system we reached the breakwater. A hotel stood on the last piece of solid land, its restaurant and terrace looking out over the grey and choppy waters of the bay. A sea mist had rolled in and as we walked along the breakwater we could see nothing of Rügen or where the bay opens out into the Baltic. More gulls sat atop the rolling waves. Cormorants dived and a family of swans swam close to the shingle beach by the hotel terrace. Between the mist and the leaden waters there was not much colour in the scene, just a few red fishing flags planted in the bay and the fluorescent jackets of the fishermen on their boat as it chugged its way in towards the harbour. I was happy they were there, happy that there were still some people working the bay in this settlement by the sea that still called itself a fishing village in the tourist brochures, and yet where most of the boathouses, the workshops and the stables had been converted into holiday apartments and guest houses. As a light drizzle began to fall the boat slowed, so that one of the brightly-dressed figures could lean forward and pull some nets in.

Still, they were moving steadily towards the shore and I wanted to watch them land their catch. We hurried back along the breakwater and across the wooden bridge. By the time we reached the harbour they were ashore, hauling plastic boxes from the boat across a short stretch of tarmac to a garage space beyond. Rolling doors had opened to expose an interior filled with refrigeration equipment and polystyrene transportation boxes. It smelled of plastic and fish guts. At the garage door the men in bright jackets dumped their boxes on scales, whilst another man made notes on the clipboard.

Are they from the bay? I asked.

Both me looked at me. There was no reaction at first and then one of them nodded. His whole demeanour was easy to read. Not only was it a stupid question, but who the fuck was asking? I looked down at the fish in the box as if that would give me a clue to what they were, but something about the way the two men looked at me intimidated me into silence. I didn't ask and instead backed away as two other men approached, each lugging their own heavy boxes to be weighed and recorded. I stood to one side and pulled out my notebook. Despite the less-than-friendly response of the fishermen and the drizzle that was falling, it was, with the boat and the nets and the fish just landed at the harbour, something of a perfect scene.

Don't romanticise, I scribbled in the margin, but it was too late. Greifswald will do that to you.

*

Not far from the harbour and the wooden windmill, on a road that leads from Greifswald along the coast and through the collection of detached houses we had seen across the fields, stand the ruins of Eldena Abbey. This is the place I had first spotted in the top-floor room of Berlin's Old National Gallery, Casper David Friedrich's painting *Abtei im Eichwald* hanging alongside the monk by the sea as I started this journey to the coast, before I even sat down on that bus to Lübeck. It is Friedrich who made this ruin – which he painted a number of times – famous, and it continues to draw bus tours to this little corner of suburbia where the ruins stand surrounded by well-tended middle-class gardens, complete with their collections of patio furniture and trampolines. Perhaps it was the drizzle that moved in off the bay as we arrived, or the steady stream of traffic that passed by beyond the brick walls, but the ruins in person had nothing on those of Friedrich's paintings. On canvas, with the sawn-off tree stumps and hooded figures gathered beneath red-brick ruins in the snow, it looked like a Harry Potter stage set or the land beyond the back of the wardrobe. The reality was more prosaic.

Earlier in the day, at the bookshop where I bought the postcards of a very different set of ruins – 1980s Altstadt – I had found reproductions of a number of Friedrich's paintings. *Greifswald im Mondschein* was painted in 1817 and depicted a gloomy, desolate scene of low waters and mudflats, and a murky view across to the spires and towers of the Greifswald skyline, still recognisable almost two hundred years later. *Kriedefelsen auf Rügen* was also from 1817 and depicted another Baltic scene. This time a couple of figures looked down above the chalk cliffs of Rügen, down across the jagged, white brilliance of the rocks to the blue waters of the sea beyond. *Der Wanderer über dem Nebelmeer*, created a year later, offered up an epic image from the south. But there remained an element of the coast in this image of the forests and hills of the German interior. The solitary walker stood above a sea of fog, resting on a rocky outcrop as hills and trees emerge as if on islands from the wispy clouds. I bought all the postcards, taken as I was in Berlin with these paintings and the story of the man who painted them; another, once-living example of the contradiction of the coast.

Casper David Friedrich was born in 1774 in Greifswald, a city still living under Swedish rule, the son of a candle-maker and soap-boiler who lost his mother and two of his sisters to illness in the early years of his childhood, before witnessing the death of his brother as he fell through a frozen lake when Casper David was only thirteen. Spurred on by his losses, Friedrich studied art in Greifswald and Copenhagen before settling in Dresden, but he would continue to return to his Baltic coast for inspiration as he developed a body of work that reflected a sense of unease with the materialism of modern society, which in turn resulted in a focus on the natural world and the beauty of landscape that was a feature of art across the continent in the early decades of the nineteenth century.

Friedrich died in 1840, before the revolutionary convulsions of 1848 that saw the first stirrings of the liberal German nationalism that would develop into the more reactionary version that came with German unification under Prussian rule in 1871, and which would later be satirised by Heinrich Mann. This was a period of rapid industrial growth in Germany, and there were many who, in attempting to develop the national myth around which they could unify the young nation, were also ill at ease with the developments of industrial society. Friedrich's paintings were jumped upon, representing for many the romanticism at the core of German-ness; the evocative forest and the seashore that stood at the heart of German mythology and folklore, and which Friedrich had captured perfectly. In the 1930s the Nazis would return to these ideas, and it is said that Casper David Friedrich was Hitler's favourite painter, much in the same way that Wagner was his favourite composer.

Hitler. The first, and for many the only necessary, piece

of evidence for the prosecution. You need to do a lot to live down being Hitler's favourite painter, and yet Friedrich's images of the world between and above the trees, of the beauty of the Baltic coast and the ruins of Eldena Abbey, were painted at a time when German nationalism and identity, such as it existed, were seen more as a force for liberation from Napoleonic rule than the expansionist, chauvinist ideology it would later become. At the same time, it is not hard to see the appeal of these paintings for those creating a cultural identity forged on notions of purity and individual insignificance when faced with the glory of nature, of the misty limestone mountains, chalk cliffs or the deep, dark mystical German forest of the fairy-tale imagination. Like so many of the ghosts along the Baltic shore, the subject of Casper David Friedrich is – even before we have had the chance to decide if we *like* the paintings or not – more complicated than simply the taste of a failed Austrian artist who would become the shorthand for evil in the twentieth century and beyond.

I flicked through the postcards, at the bookshop and then later, back home in Berlin. I do like these paintings. The ruins and the mountains. The forests at dawn and the mudflats at dusk. And I am not alone. Despite Friedrich's reputation and what his art would come to represent, in the aftermath of the

Second World War and the genocidal catastrophe wrought by the Nazis, young artists were searching for new ways of imagining what it meant to be German when faced with a combination of recent history and the two Germanys being built out of the ashes – the bland, pro-American consumerism of West Germany on one side of the fence, and the drab conformity of the Soviet-controlled East on the other.

In attempting a re-evaluation of the eighteenth-century painter, the art critic Jonathan Jones was clear what artists such as Gerhard Richter or Werner Herzog were up to.

They, he wrote, *went looking for Germany, and what they found was Friedrich.*

It would shape their own work, not as a celebration of the power of nature and of landscape, but as a warning. What those artists saw in Friedrich was what others saw in the satire of Heinrich Mann's *Man of Straw*. A satire on the hubris of human territorial ambition. In 1814, a century before the First World War and the publication of Mann's novel, a century before the trenches and the defeat of a Germany built out of Bismarck's blood and iron, Friedrich painted *Der Chausseur im Walde*. The lost French soldier of the title was retreating through the central European woods following defeat at the gates of Moscow, passing through once-conquered territory that was now filled with enemies. It may have seemed only populated by trees, but it was no less threatening for all that. The nationalists that followed Friedrich saw in this painting the mythology of German power hiding behind those protective boughs and branches. But perhaps they were not reading it properly. Like Napoleon, the Nazis would founder on the wide-open spaces of the Russian plains. Maybe they should have looked a little closer at the paintings they so admired.

*

In the drizzle we picked our way through the ruins. The abbey was built in 1199 and dissolved during the Reformation in 1535. A century later and the Thirty Years War left it devastated, like much of northern Europe. In the decades and centuries that followed more and more brick and stone was plundered from the site. It has been a ruin far longer than it was ever a working abbey, and it was in the ruins that Friedrich felt the symbolic power of the place.

I didn't. Perhaps it was the steady sound of the rush hour traffic on the other side of the wall. Perhaps it was the squeak and shout of children playing on that garden trampoline on the other side of the fence, oblivious to the gentle rain. Perhaps it was the squawk of yet more hooded crows and herring gulls. The ruins of Eldena stirred little in my imagination, except for the suspicion that as a location for a game of hide and seek, it would be hard to surpass. I got bored of the old abbey long before Katrin, who was happily taking pictures of the crumbling brickwork and trees growing where Mass was once heard. I wanted to go to the pub.

*

We found one back at the harbour, a tiny watering hole with its own smokehouse and outdoor seating that was empty in the light rain save for some smokers. We went inside to discover a dark and small pub, nothing more than a bar with six stools and a single table in front of the twin toilet doors. There was no question that we would be sitting at *someone's* spot, but none of the three men nursing beers at the bar flinched as we sat down. We ordered a couple of beers and a couple of fish rolls. The bartender moved slowly, sighing at the extra work. Two pre-sliced rolls were topped with iceberg lettuce, smoked fish and a dollop of white sauce from a jar. A single slice of cucumber for garnish. But the fish was soft and only gently smoky and the beer was cold. The rain was falling harder now, hammering at the windows. The pub was cosy. We settled in.

The one thing our fellow drinkers seemed to have was time. Each statement was considered, the replies carefully formulated. Sometimes the interlude would involve a couple of sips of beer. Another round of schnapps. A visit to the bathroom. During these breaks in the conversation I looked around the rest of the pub, my eyes becoming accustomed to the gloom. Nets and buoys. Weights and anchors. Photographs of the harbour on days of extreme weather – snow or storm – with ice on the beach, the Bodden frozen.

One of the drinkers saw me looking at a newspaper report pinned to the wall by the door.

You could drive to Rügen, he said. And then, as an afterthought: *Miserable.*

We finished our beers and ordered another. This time the bartender made the round without getting down from his stool. He was about nineteen or twenty. As he placed the drinks in front of us the door opened and a young woman walked in. She said something as she sat down, a handful of words that told us she was his sister, and that they were both children of the owner. She ordered a hot chocolate.

Make it yourself.

Their father arrived a minute later, sitting down on the only empty stool in the pub, next to me. He was wearing a soot-blackened apron and smelled of woodsmoke.

What have we got today? one of the drinkers asked him.

Butterfisch. A pause. *Und Aal.*

The drinker nodded but it was clearly a question for form's sake. The men turned instead to gently tease the young woman about potential boyfriends in the village. Her father ignored the conversation, staring instead at the foam slowly settling in his glass. One of the drinkers stood up to push aside the curtain and look outside. The rain continued to fall as darkness approached.

Through the window and across the river I could see a fisherman roll down the shutters and lock the garage door, checking the lock of the tiny boathouse as he passed. The rain forecast for the morning was falling steadily now, but he did not seem to care. He paused for a moment, looking across at the lights shining from the pub window, contemplating a drink, but it was not for him tonight. Not the same old questions, the same old conversations. The same old stale fish rolls and the same four litres of beer.

He walked instead along the quayside past the restaurant. They were perfectly located, these establishments, facing the boats and their nets. A subliminal message to potential customers.

Look how fresh our fish must be!

And because no one asks, no one learns that the fish on

their plate comes from the North Atlantic or the Philippines, delivered in freezer bags or massive polystyrene trays of ice. He kept walking, down to the path by the river that led towards the estate. An apartment looking back across the fields, to the harbour and the Bodden beyond. In the winter the bay sometimes froze, and an ice breaker would have to clear them a path. Some of his friends must have wondered why he did it, on days like these, but that was the job. Better than propping up the bar, crying over a life ruined by schnapps rather than salt water. There were not many of them left, but if there were still fish to be had, and people to buy them, they would still follow the ice breaker.

In the gloom he disappeared, lost to a low mist rolling across the marshland to the north and in off the bay. It was warm in the bar but still I shivered. We were in for another round, and the one after that. Turning back to my empty glass I looked up, and caught the bartender's eye.

X

The Possibilities of Islands (Rügen & Hiddensee)

Through the Granitz woods – The forest and the German imagination – The days the whale came – The mythology of Rügen – English boys at the seaside – The Goethe Oak – The Colossus of Rügen – Strength through Joy – The New Prora – Erasing the past – Gerhardt Hauptmann and Hiddensee – The unknown island – Seven writers on the shore

From the moment I left the beach and entered the woods the path began to rise, the start of a rollercoaster of a route that undulated along the sea cliffs and through the ancient forests that occupied this corner of Rügen, Germany's largest island. This landscape was formed during the Ice Age, the earth and stone moved and shaped by the slow progress of a giant glacier, bulldozing everything in its path to leave behind something lumpy and uneven, like the finger-pushed crust on an otherwise smooth pizza base. When the ice retreated these small hills were left as evidence of its furthest advance, and having spent most of my Baltic explorations following sea-level paths behind dunes or the straight-line routes along the crest of the man-made dykes, the forest path of Granitz felt almost mountainous; the views down from the cliff-top to the Baltic waters below positively vertiginous.

I had come to Rügen both to explore these forests and because this island – of all the places along the shore between Lübeck and the Polish border – seems to have captured the German imagination more than any other. In this place Caspar David Friedrich had painted some of his most iconic works and, as I stood at one of the lookout points in the Granitz Forest, the chalk cliffs of Jasmund winked at me across the bay in wintery sunshine. Those paintings began a rush to the island in the early years of the nineteenth century and it has continued ever since. As one of Germany's most popular tourist destinations, Rügen is responsible for a quarter of all visitors to Mecklenburg-Vorpommern. It was also the place that the Nazis chose to build an enormous holiday camp for the German workers, and the remnants of their grandiose totalitarian dreams still stood, down there in the trees along the sweep of the bay. But that was for later. First I was walking the woods.

The beech trees of Granitz tell the story of the German lands before people began to interfere and shape the landscape to their own needs. Such beech forests once covered almost 70% of what is now Germany and today, after thousands of years of human settlement, clearance and farming, they have been reduced to one twentieth of their former expanse. Despite this, or perhaps because of it, the forest has remained a powerful symbol with a central place in German cultural identity. This probably began with the Romans, and the victory of German tribes at the Teutoburg Forest in AD 9. It continued through the centuries to encompass fairy tales and folklore, works of art and literature. The forest was, at the same time, a place of leisure and of refuge. It was both real and a place of the imagination.

Whenever I walk in the forest I take with me my own cultural baggage, one that induces a low-level sense of unease. The forest is a place of robbers and bandits, where the Blair Witch lurks with twig sculptures created by the hands of a demonic Andy Goldsworthy. In the mythology of the Germans, the forest means something slightly different: a place of sanctuary in which to hide or from which to launch attacks against the enemy. A place that may be disturbing and discombobulating, but only to the outsider. A place where Caspar David Friedrich's soldier stands alone as the trees loom, attempting to make out movement or the blinking of an eye in the gloomy shadows.

The path followed the high cliffs of the glacial moraine that stands between the seaside resorts of Binz and Sellin. I walked to Sellin along the high path, before returning through the lower forest close to the single track of the tourist steam train, whose whistle accompanied me as it echoed through the trees at periodic intervals. Although it was winter, both towns were fairly busy with off-season bargain hunters, but for most of the walk in the forest I had the path to myself. The air was still, and the only movement came with a flash of colour from a jay or the scurried hurry of a woodpecker spiralling up a tree trunk. At one point the forest path turned into a cobbled street, leading up through the trees to the highest point of the walk, the hill topped with an Italianate hunting lodge complete with beer garden and stands selling mulled wine and hot chocolate. Here there were people, and I soon continued on my way, back down the path and into the trees, embraced by the protection of the forest.

*

Long after the defeat of the Romans it was the turn of the Brothers Grimm, who followed the paths through the trees to collect the folk tales that had been passed down from the generations and which would, later, provide the Disney Corporation with a ready supply of stories upon which to base an entire merchandise and theme park empire. But for the Grimm brothers, as well as the likes of Friedrich and the poet Hölderlin, the forest was more than stories told around a campfire. The mythology and legends of the German forest were crucial to the forging of a distinct, national identity in the aftermath of the Napoleonic wars. Trees, and in particular the oak, would come to symbolise the strength and the solidity of the Fatherland. For the likes of Goethe, the forest was, in aesthetic pleasure and in its beauty, a means of defining German-ness as something different and distinct within European cultures. To Goethe, the forest was organic, natural and wild – especially when viewed in contrast with the order and neat lines of a palace garden. And were not those palace gardens somehow French? Or at least French-inspired? Well then … the forest was, by definition and by virtue of it not being as planned, sculptured and landscaped as a garden, something most definitely and distinctly 'German'.

This symbolism, born out of opposition to imperial forces, would be later adopted by the Nazis, who had expansionist ambitions of their own. During the Third Reich the first areas of natural protection were created for these places that were 'truly German', and the forest had a visual appeal for the Nazi propagandists as well. In Nuremberg, as Albert Speer made his plans for the mass rallies of strength and might, a new forest was imagined; a *Fahnenwald* of banners and flags beneath the spotlight beams that cast trunk-like columns of light into the night sky. There was no escaping the imagery, and there still isn't. At an information board at the entrance to Granitz I read the German word for beech forest, a very normal descriptive word that now carries the weight of a very different meaning: *Buchenwald*. The name of the extermination camp at Auschwitz? *Birkenau*. Birch meadow.

Back in Binz, I followed the path along the edge of the

forest towards the town and the pebbled beach where I had started the walk. Signs warned of the dangers facing the forest, of the rules to obey if one wanted to follow the paths through the trees, as I had done. The warning signs were understandable: lose 95% of your beech forests and you have to look after what remains. Indeed, it was the fear of such 'forest death' in the second half of the twentieth century, at the hands of pollution and acid rain, that became the rallying cry of a Green movement that would become one of the first in the world to be elected into a governing coalition. As the Greens were building support in West Germany, in the East whole swathes of forest were inadvertently protected through designation as military, or otherwise restricted, zones. And once again, almost two thousand years after the victory over the Romans, and if only for the elites, the forest became a place of sanctuary and refuge once again. In the aftermath of the 1953 uprising in the GDR and the 1956 Hungarian Revolution, members of the GDR Politbüro decided that their villas in the north of Berlin were not safe enough from the unruly workers they professed to represent. Fleeing north, they moved into a fortified compound in the forest, just outside the town of Wandlitz, where they lived out the next thirty-odd years of the GDR, cheek-by-jowl in a gilded woodland prison of their own making.

*

On the beach, with a view across to where people walked along the pier or followed the promenade between the row of hotels and the sands, I sat down on a large rock close to the water's edge; another remnant of the glacier's slow and steady push all that time ago. As I sat a couple walked carefully over the rocks and pebbles, stepping around the rock pools, poking at the floor with long sticks. They were looking for amber or 'Chicken Gods', those rocks with holes right through them that are a symbol of good luck. As they passed, the man caught sight of a cormorant on the rocks beyond the promontory. He paused and pulled out a notebook, hurriedly scribbling what I imagined was a description of the scene, here where the bay began its sweep around past the Nazis' holiday camp and the ferry port to the white cliffs of the Stubbenkammer.

Was this a habit only for the seaside? Or was his notebook filled with descriptions and observations of all the places of his life? The moans of railway workers on the night shift as he headed home from a play. The chatter of his neighbours who could remember when their apartment block had no elevator and the flats were still warmed by coal ovens in the corner of each room. The morning rush on the S-Bahn.

The quiet of a cavernous furniture showroom on a midweek afternoon. His street, observed from above from the living room window.

How long had they been coming to Binz? They had the aura of outsiders, but outsiders who are nevertheless at home in their surroundings. They looked like a couple that had been coming here for years, travelling north from their apartment in the city to a house by the sea. How things had changed since they first came. The hotels and the restaurants, the cars in the car parks and the flags flying from the flagpoles. One summer, back in the 1980s, a whale came. He took a wrong turn through the Øresund and there he was, stuck in the Baltic. Back and forth he swam, between the GDR and the Soviet Union, from Sweden across to Poland, over to Finland and back to Rügen. Crowds wherever and whenever he came within sight of land. And then one day, he was gone. He'd found his way back out through those straits where a bridge now stands, back into the open waters of the Atlantic. Yes, things change. But here, down on the beach, sheltered by the canopy of trees that stands above the Ice Age rocks, things change slower than elsewhere along the shore.

*

In the Jasmund National Park, on the opposite side of the bay, a steady stream of visitors was making its way through the woods, either on foot or using the shuttle bus that links the car park with the visitors' centre on top of the Königstuhl – the most famous of Rügen's chalk cliffs. Like Granitz, Jasmund is predominantly a beech forest. Unlike Granitz, the paths linking the car parks to the top of the Stubbenkammer cliffs are often busy, regardless of the time of year, thanks to their popularity with visitors. They come because of those paintings by Caspar David Friedrich. They come because of the forest's listing as a UNESCO World Heritage Site. They become because it remains, despite the crowds, a beautiful corner of the world.

Rügen's role as a place of almost pilgrimage-like devotion for poets, artists and writers as they attempted to shape a sense of national identity reached its height during the eighteenth and nineteenth centuries. As with Goethe and his view of the organic forest in favourable contrast to the prim, manicured garden, this was identity born out opposition, namely to the events of the French Revolution and the Napoleonic wars. As the nineteenth century progressed, so too did the vision of a unified Germany, pulled together from all the disparate kingdoms, principalities, duchies and other territories that made up the Holy Roman Empire.

All nations need founding myths, and for the artists, poets and thinkers searching for a physical space upon which to 'create' their mythology, Rügen was the ideal place.

It might have seemed an odd choice at the time. After all, if Rügen was the centre of anything, it was the old pan-Slavic religions of Svantevit whose temple stood on Kap Arkona. Also, throughout the eighteenth century and into the nineteenth, Rügen remained under the control of Sweden. Not only did neither of these things matter, the fact that the island was under foreign occupation actually helped. Its remoteness fed the idea of a place apart from the developments taking place on the German mainland, and the rise of German nationalism can be seen as much as a reaction to modernity as it was to a rivalry with the French. The first writers and artists who made their way to the island saw themselves as explorers in search of a repository of true 'German-ness' that had been lost elsewhere. On the cliffs of the Stubbenkammer, and in particular the Königstuhl, and in the paintings of Caspar David Friedrich, the essential elements came together. This was the high point of the Rügen myth.

By the end of the nineteenth century, with Germany indeed unified, the writer Theodor Fontane had his legendary character *Effi Briest* reject Rügen as being overly melancholic. It seemed as if the myth had already been shattered. But as tourism developed all along the Baltic coast, into the twentieth century, it proved to be enduring. One summer I travelled with Katrin to Rügen, to walk through the forest and take our place atop the Königstuhl at this ground zero of German national identity. We wanted to look out at where the Romantics once gazed. Deep in the ancient beech forest we came to a turnstile. It seemed that if we wanted to see what Friedrich had seen, we would have to pay. Standing to one side of the queue, an old man with a white moustache sidled over and told me that a little way down the path along the cliffs we would come to the Victoria lookout point, with a view that was absolutely free.

Walking away, I tried to think what the queues reminded me of, and as I looked back at the line of people standing in the shade of the forest, it came to me: the line of people that once snaked out from Lenin's mausoleum and across Red Square. Those queues don't stretch quite as long as they once did, which suggests that the power of the founding myth can fade. Judging by the line on a sunny summer's day in Jasmund, that time had not quite yet come for the Königstuhl.

*

Even if Theodor Fontane's characters were not so enamoured by Rügen, the island continued to attract writers and artists beyond the height of German Romanticism. In the summer of 1931 it was the turn of two English writers to travel north, accompanied by a German friend, for a summer holiday and an escape from the heat of Berlin. Christopher Isherwood and Stephen Spender were both living in Germany at the time, and their holiday at the seaside would be immortalised – and fictionalised – as the chapter 'On Ruegen Island' in Isherwood's *Goodbye to Berlin*.

In the book, Stephen's character is called Peter and the chapter opens with a bucolic description of the view from the veranda of the boarding house they were staying in. Although, in reality, it appears that the German character 'Otto' was actually Isherwood's companion on the trip north, in the book the narrator is caught between Peter and Otto – two unhappy lovers. But despite the tension between Otto's restlessness and Peter's possessiveness that makes up the emotional core of the chapter, the writing is still infused with the atmosphere of carefree days by the sea that stands in contrast to the poverty and political tensions they had left behind in Berlin. That is, until you begin to notice the warning signs that are barely remarked on by Isherwood's self-centred characters but which can be read throughout, for the summer of 1931 is only eighteen months before Hitler's appointment as Chancellor and the Nazis had long been on the move. The narrator describes the scene on the beach:

> Each family has its own enormous hooded wicker beach-chair, and each chair flies a little flag. There are German city-flags – Hamburg, Hanover, Dresden, Rostock and Berlin, as well as the National, Republican and Nazi colours ...

Sandcastles are decorated with swastikas and young children carry Nazi flags as they sing 'Deutschland über alles'. The young men are befriended by a bigoted doctor who describes communism as a mental illness and declares that Otto has a 'criminal head' and thus should be in a labour camp. In a neighbouring town, the narrator meets some Nazi boys who discuss how they are preparing for war. Despite the hot weather and the relationship between Peter and Otto that is played out on the pages, it is clear that the storm clouds are gathering.

What is true for *Goodbye to Berlin* is true for Spender's own book about his time in Germany, *The Temple*. The question that you ask as the reader of both works is whether the sense of threat and foreboding that we can take from the doctor's attitudes, or the children singing songs on the beach, are a result of what we know now. Do we read books like we read a place? If we are not alone as we follow the shore, are we also not alone as we follow the words on the page? What is interesting about the likes of Stephen Spender and Christopher Isherwood, with our knowledge of what was to come, is the fact that these are two men who moved to German precisely as a means of escaping the stifling atmosphere back home:

> For many of my friends and for myself, Germany seemed a paradise where there was no censorship and young Germans enjoyed extraordinary freedom in their lives.

This censorship-free paradise Spender was describing would be soon become the very place books were burned on a square in Berlin only a few years later; a country where Otto and Peter could and would have not only ended up in the labour camps of the doctor's bigoted imagination, but in places that were much, much worse.

*

Just outside Binz I followed yet another path between the trees, much like the one the characters in 'On Ruegen Island' used to get from their guest house to the beach. Here, in the beech forest on a narrow strip of land between the Baltic and the Bodden inland sea that lay behind the town, a huge wooden and steel construction climbed high above the trees. This walkway was part of a new nature centre, and from the top of the tower it offered spectacular views across the island in all directions.

At the top, a little uneasy in the wind, I could see across to Jasmund and the Stubbenkammer cliffs. The pier of Binz pushed out into the Baltic where coastguard ships patrolled the bay. Close to Sassnitz and the ferry to Lithuania waiting at the dock, where once huge container ships linked the friendly nations of the USSR and the GDR, two countries that no longer existed. And, down below and immediately before me, stretching out for kilometres between the port and the first houses of Binz, the so-called 'Colossus of Rügen' at Prora. These were the remains of the Nazis' huge holiday camp, erected along one of Germany's most beautiful beaches. On the top of the tower I read an information board about White-Tailed Eagles. With Prora in the background, a descriptive word for the forest jumped out at me again.

Buchenwald.

From a Buchenwald on the northern shore of Germany to the Buchenwald of its interior: a concentration camp that occupied a site in the woods just outside the town of Weimar. At that very point stood an oak tree under which, it was reputed, Goethe sat to compose some of his greatest works. The Goethe Oak would later be enclosed within the confines of the Buchenwald camp, destroyed by an Allied bombing raid. The very best of Germany surrounded by the very worst. In his book *The Bells in Their Silence*, the writer Michael Gorra is faced with the question that all of us must ask as we make our way through these lands, whether the rolling hills of Thuringia or along the Baltic shore:

> Any student of German culture must learn to negotiate the contradiction and connections that the Goethe Oak implies; must worry at the question of how one may get from the poet to the prison, and back again; must worry at the question of their coincidence in something more than space.

Above the trees of Rügen I looked out beyond the rooftops of Prora to the Baltic sea, and then began my descent to the forest floor. Down there, among the trees, is both light and dark. On the other side of this narrow strip of woodland, Prora was waiting for me. As I crossed the street and the railway tracks to find the entrance to the complex, I thought of the children in Isherwood's book carrying the Nazi flags and the little boy in Katrin's grandmother's photograph. However we move along the Baltic shore, the swastika flag will eventually come back into view. The Nazis were only in power for twelve years, and yet their legacy has so tainted our idea of Germany that it is used to understand not only what happened during the years from 1933 to 1945, but also – whether we like it or not – what happened before those twelve years, from Friedrich's paintings to Goethe's oak tree, and what has happened since.

*

Some memories linger longer than others, and some remain clear, a continuous mental videotape with a start, a middle and an end. My first visit to Prora was in 2004, during my second visit to the Baltic with Katrin. She had taken me to Stralsund, to the apartment and the Grünhufe estate, past the theatre and the remains of the school. We had travelled on, across the bridge and on to Rügen, to see the concrete-slab apartment block in the village of Dranske that had been her first home, as a baby brought north from her birthplace of Berlin. We ended the day in Binz, where we ate crêpes and drank mulled wine by the pier as the tourist train circled empty streets. And on the way we made a stop off at Prora.

Pulling into the car park on that first visit there was no sense of the spectacular. A ramshackle building to the left advertised 'Rügen's Largest Discotheque'. Ahead, a six-storey block with a number of cracked windows was a youth hostel, closed for the winter. Otherwise there was nothing to see as the car park was completely enclosed by pine trees, their cones and needles scattered across the concrete-slab paving stones. Ours was the only vehicle parked beneath the trees, but still we fed change into the ticket machine that stood slightly dented beside the path to the disco, perhaps the victim of a tired and emotional Saturday-night reveller on their way home from the club.

We followed a path around the trees and saw for the first time the scale of the site. A road ran along the back of huge six-storey buildings, each at least half a kilometre long, stretching out along the bay towards Binz, further than we could see. Most of them appeared to be empty, with whole floors abandoned and left exposed to the elements through glass-less windows, but here and there were signs pointing the way to a number of businesses and other projects housed in this gigantic structure: a couple of small museums; a tea shop; artists' studios and pottery workshops; a honey manufacturer across the street from his collection of hives; the youth hostel and the disco. In these huge abandoned buildings a motley group of people had found their space.

At periodic points along the length of each of the buildings, archways led from the road through the belly of the structure to the dunes and a narrow strip of pine trees. Beyond these was the beach, a glorious strip of sand. On that day in January 2004, it was all the more appealing because of the sense of abandonment that seemed to blow across the sands and leak out from every cracked wall and open window. The ruins of the old pier split the beach in two, where taggers had taken their spray cans to the brick walls that had provided shelter for beach fires. All that was left were blackened circles in the sand and empty beer bottles at the water's edge. Away in the distance we could see a few figures walking on the beach at Binz, but no one had drifted this far along the shore. We had it all to ourselves.

We sat on the ruined pier and looked out across the bay – the Prorer Wiek – towards the open waters of the Baltic. It was choppy that day, beneath clear winter skies. The only sound was from the waves and the rustle of the pine trees, and then came a solitary shout from an open window of the youth hostel. It must have been open after all. A staccato sentence in what sounded like Spanish or Portuguese, the specific words lost to the breeze. A reply came, from somewhere down below. The voices drifted away, and we never saw who they belonged to. We sat there for what, in the videotape of my memory, seemed like hours. And indeed, at the moment the film proceeds and we are standing in Binz with our mug of mulled wine, it has already gone dark. Winter daylight is limited in Germany, and the fires of Prora pier had long been extinguished.

*

Within a couple of months of Hitler coming to power in 1933, all trade unions were outlawed and replaced by a new organisation – the German Labour Front – that had as its explicit goal the education of the German workers towards a *National Socialist attitude*. It would soon become the largest mass organisation in the country, and in the November of the same year it founded its leisure wing. *Kraft durch Freude* – Strength through Joy – was devoted to the supposedly free time of the German worker, but its intention, according to its head Robert Ley, was something altogether more ambitious: *Everything we do ... all, all of it only serves this one aim to make people strong, so that we can solve this most urgent problem ... that we do not have enough land.*

The joy was there to build strength. Holidays as an imperialist project.

The scale of the operation was staggering. Into production came the first mass-produced family cars, the so-called *KdF-wagon*. There were subsidised holidays offered, across the Third Reich and beyond. A fleet of cruise ships, including the *Wilhelm Gustloff*, were launched into the waters of the Baltic and North seas. And plans were laid for a holiday resort on Rügen that was to be the prototype for four further leisure complexes. They would, like the cars and the cruises, become central to National Socialist propaganda and help to both strengthen the people and build support and loyalty from ordinary, working-class Germans.

Prora was designed to house 20,000 holidaymakers at a time, in eight half-kilometre buildings laid out along the beach at Prorer Wiek. Each block would contain a restaurant capable of serving 2,500 diners at a time. There would be cinemas and ballrooms, and a landing stage for those cruise ships. Prora was so large it would have two train stations, plus swimming pools and an open-air *Festplatz* for summer evening concerts and propaganda rallies. There would be so many people accommodated at any one time that bathing in the sea would be scheduled, as with the sittings in the restaurant, to prevent overcrowding on the sands. It was to be a spectacular place, built to impress, and a sop to those workers whose trade unions had been shut down. And it would make the people strong, ready for war.

Construction began in 1937, but by 1939, with war already declared, priorities shifted. Prora was unfinished but resources that had been earmarked for the resort were allocated elsewhere. Ultimately the war ended in defeat, and as with so many of the Nazis' grandiose dreams, they did not finish the job. After the war, some of the building work was completed so that the site could be used by the East German army, and one section would indeed become a holiday camp for the family members of the East German military. The rest of the site would also be used by the armed forces, and would remain that way until the fall of the Berlin Wall. It was also used to house those young men who had opted against compulsory military service. Conscientious objectors were rounded up and sent north to Rügen, where they were used as 'construction soldiers'. For these young men, Prora was certainly no holiday camp.

With reunification, the site was handed over to the state and became a colossus in search of a purpose. The debate raged as to what should be done with this place that was, in the eyes of many, tainted by its Nazi and Communist past. Matters were complicated in 1994 when the existing buildings were granted landmark protection, preventing the obvious option that many had been in favour of, namely knock it down and start again. Instead the state prevaricated, delaying decisions or getting lost in discussions. In the meantime, portions of the site were rented out to those small and idiosyncratic businesses and organisations that had occupied parts of Prora during my first visit. In that same year, the local government finally decided they'd had enough and began the process of selling the blocks one by one into private ownership. In the words of the Documentation Centre, who still at the time of writing maintain an exhibition on the site, the state 'washed their hands' of Prora. It would become less a place haunted by its past than a place of property speculation, where there was some doubt as to whether any kind of historical link or memorial to what went before would be preserved.

*

It was through the same entrance and the same concrete-slab car park that I arrived, some twelve years after my first visit. The discotheque was still there, advertising five dance floors and three chillout rooms. The youth hostel had moved to a different block, now with its own campsite, and although it was once again winter, there was much more life at Prora. The Documentation Centre was filled with people, many of whom were waiting for a guided tour. The road that ran along the back of the accommodation blocks was bustling with activity. After all those years of inaction, things had started to move, as the private developers began the process of gutting those half-kilometre buildings down to a skeleton frame before, one-by-one, putting them back together again. This included replacing the cell-like bedrooms conceived by the Nazis with holiday apartments and plush hotel rooms, bakeries and restaurants at the ground level, with balconies fixed to the sea-facing facades to offer views across the dunes and through the pine trees to the beach and the Baltic beyond.

Construction workers moved back and forth, and behind double-glazed windows in some of the completed units the first residents and guests were enjoying the view. Unseasonably nice weather had brought a number of curious visitors to the site, enticed by the banners strung out along the road to Binz that spoke of 'investment opportunities' and the tax rebates that come with putting your money into landmark protected property. A coffee shop was doing good business with all the visitors, as was the bakery. Of the pottery studio or the honey manufacturer there was no sign. Where the beehives had once stood a larger space had been cleared in the trees to build a two-storey car park for the residents of what, the signs boldly proclaimed, was the 'New Prora'.

I stepped inside a show apartment of an otherwise skeletal block. A young man sat at a desk with a couple, patiently explaining the options, the details of studios and two-bedroom apartments, the cost for parking spaces and, of course, those tax rebates. I climbed a dusty stairwell to the apartment itself and, despite myself, was impressed. Spacious and neat, all that was visible through the windows was trees to the back and the sea to the front. Inside the colossus of Rügen you could not see it, just the woods and the water. It was easy to imagine how – as the material downstairs boasted – they had managed to sell 80% of the properties in this particular block before the building work had even begun.

Later, I visited the website of the New Prora project. I was greeted by beautiful artistic renderings and a film explaining how a 1930s construction was being adapted to meet the needs of twenty-first-century leisure time. Alongside new balconies and swimming pools would be concierge services, and once again they stressed the possibility of writing off all the renovation costs on your next tax declaration. I wondered if any would-be investors would be thinking that this all sounded a little bit too good to be true, and – if they had never heard of Prora – where this opportunity had come from. I clicked on 'History':

The first idea came up probably in 1935. It was supposed to be a huge seaside resort for the common people. For this purpose, the most beautiful beach in Rügen was selected: Prora Wiek.

I continued reading. The architect won the Grand Prix at the World Exhibition in 1937, before construction was 'preliminarily terminated in 1939'. Don't mention the war. There was also no mention of who commissioned the architect, one Clemens Kotz, in the first place. No mention of Robert Ley or of Strength through Joy. No mention of giant cruise ships. No mention of the Nazis.

From 1945 on some houses were completed and used as hotel, army accommodation, hostel, museum and artist studios.

The developers at New Prora were keen to insist that you would be buying a piece of a world-famous historical monument. They just did not seem all that keen to let you know why it was famous in the first place.

Back outside the show apartment I walked on to where a hotel housed in one of the blocks was almost finished, and made my way around the side of the building. Trees had been cleared to make space for the new swimming pool. The balconies had been bolted on to the facade. At the Documentation Centre, and in a recent edition of the local newspaper, there had been a warning that should the state sell off the one remaining building at Prora that they still held, then the privatisation of the site would be complete. Would the various new owners and developers have any interest in maintaining a memorial at Prora, a museum or indeed the Documentation Centre? Or would the hundreds of thousands of projected future visitors come each year to the site without any knowledge, or chance of gaining it, as to what the place was and why it came to be built? Sometimes, as I was about to discover, history can be eradicated and erased. But sometimes, with a splash of paint and a shiny new kitchen, a balcony and a concierge service, it can simply be hidden in plain sight.

*

From Prora I drove north with Katrin's parents, following the coastline of the island through the Jasmund National

Park towards Dranske, retracing again that 2004 journey to their old home that had stood on a narrow peninsula sticking out from the north of Rügen. The winter they had lived there – Katrin's first – was legendary. Katrin was six months old in September 1978, and the winter that followed was one of the coldest in memory, remembered in DVD documentaries sold by the local newspaper to this day. The Bodden froze. The army drove its tanks out on to the ice. The walls of snow on either side of the single road that led in and out of Dranske were over three metres high. Sometimes the snow flurries were such that as soon as you had finished digging your car out of the overnight snowfall you had to go to the back and start again.

Drankse had been an important naval base since before the establishment of the German Democratic Republic, but in East German times it was expanded, necessitating the building of new housing blocks for the officers, sailors and their families. As with elsewhere in the GDR, these were the new-style blocks, built on the edge of the old fishing village. As well as the apartment buildings there was a squat central supermarket, schools and doctors' surgeries, and all the other infrastructure needed for what amounted to a new town among the fields and dunes at the very edge of the country. The first time we had come to Dranske some of the blocks were still standing, but now there was very little evidence of the GDR period remaining. Just the school still stood, a hollowed-out ruin awaiting demolition. The supermarket was gone. As were the doctors' surgeries, replaced by new detached houses. All the apartment blocks had been cleared, leaving only a grassy field. The estate, the new town, where Katrin had spent the first winter of her life, had almost disappeared without trace.

Our building was there … Jürgen lived over there … the Müllers just there. The kindergarten was on that corner … No, it was the other one …

Gabi and Fritz were pointing through the windscreen at empty spaces. They could see their Dranske as they showed it to me, but I was left with just grassland and neat, boxy detached houses. I had no access. We moved on, past the football club that had changed its name and the old naval club – where they had gone drinking and dancing, for film nights and other cultural activities – that was now a hotel, looking out over the harbour and the Bodden, making the best of Dranske's lonely isolation and wild beauty.

We turned down past some allotment gardens and the peninsula narrowed, barely ten metres across between the Bodden and the Baltic. The car rocked and rolled over the concrete slabs. We were surrounded by water and yet couldn't see it, our view blocked by the dunes and tall grass. This had been Fritz's way to work, heading down the lane from town to the base at the very point of the peninsula. Just before the peninsula opened out again we came to a halt. A lonely bus stop and a tight turning circle. A locked gate behind a striped red and white barrier protruding from a guard's hut. The glass was shattered, the barrier slightly bent. This was not the most northerly point in the GDR – that honour belonged to Kap Arkona, where Friedrich's monk had once wandered the hilltop – but it was this place outside Dranske that really felt like the end of the road.

We turned and drove on, to Kap Arkona and Schinkel's lighthouse where I searched in vain for traces of what I saw in the painting that hung in the Berlin museum, but my mind was occupied by Dranske. Beyond that barrier was the remains of the base, where there had once been barracks and drill halls, boat clubs and a swimming pool, a theatre and a running track. Faced with the gate it felt like a lost world, accessible only through Fritz's stories and those of others who remembered it. At Kap Arkona there was no monk standing on the cliff top. At Prora and Dranske I was also moving through scenes of much more recent history that were slowly disappearing from view.

Back at the apartment in Binz I logged on to Google Maps,

trying to see from above what had been hidden from me at ground level. Among the trees and framed by sandy beaches, the peninsula was populated by a few grey buildings next to neat patches of wasteland where the others once stood. The harbour, from which Fritz had gone to sea, was still in place, its dark waters and piers protected by sea walls sticking out into the Bodden. And then, further down the peninsula, there was nothing more than dense trees and the outline of paths and tracks. No more buildings, just the forest before it gave way to grasslands leading down to a narrow channel. If I could have walked beyond that locked gate it would have taken me about an hour to reach the very end of the peninsula, to that sliver of beach beyond the forest and the grassy fields. That channel, through which the GDR navy boats once sailed on their way to the open waters of the Baltic and safe harbours in the Soviet Union, separates Rügen from a sandbank of its sister island. It is a place I have only ever seen once, and only from a distance. An island whose very name evokes mystery, at least for English speakers: the island of Hiddensee.

*

Gerhart Hauptmann first visited Hiddensee on his honeymoon in 1885. The playwright and novelist would later return many times, spending all but one summer on the island between the years of 1916 and 1938. In 1930 he bought a house on Hiddensee that would become his refuge, a place of work and contentment, a place of peace even during those final four summers, from 1940 to 1943, when war raged across Europe.

By the time Hauptmann established himself on Hiddensee he was already famous. Born in 1862, in what is now Poland, he wrote his first play for his brother's wedding, and following some years of travel and study in places as varied as Rome, Dresden, Jena and Berlin, he found his calling. Three plays – *The Reconciliation* (1890), *Lonely People* (1891) and *The Weavers* (1892) – made his reputation as a playwright of both talent and social conscience. In 1912 he was awarded the Nobel Prize for Literature, although this accolade did not reflect the opinion held of him by the establishment in his own country. Kaiser Wilhelm II disliked his work so much that he personally vetoed any further awards for Hauptmann until the outbreak of the First World War, when, like his fellow writer Thomas Mann, he supported military action and finally gained official recognition. After the war he was a supporter of democracy and was even, at one point, offered the position of Chancellor. But by this point Hauptmann was enjoying his position as the distinguished grand old man of German letters, making plenty of money in the fledgling film industry while spending his summers hidden away at his island retreat on the Baltic coast.

If it was the isolated beauty of Hiddensee that first attracted him to the island, it was his fame that kept him coming back. To this day, cars are banned from the island and the population is limited by planning restrictions and the need to get a ferry over there. For a man like Hauptmann it was a place to escape from the attention and responsibility, and I could imagine him stepping on to the ferry from Stralsund or Rügen with a sigh of relief, watching as everyday life retreated in the churn of the waters off the back of the boat as the low, flat, silent island of his summers came ever nearer. On Hiddensee he could work without distraction and then take to the garden, to breathe in the clear, Baltic air.

But as the Nazis rose to power everything in Germany changed, and Hiddensee would be no different. By the mid-1930s the island had become something else.

In the beginning Hauptmann made his peace with the regime, signing an oath of loyalty in 1933 even though he believed himself above politics. This was, like Thomas Mann's earlier vision of himself as a non-political man, a ludicrous position at any time, but especially as the Nazis tightened their grip on the country. Like Hans Fallada, he stayed in Germany throughout the period of the Third Reich and the Second World War, sometimes finding his work censored but at other times finding himself celebrated. During his eightieth birthday celebrations he was feted by leading members of the Nazi Party, and in 1944 he was granted the status of 'irreplaceable artist' which meant that as total mobilisation approached, even this genuinely old man of German letters was exempt from combat.

Hauptmann survived the Nazis – only just, dying of bronchitis in 1946 – but his accommodations with the murderous regime threatened his reputation and his literary legacy. But as with Hauptmann's own motivations during that period, working out what Hauptmann meant to German literature and society when he died was not a simple matter. Despite his generally accepted status during the Nazi period, he was considered an important part of the literary tradition in the German Democratic Republic thanks to plays such as *The Weavers*, and his funeral was attended by the GDR President Wilhelm Pieck. His Hiddensee house was turned into a museum to this writer of social conscience and it remains so in the second decade of the twenty-first century.

But Gerhart Hauptmann is still a controversial figure. After all, this was a man who joined Goebbels'

Reichstheaterkammer while trying to do his best by his Jewish friends, including attending the funeral of one of his closest colleagues despite being expressly forbidden to do so by the regime. When thinking of Hauptmann, the same question comes to mind that always appears when considering stories like this: what would you do? Heinrich Mann or Thomas Mann? Hans Fallada or Gerhart Hauptmann?

I tried to imagine Hauptmann in the summer of 1941 or 1942. The war was turning and he must have known, should defeat come, that the compromises he had made with the regime would surely come back to haunt him. And not only in his lifetime, for he was already well into his seventies, but in his reputation long after his death. He knew the books of his contemporaries had been burned on the streets of Berlin, and perhaps that elsewhere, not far from where he was born, Heine's prophecy had come to pass and people were being burned too. He must have seen that island in the Baltic as a true escape then, a utopia located far from the flags and the slogans and the hysteria of the city at war. Untouched and untouchable, like Fallada's house at the end of the lane. How nice for them.

In any event, utopias don't exist. There is always another ferry, another newspaper to land on the mat. The sanctuary of the sea can only ever be a temporary one. Reality, and its judgement, will come. I think of Hauptmann on Hiddensee a few years earlier, in 1937 or 1938, walking the dunes as Thomas Mann had been doing in Nidden all those kilometres to the east. Hauptmann could never really escape on Hiddensee. As Mann found, the only true escape was exile. And in the landscape of the mind and the imagination, not even then.

*

I have only ever seen Hiddensee from across the water. On the island of Ummanz, attached to Rügen by a bridge, I walked through a marshland landscape past a campsite and a kitesurf school, the water glassy in the still of an early evening. It was summer, on a trip north that I barely remember. A school group had set up an encampment on the edge of the site, and the kids were down by the sliver of beach, squealing with mock fright as they dipped their toes in the Baltic waters. From a vantage point just above the beach I could see beyond them and across the straits to Hiddensee.

Despite having never been there, the island has long fascinated me. I had seen pictures of low-lying grasslands and empty spaces, the rolling dunes beneath big Baltic skies. I had heard how there were no cars on the island, and of the quiet and the absence of light pollution at night. I scrolled along its length on Google Maps, imagining walks and what it would have meant to know this place as a kid. To name the slight rises in the landscape and the bays and sandbanks; to camp out at night on the beach, as we did on Anglesey when we were younger. This self-contained world. This is the possibility of islands, and I have been in love with the very *idea* of islands ever since I was young and read *Swallows and Amazons* for the first time. Islands were places of exploration, but ones which you could map and know in their entirety. They had defined boundaries – small, orderly worlds – upon which to base your stories and your adventures. With Hiddensee there was also its remoteness to consider, something shared with Scottish islands but not so much those along the German Baltic coast. I once used it as a setting for a short story, centred on the delirium of a Stasi agent a long way from home and the morality of spying on our neighbours. And yet, despite my interest in the place, I had never been. What had stopped me stepping on the ferry to make the short crossing? As I stood on Ummanz I did not have an answer, and I do not have one now, other than to say that it is perhaps my fear that it cannot live up to what I imagine it to be. That is all I have, and it is not very much. There is no real excuse not to catch the boat, although part of me does enjoy the fact that – for now – it exists only in my imagination.

At the campground the kids were called back from the beach by a teacher's whistle, their place taken by a couple of local lads on bicycles. One had a bag of charcoal strapped to the back of his bike, the other was transporting a case of beer. Gathering rocks on the beach they quickly built their barbecue, using twigs and a television listings magazine liberated from the coffee table at home to get the thing going. They sat back with their beers, smoking cigarettes and talking in a low murmur until the coals were hot and two further friends had arrived with the grill and the polystyrene trays of shrink-wrapped meat. I wondered if any of these boys had been to Hiddensee, just over there, across the water. There was every chance that they had not, and every chance that it had never occurred to them. As they began to eat, I left them to their meal.

*

Seven writers on the shore. Spender and Isherwood, sunbathing in the shadow of swastika flags, soon to leave this country that had seemed like such an escape behind them. Günter Grass in Danzig as the war rages, soon to make a decision he will hold close to his chest until the final decade of his life. Heinrich Mann in exile, his books burned in Berlin as Goebbels delivers a speech, mentioning the son of Lübeck by name as the works of Fontane, Marx and the rest go up in flames. His brother Thomas, also in exile, although wary so long as his books remain in print. And Fallada and Hauptmann, in their corners of the country, internal exiles who can never escape. Again the question: what would we have done?

If we don't march behind the flag and the burning torches then escape and exile, one way or another, is the only choice we have. But in truth, it is not a question we can hope to answer. Not among the gentrifying ruins of Prora where the only danger is that the memory fades, nor on the beach at Ummanz amidst the buzz of mosquitos, the crackle of the fire and the view across to Hauptmann's utopian island; a softly-lit smudge in the evening light, between the sky and the sea.

XI

Falling from the Sky
(Usedom)

Outside the ice cream shop – First impression of Peenemünde – Wernher von Braun and dreams of space – The ambivalence of technology – Golm and the graves of Swinemünde – East Prussia and the lost Baltic – Salt Huts of Koserow – The Amber Witch

At Karlshagen, a couple stood outside the small row of shops across the street from the campsite. At this time of year they hadn't expected it to be open, but when they pulled off the road in the dark the evening before the barrier had lifted, and they were given a spot down where the pine forest met the dunes. A couple of static caravans had lights on, and a Dutch camper van was parked a few pitches down. But otherwise the site was empty. In the morning they had walked through the town, past the neat rows of thatched cottages and new-build holiday apartments close to the marina. The bakery was open, and the ice cream shop, but the town felt depopulated, recently abandoned.

They kept walking, following the road that led them out of Karlshagen to the north. Once the pavement gave out they followed the bicycle path, running parallel to the street with a neat strip of grass and saplings between them. On the opposite side of the path the forest had closed in, lined with signs at frequent intervals.

MILITARY ZONE! DO NOT PASS THIS POINT! DANGER OF DEATH!

There was to be no drifting, no cross-country explorations through the trees. Stick to the road or turn back. One of the couple pulled out their phone, shading the screen from the weak sunshine as they waiting for the GPS satellites to home in on their location. The blue, flashing circle had picked them out on the narrow strip of grey surrounded by green. Scrolling in, it was as if they were attacking themselves from above. What lay beyond those trees? Paths and tracks criss-crossed the forest they were forbidden to enter, leading to and from faint circles in the earth. Alien landing sites? They flipped back to map view with a tap of the finger.

Prüfstand 11.

Prüfstand 13.

No further information.

Testing facilities. Military warning signs. A railway line disappearing off, into the trees. It was still a few kilometres to Peenemünde and there was a chill in the air now. A movement in the branches above. An involuntary shiver. They decided to turn, to walk back the way they came, back to Karlshagen.

*

Slowly, we drove through Karlshagen, past the campground and the bakery and a young couple arguing in the winter sunshine. Katrin was driving, taking her time on the empty streets. We drove through the forest, past the military warning signs and a patch of felled trees being loaded on to the back of a trailer, the only sign of activity before we reached the town limits of Peenemünde. Here we crossed railway tracks and came upon a collection of GDR apartment blocks and the crumbling remains of the red-brick *Sauerstoffwerk* – a place where liquid oxygen was prepared for the V2 rockets that, for a time, were built at this end of the island of Usedom. It was the first of many such ruins scattered around Peenemünde and the surrounding countryside.

A minute later we reached the harbour and the end of the road. Large signs announced new housing developments, with pictures of happy, smiling nuclear families standing in their sunshine gardens beside a swanky new marina. Behind the sign a slowly-rotting submarine sat high in the water of the old harbour. Despite a line of kiosks selling *U-Boot* memorabilia, access to the submarine was currently restricted, the fence to the metal walkway padlocked. There was no parking at the harbour, so Katrin swung the car around and followed the signs to an open expanse of wasteland where seven or eight other cars were parked, clustered around the ticket machine.

Climbing out the car we looked across towards what was left of the Peenemünde research and development factory, a place built to create the rockets that would rain terror down on the cities of Europe and win the war for Nazi Germany. There was not much left: a couple of squat buildings including the old control room; the medical block (abandoned and boarded up); some warehouses, now home to a UV-lit crazy golf course and, as with Prora, a disco. Dominating the scene was the hulking presence of the former power station, built to provide energy for the research and manufacture of the rockets, and which would be later used to create energy for the general grid of GDR. The power station stood at the water's edge, where barges from Silesia delivered coal to be fed into the ever-hungry furnace at the heart of the building.

*

It was Wernher von Braun's mother who recommended the fishing village of Peenemünde as *just the place for you and your friends* to create their new research and development facility in 1936, working for the Reich Air Ministry who purchased the entire north of the island for that end. It was the start of a project that led to the deaths of countless Europeans and, eventually, led von Braun to another country and another flag, where he would put a man on the moon.

Not that any of his teachers would have predicted such 'achievements', especially not those who found him sitting in their classrooms in Berlin at the age of twelve. He was a mediocre student at best, even if his music teacher detected the trace of a talent, but what he lacked in ability he made up for in confidence. That he had, his teachers would disdainfully admit, although it was no real surprise. Wernher von Braun was the son of a nobleman, descended from the Junker class of Prussian landowners that had come to dominate the military officer corps and the civil service of the newly-unified Germany at the end of the nineteenth century. His mother could trace her own lineage through various strands of European royalty. So, yes, young Wernher had the confidence of his social status, but destined for great things? His teachers hardly thought so.

Not that Wernher really cared. Like many young boys he had developed his own obsessions beyond the rules, restrictions and conservatism of the classroom, not unlike Thomas Mann in Lübeck. For Wernher, rockets were the thing, an obsession that developed not long after his father had moved the family to Berlin in order to take up the job of Minister for Agriculture in the Weimar Republic. The young man had become fascinated by the new speed records being set by rocket-propelled cars, and so he decided to carry out a speed experiment of his own. Attaching fireworks to a toy wagon he lit the fuse and stood well back. It performed better than he had dared to dream, flying off down the road with fire trailing behind it, a dramatic performance of smoke and noise that shocked onlookers and led to the exhilarated Wernher's arrest by a policeman who had arrived on the scene just in time to see the majestic, calamitous conclusion to the young man's curiosity. But despite the new Republic that was emerging from the desolation of the First World War trenches, background still counted for something, and he was soon released into his father's custody.

Later, as an older man on the other side of the ocean, von Braun would reflect on the fact that his twelve-year-old self was unknowingly channelling the inspiration of a sixteenth-century Chinese visionary by the name of Wan Hoo, who had seen the possibility of using rockets to deliver humanity to the moon. Unfortunately, Wan Hoo's early attempts at space flight proved to be spectacularly unsuccessful. Attaching a kite to sedan chair, Wan Hoo then added almost fifty solid propellant rockets. His mistake, it turned out, was to take a seat on the contraption as his servants lit the fuses. There was a lot of flame, a lot of smoke and a lot of noise … and when it all dissipated, Wan Hoo was no more.

But despite this tragic failure, Wan Hoo's dreams of discovery, of ascending high above the heavens, would continue to stoke the imagination long after his servants and horrified onlookers had cleaned up the mess. A few months after his own rocket-fuelled experiment, Wernher von Braun turned thirteen and received a telescope for his birthday from his mother. Through it he could gaze upon the stars, high above the tumultuous streets of the Weimar capital that had, by the 1920s, grown to become one of the great metropolises of the modern world. Now Wernher grasped the possibilities Wan Hoo had seen for himself some three hundred years before, and he became gripped with the certainty that space flight was possible. Not that this conviction would help his school record very much. Although he began to show some improvement in Maths and Physics, those subjects that might help him achieve this new, incredible goal, his performance elsewhere was never more than satisfactory.

In 1929 the Wall Street Crash rocked the world's financial markets, and sent a shock wave through a Germany still counting the cost of the years of hyperinflation that had only recently come to an end. A year later the National Socialist Workers' Party of Germany entered the Reichstag for the first time. Berlin's streets became the scene for bloody street battles between the Nazis, the Communists and the authorities. By this time, the fifteen year old Wernher had been sent to a boarding school on a North Sea island, far from the chaos of the capital, where he read the novels of Jules Verne, worked on his music compositions and continued to daydream of journeying to the stars. It was in his room at boarding school that he would make the sketch that he kept close to him for the rest of his life.

The outline of his drawing was a teardrop shape and inside it, the cross-section of a space capsule. The sketch was precise, neatly shaded, and labelled in von Braun's schoolboy German handwriting:

Food for 100 Hours
Photographic Equipment
Astronomical Telescope
Radio Equipment
Gyro (can be turned off)
Magnesium supply (for signalling purposes)
Oxygen for 120 hours …

Only a few years later and von Braun was back in Berlin, a keen member of the *Verein für Raumschiffahrt*, an amateur rocket society. His enthusiasm and talent caught the attention of an army ordinance officer called Dornberger, who saw something in the young man and, more than that, saw something in the rocket technology these happy amateurs had developed. Seeing the military application of the technology, Dornberger arranged for Wernher to be given a university place in order to continue his research in a more formal setting. As he completed his first year of studies for a doctorate as a precocious twenty-one-year-old, Germany changed in a way that would have a massive impact on Wernher's future: Adolf Hitler came to power.

A year later he was finished and began to work for the German Army. His mother's advice led to the establishment of the facility at Peenemünde where, via a series of circular launch sites carved out of the forest and a newly-laid airstrip, Wernher von Braun and his team of visionaries could launch their rockets into the sky to fall harmlessly into the Baltic Sea. They would perfect the technology and develop the V1 and V2 rockets to be aimed at the cities of Europe. And later, much later, Wernher von Braun would achieve Wan Hoo's dream and put that man on the moon. But in Peenemünde, whether he liked it or not, Wernher von Braun was now working to further the goals of Hitler and the Nazi Party. He was no longer channelling the tale of a Chinese visionary, but that of Faust – a story much closer to home. It was only near the very end of his life that he would come to terms with his own pact with the devil.

*

We entered the former control room at Peenemünde and paid our admission. The museum, both inside and out on the grounds, was designed to provoke. From the first displays we were expected to ask questions about the ambivalence of technology, about how schoolboy dreams of space flight led to delivery vehicles for death. Those rockets stood as replicas in the grounds between the control room and the power station, bilingual signs reminding us of the numbers.

V1 Rocket: Fired 22,000 times.

V2 Rocket: Fired 3,000 times.

And the details of what this meant. The deaths in Antwerp and London. The destruction of cities. The miracle weapon supposed to end the war in Germany's favour but which never did. The slave labourers who built these rockets and were killed in their construction. More of them, in fact, than ever died in their operation. And in Peenemünde, among the trees on the edge of neighbouring Karlshagen, where the bakery and the ice cream do off-season business across the road from the campsite, there lived not only the engineers, the scientists and their families, but also men and women housed in a concentration camp that opened in 1943; an extension of the infamous Ravensbrück camp in Brandenburg.

With this knowledge we explored the site. Katrin took photographs and I took notes. Later we discussed how we could talk about this place with our daughter. Lotte was not yet ten years old. She had no understanding of the meaning of the word 'Holocaust'. Was it possible we could wait a little longer?

We continued to walk the site. In truth, Peenemünde as we found it was little more than a memory, with much of what was once part of the research and development site long gone, thanks to the bravery of a couple of Polish slave labourers who were held in the nearby Trassenheide camp. In 1943 they managed to smuggle maps and sketches of the facility out of the camp, passing them through the hands of the Polish resistance and British intelligence until they reached the RAF. Now it was not only the rockets falling from the sky, harmlessly into the gentle Baltic waves, but enemy bombs. The facility was evacuated in a rush as Wernher von Braun and his team decamped to the south and a set of underground factories in the Harz mountains, just a short distance from where the witches dance in Goethe's tale, gathering on Walpurgis Night on the slopes of the Brocken mountain.

Do rockets bring us closer to heaven, or hell?

The exhibition at Peenemünde asks this question up front, and in bold letters. Ask Wernher von Braun, whose talents helped the Nazis destroy Antwerp and huge swathes of

London, and yet also saved him from the normal fate of an SS officer in post-war Germany as he was, instead, spirited away to the United States in order to work for NASA, to lead the Apollo missions and put that man on the moon. From an underground lair, working for Hitler, to an iconic, inspirational glimpse of the future. It turned out that it was not such a long journey after all. From Nazi Party member to American citizen. From working for Adolf to working for JFK. But however much his reputation was rehabilitated on both sides of the Atlantic, the thought remains: he may have sat in that boarding school at the North Sea and dreamed of the moon and the stars, but he built rockets that killed civilians in their sleep. No wonder Peenemünde was an unsettling place. At the chain fence, where the coal was lifted from the barges to be taken to the power station, I looked back across the wasteland car park towards the harbour and the billboards for the new developments around the marina. A second home, here?

Back in the car park it seemed as if Peenemünde was not only populated by ghosts, but by ghouls as well. Gathered in the car park a group of men, all shaven heads and steroid-pumped muscles, swigged from cans of energy drink that rested on the roof of a car plastered with stickers pledging allegiance to a band with a notoriously neo-Nazi fan base. What were these boys doing in Peenemünde? Had they come to debate the ambivalence of technology, or the contradictions of Wernher von Braun's life and work? I should have stopped to ask, but I was a coward in the wintery Baltic sunshine. Instead I followed Katrin, who had unlocked the car, and we climbed inside. Despite the closed and locked doors, we did not start to talk until we had left the wasteland and driven past the red-brick ruins and the holiday homes, the railway lines and the concrete-slab apartments, and we were once more surrounded by the safe embrace of the forest and the road to Karlshagen.

*

At the other end of the island we pulled into a sandy car park at the end of a lane. The sun had gone now, lost behind heavy clouds. Alongside the car park was a pub. A sign on the gate told us they had gone on holiday; annual leave for the innkeeper. At the edge of the car park a raised path led out across a strip of wetland, perhaps 250 metres across. On the other side of the marsh: Poland.

The last three kilometres of Usedom Island are part of Poland and have been since the end of the Second World War, when the town of Swinemünde – the largest settlement on the island – became Świnoujście as part of the transfer of lands and the expulsion of populations as the maps of Europe were redrawn by the victorious powers. The wooded slopes of Golm, just outside Swinemünde, were once a popular Sunday excursion for the population of the port and spa town. After the war it was separated from Świnoujście by a heavily fortified border strip. Now, with both countries in the European Union and part of the Schengen agreement, Sunday strollers and cyclists can once again move easily between the two, with only a stretch of peat bog and a couple of painted border posts to mark the dividing line.

It was not time for us to cross the border. Not yet. Instead we turned away from Poland and followed a gravel track, gently rising towards a wooded hill. The wind had dropped and there was no sound from the trees. No sound, indeed, from any birds. Just our footsteps crunching in the gravel. Across the bog we could see smoke rising from the chimneys of the houses in Poland, but otherwise there was no movement to catch the eye. The hill we were slowly climbing was the highest point of the island, standing at 59 metres above sea level. It was this vantage point that had made it such a popular destination before the war, but we had come for a different reason.

The hill stretched out in front of us. Wooden crosses scattered up one slope. A collection of granite headstones across another. And beneath the earth and the trees and the handful of markers, the remains of thousands of victims of one of the most deadly single nights of bombing during the entire Second World War.

When the *Wilhelm Gustloff* was sunk in the Baltic a few hundred kilometres to the east of Usedom, some of the survivors pulled out of the icy waters were landed in the town of Swinemünde where they joined thousands of other refugees from the east, many of whom were housed in a camp that spread out across the spa grounds between the harbour and the beach. Joining them in this makeshift accommodation were wounded soldiers from the fighting, as the German Army fought what would be a futile rearguard action against the relentless advance of the Red Army towards Berlin. This was the scene, overcrowded and desperate, some six weeks after the sinking of the former KdF cruise ship, when the 8th US Air Fleet launched an attack on the naval marshalling yards of Swinemünde. On 12 March 1945, some 670 bombers dropped nearly 1500 tons of bombs on the town, with a direct hit on the refugee and hospital encampment. The death and devastation of the raid is barely imaginable. As the town burned, survivors began the process of transporting the dead to what had become a military cemetery on the slopes of the hill at Golm earlier in the war. No one really knows how many people died, with estimates varying between 5,000 and 23,000, and with the confusion of wartime and the countless refugees in the town it is unsurprising that accurate records were not kept. Bodies were loaded on to horse-drawn wagons and trucks and transported from the town to Golm. Those who could be identified were buried in one part of the cemetery, their names recorded on plaques or individual headstones. The vast majority, however, could not be identified and they were buried in mass graves.

Standing at the Golm cemetery I looked out across the peat bog, beyond the Polish gardens to the tower blocks and cranes of Świnoujście in the distance. I tried to imagine the city burning, the smoke rising from all those bombs that had fallen from the sky and the procession of survivors bringing their dead – known and unknown – to this beautiful spot where once they had gathered in the beer garden or enjoyed the view across the island to the blue Baltic waters beyond. And as so often on these trips north, I found my imagination failing me. Oh, I could picture the scene; I could conjure the sounds and the smells. I imagine no birds were singing on that March morning either. But what I could not summon was the emotion of that moment. The grief of loss and the relief of survival. The fear of what was to come next. Of what would fall from the sky or appear over the horizon. And I wondered, again, whether the people ferrying their dead from the town to the hill beyond had any sense that this was something they as a people had brought upon themselves. Is that how they thought? Did they look down upon the smouldering ruins of Swinemünde and think about Wernher von Braun's rockets landing on Antwerp and London? Did they hear horrific stories of the Soviet advance from the refugees camped in the spa grounds by the beach, and wonder at what crimes had been committed in their name to reap this terrible and terrifying revenge? It is here that my imagination failed me, as I pulled away from the edge and continued to walk the cemetery grounds.

At a memorial in front of the site of one mass grave of identified victims, a small sign told me that because of too many thefts, the bronze plaque had been replaced with a plastic one. The list of names that had been carved into this non-precious plaque reflected the cultural mix of the Baltic lands, where a Polish name could belong to a German-speaker, or a German name belong to the son or daughter of Polish-speaking parents:

Else Busch

Albert Fenski

Ladislaus Kaspachack

Anna Krause

Wilhelm Mundt

Otto Pinkowski

Karola Scheusky

Hermann Schmidt

Stanislaus Zajock

Individual names lifted out from the anonymity of statistics numbering in the thousands. On the hillside a granite statue stood, the *Freezing Woman* by Robert Leptien, surrounded by wreaths bearing the colours of Germany, of towns like Neubrandenburg and Ahlbeck, of communities in Mecklenburg-Vorpommern and the refugee associations from East Pomerania and East Prussia, those lands which are now part of Poland or the Russian Federation. The statue was of a life-size woman, pulling a heavy overcoat across her chest, eyes cast down towards the ground. A picture of grief. At the top of the hill was a circular memorial to all the victims of the raid, the named and the unnamed. But where letters once hung within the circular structure, there were only the fixtures. The letters too had been stolen. What should have been standing there was a line of text from the old GDR anthem:

That never again a mother mourns her son.

But the letters had been taken, and like the stolen memorial plaque, the fact of the theft was more unsettling in the here and now than the knowledge of all those dead buried beneath my feet as our voices and footsteps echoed in the empty memorial.

*

The first wave of refugees from along the Baltic shore began to move west from the middle of 1944, as the Soviet Red Army pushed on through East and West Prussia, East Pomerania and German-occupied Poland towards their final destination, the capital of Nazi Germany in Berlin. This was a flight driven by fear. Fear of reprisals for what German troops had done on Soviet soil. Fear of the stories of death, rape and forced labour filtering back from territories already taken. Fear of what the historian Klaus-Dieter Henke would describe as, *a tempest of reprisal, revenge and hatred*. Once Berlin was taken and the victorious Allied forces gathered in the villas of Potsdam, the facts on the ground were formalised, the borders of Europe redrawn.

Included in the agreement was the so-called transfer of the German-speaking populations of those German territories that were now to be part of the Soviet Union, Poland and Czechoslovakia. Altogether some 14 million people were forced to leave homes and communities that had been established for centuries. Along the Baltic coast the total number was 7 million – 4 million had already fled during the war, with a further 3 million 'transferred' in the years that followed. The Allies agreed that this transfer should take place 'in an orderly and humane manner'. The reality was somewhat different.

Some were killed in their own homes, victims of the same form of violence their compatriots had unleashed further to the east and which had rebounded on them. Some ended up in Soviet labour camps, with many never to return. Some Nazis committed suicide, while others burned their uniforms in an attempt to hide themselves in the civilian population. In the icy Baltic waters, 9,000 died as the *Wilhelm Gustloff* went down. These territories east of the Oder river became Germany's 'lost Baltic', and the survivors of the transfer – somewhere between 600,000 and 2 million people died in the process – were scattered throughout the Federal Republic and the GDR. They arrived in a country not particularly willing to even acknowledge what had happened to them or their loss. Beyond Germany there was even less sympathy. In the millions upon millions who had died in the war, from the battlefields to the bombing raids, in the concentration camps and the extermination camps of the Holocaust, the plight of the German refugees was not only seen as far, far down the list of tragedies, but even as some kind of justice. After all, hadn't these sorry figures trudging through the burned and blackened landscape been the very same who had lined up triumphantly behind the swastika flag?

Within the two new Germanys that emerged from the conflict there was also little interest in the plight of their fellow countrymen and women. It was the same as with the victims of the bombing raids of Hamburg and Dresden, where, as W.G. Sebald wrote, *it seems to have left scarcely a trace of pain behind in the collective consciousness*. As Germany emerged from the ashes and defeat, the direction of gaze was forward, not back. From a hilltop in Golm there was nothing to be gained by looking across the peat bog to that land that was now another country. The danger was, as the expellee from Danzig, Günter Grass, acknowledged in *Crabwalk*, that the silence did not lead to forgetting, it just surrendered the subject to the Far Right. In his novella, the sinking of a ship became a rallying call around which anti-Semites and neo-Nazis could gather on the Internet, feeding their own grievances in the late twentieth century with stories from fifty years before. It is why for so long the anniversary of the firebombing of Dresden, an act that brutalised a city and its people beyond any military justification, was marked by skinheads parading through the city. In the back rooms of pubs and chilly conference centres, off-season and often by the sea, survivors of the expulsions and their descendants gather, to reminisce of places many of them have never seen and those that have can barely remember. It is hard to imagine what they expect to achieve. The lands are not coming back. For many, it is just about keeping the memory alive.

Max Egremont, in his travels to what he calls this *Forgotten Land*, lists some of the names people had for their lost Baltic. It was the *land of amber*, the *land of dark woods and crystal lakes*, a place populated by people and horses, *a distant land*. This is how the expellees thought of the place they had left behind and to which they would never return.

It's partly consoling, Egremont writes. *The land, at least, remains where it was: your other country – although lived in by others.*

The land is still there. The rest, the culture and traditions that reflected some of the best and worst of Germany – the thought of Immanuel Kant and the art of Käthe Kollwitz versus Junker landowners, militarism and chauvinism – exists now only in nostalgia-laden DVDs and recipe books, in recreations of maps and the complete Königsburg telephone directory, reprinted.

For many survivors, and even their descendants, the sense of loss that they could articulate was the loss of their landscape. Those snow-covered forests, frozen lakes and rivers. And, of course, the sea: the Baltic behind the shifting dunes, a stage set for melancholy retelling of childhood memories, like Thomas Mann dreaming of Travemünde in his American exile. Since 1989 there has been good business to be made in offering nostalgia tours to Gdansk and Kaliningrad. I always wonder what the locals made of these: as harmless as the Bostonian visiting his ancestors' stomping ground on the Dingle peninsula? Or an advance party intent on reclaiming territories lost? But in these slight returns, partnerships have also been formed. In Nida – once Nidden – at the house where Thomas Mann's son Klaus heard the Nazis' songs drifting across the dunes, a museum has opened co-funded by the Lithuanian and German governments. An aid to remembering where, for so long, the expectation was forgetting.

In Golm I moved up from the memorial and where the

headstones and wooden crosses stood, half-submerged in fallen leaves, to the very top of the hill. Here I could see the former checkpoint at the border, now permanently open. More of Świnoujście stretched out to the horizon, the tower blocks and detached houses giving way to allotment gardens, polytunnels and Polish flags the closer it got to the border. I was standing at the site of the old pub that had once been the Sunday tripper's destination of choice. I imagined the writer Theodor Fontane, who had lived in Swinemünde from the age of seven to twelve, climbing the hill with his chemist father. Just down the hill the Berlin to Swinemünde train stopped at Golm, before the bridge to Usedom was detonated by the SS at the end of the war. It was never rebuilt. By that point the pub had already closed, the military cemetery already established, ready for when the thousands of dead of Swinemünde would be laid to rest closer to their hometown than the survivors of the bombing raid would eventually be allowed to live.

And yet ... In writing these words and remembering that afternoon on the hillside in Golm, I remind myself that what was 'lost' in the German Baltic did not begin with the first refugees fleeing the Red Army or with the redrawing of the borders in Potsdam. The process had already begun well before that. I think of *Kristallnacht* and the burning of the synagogues and attacks on Jewish businesses. Of the Jews of Königsburg, as elsewhere, forced to wear the Star of David. Of the concentration camp at Soldau where 10,000 people were murdered. Of the camps at Stutthof and Königsburg. And of Palmnicken, East Prussia and death on the sands.

The *Wilhelm Gustloff*, again. The day after the ship was torpedoed, SS officers arrived in Palmnicken where a group of some 5,000 prisoners from the Königsberg concentration camp had been taken, following a death march that had begun a week or so earlier and which had already cost 2,000 lives. Forced on to the beach late in the evening, the guards began taking people in groups, forcing them into the icy waters where they were then shot, seemingly in retribution for the sinking of the ship. When the bullets ran out, the guards murdered the remaining prisoners with grenades. Of the 7,000 prisoners of the camp, only 15 survived the death march and the massacre on the sands. When the Red Army entered the town, the beach was covered in bodies.

Reprisal, revenge and hatred. What was lost, indeed.

I walked back down from the hilltop, through the cemetery towards the gravel path and the car park, still struggling with the thoughts this place inspired and the fact that the memorial and the plaques had been desecrated, stolen. I found it both hard to comprehend but also hard to imagine happening elsewhere, where the victims of the Second World War were laid to rest. It was easy to imagine the outcry, if it did.

They had it coming.

Half a question I asked myself, half a statement of fact.

Sometimes the ghosts of the Baltic shore threaten to overwhelm you. The car park was empty. The pub closed. On the other side of the bog someone in Poland was burning leaves, the smell drifting across the border to where we stood.

*

All places have stories, and all are haunted in their own way. In the resort of Koserow, halfway between Golm and Peenemünde, I wandered through the *Salzhütte*; thatched wooden cabins that occupy a hollow just behind the pier, a remnant and a reminder of the pre-tourism industry of the island when Baltic life was concerned predominantly with the twin goals of harvesting the produce of the fields and the sea. The huts were erected in the nineteenth century, close to the beach where the fishermen would land their catch. In the early 1800s the Baltic herrings which were pulled from the sea in their millions were caught under royal license, and in these huts they were packed in salt before being transported across the German-speaking lands and beyond. It would not be long before the herring industry declined in step with the rise in tourism, but as is often the way in such places the huts were retained along with a small fishing fleet as a token gesture towards the past. It is not only exiles who deal in nostalgia, and the Koserow Salzhütte offered some Baltic authenticity for the traveller sick of the identikit bathing resorts now strung out along the coast. The cabins today are home to souvenir stalls, as well as a fish restaurant and smokehouse, the historic location allowing the proprietor to add a euro or two to the price of each dish. Business was slow on the day I was there, and an open door to the storeroom gave me a glimpse of the chef, smoking a cigarette among the stacks of tinned and dried goods.

Koserow was a town of modest charms, but after a missile factory and a graveyard it had a normalcy that was immediately appealing. Beyond the *Salzhütte* I walked through row after row of neat detached houses, some of which were clearly lived in, while others were second homes – locked up and shuttered during this off-season midweek. There were hotels and apartments, a football pitch and a church. I had left Katrin at the bungalow we had rented to go for this walk but picked her up again as I passed by the cabin close to the woods on the edge of town. Together we walked, trying to make sense of the place. There was a crazy golf course and bike rental companies, hotels with banners advertising Bundesliga on SKY and restaurants primed for the mid-afternoon trade in *Kaffee und Kuchen*. At the same time there were also boys and girls returning home from school, the groundskeeper preparing the pitch for the game on Saturday and familiar conversations in the bakery queue and at the supermarket checkout. It was a place that, in the highest of seasons, must be dominated by outsiders, and yet among this transient population lives a core of locals for whom this is home.

*

The next morning we crossed the track from the cabin and followed a sandy path through the beech trees, making our way to the top of the Streckelsberg. This 58-metre hill is the third-highest point on the island and was once much higher. The winds and waves coming in off the sea have cost the Streckelsberg height, as well as eating away at the cliffs despite the best efforts of locals to counteract erosion. In the early decades of the nineteenth century, around the same time the *Salzhütte* were being built to deal with the volume of herring pulled from the Baltic, a certain Forester Schrödter planted beech trees on the slopes of the Streckelsberg in an attempt to prevent it collapsing into the sea. Now he is remembered by a memorial stone, next to which cyclists following the Usedom bike path use the shade of Schrödter's trees to take a break, and Nordic walkers rest their oversized poles to one side in order to stand, hand on hips, as they read the dedication.

It is not much of a mountain, but the path was steep as we climbed the steps cut into the sandy soil to reach the lookout point. Here scientists from Peenemünde would come during Wernher von Braun's testing phase in order to observe the flight and the trajectory of the rockets launched from the north of the island to fall into the sea. Locals would also gather to watch the show, and I couldn't help but wonder what it was they thought they were watching, and whether they considered the consequences of those rockets falling elsewhere; not into shallow Baltic waters but on to the streets of British and Belgian cities.

The legends of the Streckelsberg are older than the rocket scientists of Peenemünde or the trees planted by Forester Schrödter. They come instead from the time around the Thirty Years War, another recurring trauma that I seemed to be returning to time and again on my journeys along the coast. This was a time when much of the continent was decimated by the foraging and pillaging of retreating armies, the droughts and famines that led to crop failures, and the sporadic outbreaks of the plague. Up to forty per cent of the population of the German provinces was wiped out by the conflict and its aftermath, and the fact that this period still features heavily in the folklore of the region suggests that the memory of suffering can be passed down through centuries, the effects of war and famine lingering longer in the cultural memory than the simple thirty years of the conflict. At the time the continent collectively lost its mind, driven into madness by decades of war, death and despair, and the blame soon landed at the feet of witches. The witch-hunts that followed the Thirty Years War were like nothing seen before or since. Two hundred women were burned at the stake in Würzberg. Six hundred in Bamberg. It was in Fraconia that the hysteria began, but it soon spread, eventually reaching the limits of the land and the shores of the Baltic, on the island of Usedom.

It was on the lower slopes of the Streckelsberg, much larger then, that a young pastor's daughter by the name of Maria Schweidler combed the beaches for amber during the years of starvation that followed the war. Those pieces that she found were sold in order to help support her family. Her misfortune was to become the object of desire for the local sheriff who, when he found his advances rebuffed by young Maria, made the claim that her supposedly 'unexplainable' wealth must surely be, could only be, the product of witchcraft. Maria was charged and found guilty, sentenced to death. On her way to the execution, and in the way of all good fairy tales, she was rescued by a local nobleman who she then married and they lived happily ever after. But the legend of the *Bernsteinhexe* – the Amber Witch – is less a story about what took place in a war-ravaged continent some 400 years ago than it is about the literary tastes of a much later era, not only in the German-speaking lands but also Victorian Britain.

The *Bernsteinhexe* was a literary hoax, not a story passed down through generations as part of that cultural memory of war and its aftermath. It was the creation of Wilhelm Meinhold in 1838, almost two centuries after the events were supposed to have taken place. Meinhold claimed he discovered the true tale in an old manuscript found amongst the rubbish of the local church. He published the story as a genuine historical document, putting his own name only to the introduction, and it became one of the bestsellers of its time all across Europe. At a certain point, though, Meinhold wanted some credit for dreaming up and pulling off such an elaborate and successful hoax, so he came clean and admitted what he had done, that he himself had invented the story of virtuous Maria, the randy and scheming sheriff, and the dashing nobleman. Unfortunately for Meinhold, the literary world and the reading public were not willing to admit to having been taken in by such a trite and clichéd tale. They simply refused to believe him.

It took a while, but eventually Meinhold managed to persuade the world that he had indeed invented the whole story, but it did little to diminish the popularity of the tale. The novel remains in print to this day, and there are many versions of the legend for sale in the bookshops of Koserow and elsewhere along the coast. At the top of the Streckelsberg, where the scientists and the villagers gathered to watch the rockets fly, an information board tells the story as fact. Looking out across the water we pondered the blurring of fact and fiction, of how truth becomes legend to be repackaged as truth and once more exposed as invention. I looked left, along towards Karlshagen and Peenemünde, and beyond to Greifswald and Rügen, Fischland-Darß-Zingst and Kühlungsborn, Travemünde and Lübeck. I could see the coastline straightening and stretching out; the bathing resorts and the cities; the whitewashed villas and the water-stained *Plattenbau*; sites of personal memory, of mine and Katrin's, and the sites of remembrance, where plaques are laid and museums built; and then those where the only acknowledgement of events is in your own head, thanks to your own knowledge of what happened. But what happens when you are gone, and there is no one left to remember?

I looked right. The same coast, stretching out now. More bathing resorts. More villas. More *Plattenbau*. The dunes between the beach and the lagoons. The forests and farmers' fields. Beaches for dogs and beaches for nudists. Campsites and a drive-in cinema or two. Beer gardens and stalls selling fish rolls and little plastic messages in a bottle, that you can throw from the pier or affix a stamp to and chuck in a letter box. There are many stories along this Baltic shore but sometimes it feels like the same scene repeats itself time and again: wicker beach chairs and sandy volleyball courts; the trickle of an ice cream down an arm and a cold pilsner to the lips. Only now, the scene to the right of me was limited by a line in the sand, even if I could not see it. I knew that the German Baltic was about to come to an abrupt end, only a few kilometres from where I stood, and a long way short of where it would have done had I been standing here with von Braun's scientists watching the rockets fall from the sky. The sea was calm, glassy, disturbed only by the cormorants as they dived from the surface, the waves tiny against the beach at the foot of the sandy cliffs. Down the coast, around the corner and just beyond the town of Ahlbeck, the waves break on another country, and the self-imposed geographical limit of my explorations would be reached.

There was a chill in the air. We had been standing on the top of the Streckelsberg for twenty minutes, undisturbed, and we were getting cold. It was time now to retreat back down the path through the beech trees to the cabin. There was a train to catch. One last walk along the Baltic shore. The journey was almost over. Almost, but not quite.

XII

Above and Beneath the Waves
or
The Decline of a Family, Part Three

Halfway up the hill, when the last of the houses have retreated behind the beech trees, at the point where the summer cyclists first think about dismounting and starting to push, Maik steps from the path and carefully picks his way through the fallen leaves, branches and ferns, until he reaches the lip of the cliff. Holding on to a tree trunk for stability he leans out, a figure on the bow of a ship, looking down upon the carefully raked sands and the beach chairs laid out in neat lines, locked away for the winter, and then out across the water, the gentle waves of the Baltic as they meet the wooden poles of the breakwaters, their energy reduced enough so that when they reach the sands at the shore they make land gently, with the tiniest of splashes. Maik walks this path every day, in the early evening to his bar on the cliff top and down again in the early hours of the morning, sharing the witching hour with the owls of the beech woods and the last of his customers, as they make their steady way back down into town. In the summer he opens the bar from late morning on, catching the passing trade of walkers and cyclists, but at this time of the year it is only his small group of loyal locals who climb the path to hand over money for drinks. A few more when there is a game on. A few more still on a bank holiday weekend. But today is Tuesday and the footballers are on their winter break. He leans a little further out, feeling the gentle wind on his cheek for the first time. Lost in the view across the water he hangs there for what might as well be forever, could have been, until the moment is broken with a sound from his pocket. A message on his phone. Still holding on to the tree he pulls the device from his pocket with the other hand. Veronica is waiting. And he has the keys. She must have passed him on the path as he was hanging there. Pulling himself back from the edge he makes his way back through leaves and tree roots, scuffing his shoes and the bottom of his trousers. He doesn't care. It is always worth it, for that moment alone on the cliffs.

At the bar he lets Veronica in with an apology and she begins to prepare the counter, checking the fridges and the glasses, stacking the ashtrays ready to be placed on each table, wiping the laminated cocktail menus and turning on the coffee machine and dishwasher. Maik takes a bottle of beer from the fridge closest to him, flicks on the television, and slides on to his chosen stool at the end of the bar. He should really be working the shift himself. At this time of year, and the way the midweek nights have been going, he can't really afford not to, but Veronica needs the money and in any case he doesn't feel like working. Not today. Not most days. He likes being here though, in his cosy cabin on the hill, warmed by the neon sign hanging above the whisky bottles.

Beyond the window the sea has already disappeared into the darkness, but he knows it is there.

When he came to the town – when was it? Five years ago? More? – looking for something to keep him there, it was this location that had attracted him. Even the estate agent had been sceptical when she showed him the property. It had been a Greek restaurant. Failed. An ice cream bar. Failed. A pizzeria. Failed. But Maik had fallen in love with the view, and he knew that it was the key to making it work. So in the summer they shifted more drinks in the beer garden outside than they could keep properly cool, while he sat pretty much alone in the bar's interior. That got them through the off season when the same collection of drinkers sat at the bar with Maik, who would – once or twice an evening – step on to the terrace to look out into the black void, perhaps spotting the flashing lights of a ship heading out from Polish waters or a tanker far out at sea. If the wind was right and the waves were a little higher than they were today, he would be reassured by the presence of the Baltic out there in the darkness, and he would step back inside to the smoke and the music and the next round of beers a little more at ease than he had been when he left only a few moments earlier.

It had always been like this. When he left Greifswald for Berlin in 1990, that summer when it became clear that all the plans he had had, or those that his mother had had for him, were to come to nothing, he began twenty years in the city that, when he looks back now, were shaped by a continuous and simultaneous sense of both relief to have escaped where he came from and a homesickness for what he had left behind. Barely a month went by in those twenty years – regardless of how much money he had earned working in that dive bar in Prenzlauer Berg or the demands of whichever girlfriend was sharing his coal-oven-heated apartment in Weißensee, the one with the broken window in the bathroom that meant the condensation from the shower would freeze against the walls in the depths of winter – that he wouldn't catch the train north from Ostbahnhof (that had once been the Hauptbahnhof), usually to Stralsund but sometimes to Rostock, and from either of those stations he would take a bus to the first small village beyond the city to spend an afternoon looking at the sea. Just looking, until it was time to catch the bus and the train back to Berlin, almost always on the same day that he had left.

Once, only once, did he take someone with him. It was a girl, of course. With Johanna things had become as serious as any of the relationships back then ever became, long enough that she had seen him go off on his monthly pilgrimage to the Baltic at least three or four times. Naturally, sharing his bed and long evenings and nights at the bar, his clothes and his flatmates (but not like that), she wanted to share this part of his life as well, especially as he flatly refused to tell her anything about his mum aside from the fact that she lived in Greifswald, or his dad – who lived in Berlin but who they never saw. This trip to the Baltic which, incidentally, was never to Greifswald, was the only link to his past that Maik offered a glimpse of.

Take me with you, she said and so he did.

The train ride to Stralsund was fine, watching the Brandenburg countryside shift into Mecklenburg-Vorpommern with no way of telling, except for the fact that the graffiti in the train yards shifted from offering support for Berlin clubs like 1. FC Union, or even Dynamo, to the Hanseatic heroes of Rostock. Even though they caught the train in the morning, looking down on to the ramshackle buildings of East Berlin, many of which were still bullet- and shrapnel-scarred from the Second World War some fifty years after the fact, they sipped beers, a sense of childlike excitement of living behind the ordinary everyday. It reminded Maik of those school trips where it does not even matter where you are going. The ruins of a church. A communal farm. A power station. All that matters is the waiting bus by the school gates and the driver with sweat stains under his arms. The possibility of disruption to the daily routine. Nothing would happen. But it *might*. As soon as something is different, something different might happen. That's how it felt, that day on the train.

So the train ride was fine until Stralsund and they shared a six-pack of beer as the creaking diesel engine delivered them to their destination. They climbed down on to the platform with all the other passengers who had reached the end of the line, passing through the old station building with its mural of Rügen that reminded Maik of going on Pioneer camps and changing trains at Stralsund, and then, when they made it to the bus stop and began the short wait for their onward journey, the day began to sour. It was Johanna's fault. Although they were in Stralsund, not Greifswald, and although she had long ago learned better than to ask Maik about his past, she began that conversation people have when they are travelling together, when the bus station bench seems to bring you closer to another person than any number of nights sharing the same bed.

Why do you keep making these trips? she asked. *Is it like coming home?*

He didn't answer and she didn't press it. The bus came and they sat in silence for the thirty-minute journey north. When they arrived at the small village, Maik stood and began to walk down the vehicle towards the doors. He looked back at Johanna who asked a question with her eyes and, receiving the answer she was half expecting, stayed in her seat. Maik climbed down from the bus alone. He spent three hours in the village, walking the coastal path before retreating to a small pub close to the bus stop. By the time he was back in Berlin, back in Weißensee, Johanna was asleep in the bed. They didn't stay together much longer after that. And all because she'd asked the right question.

Travelling north *was* like going home, even though he couldn't. And things got worse, later. As his mum, with her new name and her new life, began to build successes that she wanted him to share and then, later still, when it all came crashing down around her ears. With dad it had always been strained, ever since Maik was young. Back then his mum was his ally. It was her that took him to Hiddensee, back and forth to the summer camps on Rügen or to their cottage in the lake district. She was the figure of strength and authority that his dad could never and did not want to be. As Maik got older the sense of security she offered him became something more problematic. He sensed, he thinks now, that there was something not quite right about her; that there was something hidden inside her that had damaged his father and would damage him if he did not make his escape. It was subconscious, this feeling. He can no more articulate it now than he could then, at the age of eighteen. So Moscow, with her blessing, seemed to be the first step. And when the Wall came down and Moscow retreated from view, it was Berlin. She was less happy about that. But she let him go.

Still he returned to the Baltic. Even after the years of the dive bar and the frozen bathroom, when he was managing the restaurant that was sunk in the basement of one of those concrete, glass and steel monstrosities they erected around the Potsdamer Platz and he had a bit more money in his pocket, he continued those monthly trips. And as time went on and both he and the city he had moved to in those early, exciting years after the Wall came down seemed to change, he began to formulate plans for a permanent return. Just the mention, during one of his infrequent phone calls to his mum, had her in tears at the possibility. She needed something to look forward to, beyond her weekly trips to the shops or those school visits she now made, to tell children her story and find her own way of justifying the unjustifiable.

Maik had read his own file. It was slim, of course, seeing as he was only nineteen when the whole GDR system collapsed under the weight of a thousand chisels hammering away at the remnants of the Berlin Wall. But he had applied, and been accepted, to go and study in the Soviet Union and so they had been monitoring him for a while. He went to that office on Alexanderplatz and made his request, and a few weeks later they called him back in and he was handed a folder, offered a cup of coffee in a plastic beaker, and with both on the table in front of him, he began to read. There was not much, in all honesty. School reports and grade cards. Assessments from teachers and Pioneer leaders. He realised one of his classmates had already been working for the Ministry as an IM, but they had all suspected as much at the time. Also one of his colleagues at the rowing club, which was more of a surprise. And then there were those two little slips of paper, photocopies of fragments of reports written about others but that had relevance, in the eyes of one officer or the other, to his own file. The information was harmless, about his nerves about travelling to Moscow or an opinion, given over dinner, about the behaviour of one of his teachers. But it was still a shock to read the words of his own mother, typed out and filed away in a folder that bore his name.

The only person he ever spoke to about that day was the woman in the Stasi office who had handed the file over to him. *Your own mother?* she said, in a voice that was more sad than incredulous, as if she had heard it all before – and she probably had. But it wasn't as if she had been informing on him. Not directly. In fact, he could picture how it had happened all too well. His mother liked to talk, and she would have loved the sense of responsibility, of being needed by these men in grey suits who were hanging on her every word. And when she didn't have something important to tell them she would talk about her day, as she would with her hairdresser or an old friend she had met in the supermarket queue. *Michael is pretty uptight about moving to Moscow … I told him to relax, it'll all be fine …* or *Michael doesn't think much of his new teacher. And the methods sound interesting, to say the least …* Innocuous stuff piled high to build a picture. To be used against him? Perhaps, one day. But the one day never came. The world changed. The file remained slim.

He never spoke to her about it, and although she insisted, when the whole thing came out and the local papers were camped outside her door, that it had all been so long ago, when she was a student, and basically harmless … well, he knew that wasn't true. He wasn't sure he wanted to learn any more. So no, when he came back to the Baltic after two decades in what was now, once again, the capital of his country, he kept some distance from his mother and picked a town, this town, where he had no connections, and where no one knew his name or any of his mother's.

The bar is as full as it is going to get. Four lads who work for the construction company based on the edge of town, in the small industrial estate by the Lidl and the Audi showroom, are nursing bottles of beer at the bar. A couple are sat in the corner. She has a coke with something in it. He has a half litre of beer. Veronica cleans glasses and stares up at the television screen that is silently showing a mediocre crime drama. Maik is on beer number three, rapidly reaching decision point. Does he hand her the keys and make his way home, to sleep uneasy but wake with a clear head, or does he stay, to add whisky to the beer that will allow him to sleep deeply and without feeling, but that he will pay for in the morning. Same choice every night. Tonight he pours out the whisky. Veronica watches him over the top of her glasses as he does so and he knows she is counting.

Maik put his final beer down on the mat he has been picking at all evening. The customers have all gone. He had known, when he leaned out over the beach in the last of what passed for daylight, that there was little point opening today. He should have sent Veronica home, saved the money and her time, but she had been annoying him from the other end of the bar and he had decided to make her stay to the bitter end. The third beer had become the fourth and the fifth. The first whisky the second and the third. He stopped counting, although if he asks Veronica now she can probably tell him. He feels that familiar, empty feeling inside him. No, this would not do. He did not like feeling this way. For his next birthday he would be forty-five. It was twenty years since that train ride with Johanna to the coast. She was the same age then as Veronica is now. He both wonders what his staff member thinks of him and fears finding out the answer. He decides to make peace.

Standing up from his stool he walks over to the window and presses his head to the glass, blocking out the light from the bar behind him with his hands. Outside the wind has picked up, scattering leaves across the concrete terrace of the beer garden. He cannot see it, but he can imagine the sea, the waves choppy now, the white horses scuttling across the surface, jumping the breakwaters.

Do you know the story of Vineta? he says, into the window, watching his breath form shapes on the cold glass.

What? Veronica says behind him, so he turns and repeats the question. This time she shrugs.

You either do or you don't.

Yes, then. I suppose. Don't really remember the story though. I think they told us at school …

Maik turns back to the window.

It is about here. A town from right here, on the island. Although some people think it was somewhere else. Poland maybe. No one really knows. But I like to think it was here. Where we are. Out there.

He nods, out towards the darkness. He wonders if she is even listening.

It was a town, on this island, that was really rich. They made their money off trade, buying things from one place, selling them to another. All the world passed its goods through Vineta and so it became richer and richer, more than any city before or any city since. Like New York or Dubai. Abu Dhabi! The merchants were rich but so were the ordinary people, and those who called Vineta home lived in the finest houses, ate the finest foods, dressed in the best clothes. And soon they became so rich that most people didn't even have to work any more. They could fill their days in other ways, you know? Dancing, drinking ... Orgies.

He pauses. No reaction.

Men on men. Women on women. Who knows? And then, so the story goes, things began to get REALLY out of hand. Some even say they began to eat human flesh. Some unlucky sailor who was left behind by his boat. But they didn't eat him because they were hungry ... they were rich, remember. They just did it to see what it was like. To try it out. Just because ... Probably because they had too much time on their hands, not needing to work. So they thought up all these unimaginable things. Wicked experiments. Debauched ... horrible stuff. Just to satisfy their idle curiosity ...

He trails off. He is not even thinking about Veronica now. Why had he even started to tell her this story? What is he trying to prove, to gain? He sighs and rests a flat palm against the window.

When he was a kid he was called Michael or Micha. At school and at summer camp. On Hiddensee or with the kids whose parents also had a cabin by the lake. His mum called him Micha, only using Michael when she was cross. When he moved to Berlin he changed his name. Not really, just a little. Became Maik. She changed her name too, when she wanted the hotel, wanted to be mayor. *Things happen in war,* she said, once, explaining about her father, her grandfather.

And what happened next?

Veronica's voice calls out across the bar. Maik turns again, trying to remember where he is. What story he is telling.

I ... yes ... okay. The people of Vineta, after all this had been going on for a while, well they were told that things were getting out of hand. There were some in the town who were still living under some moral code or other, and they warned the rest that they had to change or they would be punished in some way. Biblical. But the majority ignored the minority and continued with the drinking and the fucking and the who knows what and then one night ... BANG!

A force more powerful than anything any of them had experienced threw them from their beds, as if the earth had shifted, tilted on its axis. The buildings began to crumble, one by one, and started to slide into the sea. The water was black, churning and violent, ferocious with a power that those who went in simply could not swim against. They had no chance. Those who tried were dragged under by whirlpools and then drowned in the darkness. And that was it. The town was gone. For months after bodies would wash up on shore, and they were all that was left of Vineta. They should have listened to the warnings. There was a judgement day. A punishment for their behaviour. And so the story of Vineta is supposed to be a warning, you know, out there under the sea, for the future …

Veronica gives him a sideways glance, and then laughs.

Sounds like a load of crap to me. There's no town out there, under the sea.

Now it is Maik's turn to shrug.

She turns and picks up her coat from where she dropped it, hours earlier, on top of an empty beer crate.

I can go, right? This is pointless.

Maik looks at the clock. They should close in half an hour. He nods.

I'll pay you the full shift.

Veronica raises an eyebrow but says nothing. She puts on her coat and walks across the bar. As she is about to open the door she pauses, reaches out a hand and rests it on his lower arm. Just for a second, and then she is gone, out of the door and into the darkness.

Maik locks the door and turns out all the lights except for the spot above the bar. One more beer for the road. For the dusty path down the hill. Outside the beach and the waves are as lost to him now as the ruins of Vineta. He hears a voice, coming back to him from somewhere in the foggy memory of those last years in Berlin, at the dawn of a new century.

Come home. We can sort everything out.

Two weeks later he did. But not to her.

You are a Barthels too, just like me.

She wanted him to change his name. It was during the worst of that time when the truth was coming out. She called him and asked him. But he had done that once and it hadn't made the difference he had hoped. Not entirely. He took his beer from the bar and walked over to the door, opening it to the wind and the night. He could hear the waves and the straining of branches. He leaned on the frame as leaves blew in through the door. He thought of Veronica following the dull lamps that illuminated the path back down into town. He thought of Johanna on the bus and asleep in his bed. He thought of Rosa, and her tales from a lost country. Towns crumble into the sea. The Baltic remains.

XIII

Across the Border
(Ahlbeck – Świnoujście)

Winter bathing competition – the Europapromenade – Local news and the Auschwitz rift – Along the border – Searching for Swinemünde in Świnoujście – End of the journey – Kleist and The Monk by the Sea – The ghosts on the shore

On the beach at Ahlbeck, next to the pier, a crowd had gathered: a huddled mass wearing winter jackets; scarves across faces against the biting wind; steam rising from cups of coffee and mulled wine, held in gloved hands. This was the audience to a distinctly Baltic event and they were waiting for the participants to appear from a marquee that had been erected on the sands. A local radio DJ welcomed the crowd to the annual winter bathing competition to glove-muffled applause, before outlining the rules and the prizes on offer for the best costumes, as judged by a jury panel of local dignitaries. Beyond the marquee, down the gentle slope of the sands, the grey Baltic waited for them as – to the east, beyond the border – a military ship made its way out from Świnoujście towards the horizon.

Each team emerged from the marquee in turn. They came not only from Ahlbeck but from other communities both on Usedom and elsewhere in Germany. There were also entrants from Świnoujście and other towns in Poland. A solitary contestant from Denmark. Costumes included nineteenth-century bathing suits and dinner wear, sailors' outfits and bawdy, end-of-the-pier-postcard style swimsuits. The bathers greeted the cheers of the crowd with waves and fist pumps whilst the Baltic lapped gently at the shore, unimpressed. As the start time grew ever closer the bathers themselves quietened, already visibly cold as they waited for their fellow competitors to join them in a huddle on the sands. The crowds at the edge of the dunes and on the pier were growing larger by the minute, joined by a line of gulls and cormorants resting on the breakwaters with the best view of all.

It was time to begin. The competitors lined up along the beach to shouts of encouragement from above and behind. Some held hands. Others hugged themselves against the cold. A group of bare-chested lads said a toast and downed a shot of schnapps each. The jury made its way down to the water's edge.

One. Two. Three. Go!

In what seemed like slow motion they moved forward in a line, taking heavy steps through the sand. More shouts and cheers from the pier. The first feet landed in the gentle surf. Hesitation, but not for long. They were committed; there was no backing out now. *Splash, splash, splash* through the shallows and then, the water knee-deep, a fall forward in a version of a dive, each with differing levels of gracefulness. Pieces of costume floated to the surface as the once calm waters were now churned by thrashing limbs and the breathless struggle of the bathers tangled up in their clothes. More cheers. The gulls and cormorants took fright and flight.

A line of smartphones clicked and whirred in imitation of a hundred analogue cameras.

It did not take long before most of the competitors were back out of the water. Shivering and yet smiling with pride they hurried back up the beach to the tent, their clothes and a mug of mulled wine. A few lingered. The schnapps-drinking boys stood in the sea, the water up to their chests, and were joined by a team from Poland in a good-natured cross-border water fight. Shouts and laughter. A dunking or two. You got the feeling that plenty of beers would be shared that afternoon, on the long benches laid out in the marquee.

Shall we make a move?

Throughout the competition Katrin had been somewhere else in the crowd, finding the best angle for a photograph, but now she was standing at my shoulder. The tip of her nose was red in the cold. I could barely feel my feet. We left them to it and made our way out through the back of the crowd.

*

Behind the dunes we joined the promenade that ran along in front of the sea-facing hotels and apartment complexes of Ahlbeck, the last of the German Baltic resorts before the border with Poland. The promenade headed out of town to the east, a straight-line route behind the dunes and small pine forests for about three kilometres until it reached the boundary markers. Beyond those it was a further kilometre through the woods until you came to the first houses of Świnoujście, with its resort neighbourhood by the beach leading around to the mouth of the River Swine, the port and the town centre. Fittingly, for a biking and walking trail that now crosses an open border marked only by a sculpture and some painted posts in the ground, it has been named the Europapromenade in a spirit of cross-border solidarity. At periodic intervals there were paths leading down through the pine trees and the dunes to the beach. New toilets and picnic tables; bike racks and kiosks. It took us about forty minutes to reach the border, and I made the walk in an ever-changing mood that shifted between excitement and melancholy. Excitement because – as the child of an island – there remains something thrilling, even after all these years of living in Germany, about the idea of crossing a border on foot. Melancholy, because my Baltic explorations were nearly over.

Some borders feel natural. The English Channel. The Rhine. A mountain range or a river; dividing lines created by geography or geology. But in some places – the line across the Europapromenade between Ahlbeck and Świnoujście being one such example – you can feel that they have been willed into existence, that they did not develop naturally over time, that they are a product of people with their multitude of reasons and motivations. They feel both artificial and deadly certain, with a confidence in the straight line and the painted poles – black, red and gold on one side, red and white on the other – that says to the world *This is Germany* and *This is Poland*, as if it were ever thus.

Every so often on social media someone will post one of those time-lapse animations that show the shifting borders of Europe over the centuries. Countries appear, grow and then shrink, sometimes disappearing before reappearing again, slightly removed from the territory where they once stood. Sometimes they are destined never to return. Empires rise and fall. The Baltic shore is encircled, fractured. And then things come to a rest, where they stand today, and we feel certain that this is it, that things are fixed, despite the fact we have just watched a thousand years of change in less than a minute. We should know that things are never fixed.

At the border cyclists had dismounted and walkers paused, posing for photographs at the abstract sculpture that straddled the dividing line:

#leftlegPolandrightlegGermany!

A zig-zagging boardwalk led away from the Europapromenade, along the route of the border across the dunes and down on to the beach. We followed it, searching for clues on the sands as I had done a few months earlier on the old inner-German border at Priwall. Now, as then, there was nothing. We walked back and forth along the beach. At a certain point the signposts, with a warning not to encroach on the protected habitat behind the fence to the dunes, shifted in language. The numbers on the walkways to the promenade changed typeface. And that was it. Had we walked to Poland along the beach rather than the path behind the dunes, it would have been impossible to judge the moment when we crossed from one country to the next. The Baltic has no tides to speak of, but still the lines in the sand are easily washed away.

*

That morning, over breakfast at our guest house, I had flicked through a copy of the local newspaper. The bathing competition was previewed in the local news section, on the same page as a story about a candidate for mayor who had acted in a soft-erotic television show for a low-cost digital cable channel. There was little judgement in the piece, and no one seemed sure whether it would work against him in the upcoming vote or in his favour. Other stories concerned themselves with a planning permission dispute over a fish stand in one of the neighbouring resorts and rumours of political conspiracies, as the owner was also a candidate in the upcoming elections. The sports pages listed football results and the proposal for a new ice rink, right on the border, that could be shared by the populations of German Usedom and Polish Świnoujście.

For the most part these were the kinds of stories you could read in local newspapers the world over: an employment fair for young people at the local college; an open day at a nearby hospital; a new roof for the fire station. But there were others, small stories and sidebars, which spoke to the specifics of this small island shared by two countries on the Baltic shore. In Peenemünde, the former marine band of the GDR armed forces had come together for a reunion, taking part in their first rehearsals for over twenty-five years. The band had been disbanded with the absorption of the East German military into that of the reunified Federal Republic, but a quarter of a century on, the band pulled out their instruments and the yellowing sheet music from the garage and the loft and began to play those old tunes once more; rousing standards for a country that no longer exists.

On the same page a tiny article announced the latest *Heimattreffen* of the refugees – or more likely their descendants – of those territories to the east that were now also part of another country. I tried to imagine what happened at these meetings, now that most of those who can remember East Prussia or Danzig are no longer with us. Photos and recipes. Tales from a lost homeland. In Anklam, a Jewish family had returned to the town where their great-grandparents had once lived to stand outside the former family home. From this house they had been deported, murdered in the camps. A *Stolperstein* – stumbling stone – was laid in the pavement, close to the doorstep. On it were engraved the names of the couple, along with the date of deportation and their final destination: Theresienstadt.

I stood at the border and looked into Poland, the path through the trees leading to Świnoujście. How do we get from here to there? Not from Ahlbeck to Świnoujście but from Świnoujście to Swinemünde and back again. As we crabwalk along the shore we come upon those twelve years time and again, forever reminded of National Socialism and what it left behind. A divided country. A shattered country. Scars in its landscape, its people and its neighbours. In the back room of a pub, people meet to remember and talk about what was lost. On a pavement in Anklam, a family gathers to remember and talk about *who* was lost. A dozen years, and a never-ending shadow.

In 1999, during his Nobel Prize acceptance speech, Günter Grass spoke about being of that generation of writers who grew up during and after the years of Nazism and war:

We wrote by bearing in mind … that Auschwitz marks a rift, an unbridgeable gap in the history of civilisation.

In his own writing, Grass was not only doing battle with the crimes of the past but also his own sense of loss, the loss of his birthplace, and how, through his art, something of it could remain:

It could be resuscitated by the art of literature in all its grandeur and pettiness: the churches and cemeteries, the sounds of the shipyards and smells of the faintly lapping Baltic, a language on its way out and yet still stable-warm and grumble-rich, sins in need of confession, and crimes tolerated if never exonerated.

The ghosts on the shore.

*

Leaving the beach we followed the border inland, where the dividing line was clearly visible. A wide strip had been cut out of the forest, once the no man's land between the high fences of each country, floodlit and fortified like the old inner-German border or the Berlin Wall. Now, more than anything, it looked like those strips of forest removed to make space for electricity pylons and their heavy wires. We picked our way across the sandy and frosted former no man's land, an unofficial path that made its way over the uneven ground through the remnants of the border fortifications, past metal stumps and concrete posts, plus the abandoned beer bottles and other debris left behind by fellow off-road explorers. Their tracks and ours mingled with those of the creatures of the forest who now pass from one side to the other, completely at will.

We soon reached the road, where the checkpoint had once stood and where the new ice rink was to be built. Cars streamed across the border in both directions, where the dividing line was marked by a change in the road surface. Cobblestones in Poland. Asphalt in Germany. As we stepped off the sandy soil and on to the pavement we met a group of young Germans walking back from Świnoujście, swinging plastic bags filled with cigarettes by their sides. Wooden shacks advertised cheap smokes on the Polish side of the border. On the German side, across the street from the car park, a bar set back from the road made its dubious claim to fame:

The last German café before Moscow!

Crossing into Poland, we debated our next steps. From one border to the next, that had been the plan. But we were here now, and Świnoujście was just over there. We walked into town.

*

A few years before, the railway that had once stopped at the border was extended to reach the edge of Świnoujście town centre, linking the largest settlement on the island with the rest of Usedom. On the corner outside the station, beside a dentist's office that promised excellent treatment in three languages, and across the street from a McDonald's and a brand-new supermarket, a man stood with a map in his hand, looking from the paper to the sign above his head, as if confused by the street names and unsure of which direction he was supposed to walk.

What was he looking for? His past?

Later, having orientated himself, he would walk down into Świnoujście in search of Swinemünde. On his map he had marked the personal landmarks of his father's geography. The apartment and the school. The sweet shop and the doctor's office. His grandfather's shoemaking workshop and the allotment garden down by the river. His father used to watch the big ships coming in, following the narrow channel of the River Swine down through the port of Swinemünde and on to Stettin. And what about the Kurpark? Where the refugees from the east had later built their encampment only to be hit by American bombs … it had once been so lovely, on Sunday walks through the trees and alongside the lawns. They were proud that it had been designed by the same man who built the gardens for the king in Potsdam. How about that?

But the bombs did fall, and his father could never understand why they had hit them so hard. The war was almost over. But despite the devastation and the decades that had passed, his father could still close his eyes and navigate his way through a town that had been destroyed and rebuilt under a different name. And as he walked through the town, the man by the station would come to see that he need not have come to Świnoujście to find Swinemünde. He would have been better off just talking to his dad. It was a realisation that would come later. For now, standing outside the station, he just needed to know which way he was supposed to turn.

*

We walked a little way down Konstytucji 3 Maja in the direction of the town centre. We too were attempting to read the city through its buildings and its landmarks, searching for the traces of Swinemünde among what was clearly Świnoujście. The red-brick buildings on one side of the street looked Prussian. The concrete-slab apartments on the other, ever so slightly different than their GDR counterparts elsewhere on the island, most certainly a legacy of Polish communism. Newer apartment blocks, with large windows and balconies, advertised themselves for sale in as many languages as the dentist's office, and here and there – especially in the resort area of the town, close to the beach – it was clear there was money arriving in Świnoujście, and a reminder that much had changed in the decades since the collapse of communism. From the end of the Second World War, Świnoujście had been, like Priwall outside Lübeck, effectively an island, cut off from the rest of the country by a river and from its natural hinterland by a heavily fortified border strip; now the boundaries to investment had greatly reduced.

Swinemünde had been one of the Baltic coast's pre-eminent bathing resorts during the nineteenth and early twentieth centuries, and there was a sense, as we walked through the streets, that we could follow the layers of that history in the buildings as we went: Świnoujście as palimpsest. Closest to the Kurpark were the Wilhelmine villas, the grand lodging houses of the boom years when visitors would travel north on the railway from Berlin through Golm to the seaside. Next came a strip of communist-era hotels and a campsite of wooden bungalows. The hotels were boxy, with mean windows and fraying posters that advertised 'wellness' treatments that looked like they had not been updated since the 1980s. Closest to the beach we reached the new developments: brick and concrete condos, with landscaped gardens and winding footpaths that made their way between the buildings to the dunes and then down on to the beach. It was clear that most of the available space had been filled, and the next step would be to replace the communist-era structures with something more modern and appealing. What would be left would be the restored old villas and the new developments. As with Dranske on Rügen, I wondered if the future explorer of Świnoujście would walk the streets on a journey directly between the nineteenth and the twenty-first centuries, with very little remaining from the years in between.

Down by the harbour we watched the car ferries cross back and forth over the river and the huge ships waiting to make the journey across the Baltic to Denmark and Sweden.

Gunmetal-grey navy boats lined up alongside industrial barges as cranes swung in the air, high above huge depots piled with coal. From the harbour wall, men in woolly hats fished in the river or sat on benches and watched, sipping from brown bottles of beer.

We followed a winding path between the Kurpark and the river, through woods past eighteenth-century military forts built to protect the mouth of the Swine and now overgrown with bushes and trees. We were aiming for the point where the river met the sea, and one last look at the Baltic. It was calm between the trees, but unlike earlier at the border, the wind had picked up, and as we emerged over the top of the dunes it stung our faces and ears. We pulled our hats lower and pressed on, down towards the breakwater wall and the lighthouse. The beach was empty, save for a solitary fisherman standing waist-deep in the choppy Baltic waters, holding a net high above his shoulders like a boom-mic operator. I looked back down the beach, murky in the low light of an overcast winter's afternoon, and tried to make a guess as to where Poland stopped and Germany started, that line in the sand that I had decided was to be the limit of my explorations and the end of my journey.

Then I realised: this was it. If the border, back there

down the sands, had felt arbitrary, this spot at the very end of Usedom and the mouth of the river felt like the true place where my journey should end. Some boundaries, after all, feel natural, and others don't. From the Trave of Travemünde to the Swine of Swinemünde ... I corrected myself: the Swina of Świnoujście. The fisherman made slow progress away from us, parallel to the shore. As I watched him the lighthouse turned behind me, flashing out across waters that would ever-darken as the day drew to a close. Those ominous waters. I thought of our walk through the town, attempting to read the history in the streets, and the man on the corner trying to make sense of the map in his hand and that in his father's head. I thought about the bombs of 1945 and the bodies buried on a nearby hillside, in another country. Of the shifting of borders and the shifting of peoples. Of political systems and the country of Katrin's childhood, in sight and over there, and yet nothing but a memory. And I thought of ships resting on the seabed at either end of this Baltic shore, of the bodies that had been taken by these waters with only some of them returned, and of rockets falling from the sky and mythical cities falling to the waves.

*

In 1810, Heinrich von Kleist attempted to make sense of Casper David Friedrich's *The Monk by the Sea*, having viewed it in Berlin. For Kleist, the meaning of this image of the monk standing on the Arkona cliff top on Rügen was clear:

No situation in the world could be sadder and eerier than this – as the only spark of life in the wide realm of death, a lonely centre in a lonely circle …

Ever since Kleist wrote his appreciation of the painting on its unveiling, through the nineteenth century and via the Nazis and post-war Germany to the present day, reviewers and historians have argued about whether the power of the paintings comes from what Friedrich himself intended, or whether our responses are, like Kleist's, more a reflection of what we bring with us as we approach the canvas.

The core meaning of Friedrich's paintings, the art historian Beat Wyss wrote in 2008, *lies in the viewer's own interpretation, and there is nothing in them that does not already exist in the viewer's own heart and mind.*

The same can be said of place. Our understanding depends on what we know. As I stood by the lighthouse at Świnoujście, watching the fisherman as he finally dragged his catch ashore, I was looking beyond him and back down the coast in the direction of Germany thinking about the seascape and my trips up to this point. I knew that my understanding of these places was entirely based on my own experiences: what I had heard; what I had seen; what I had read.

But it was not just what I had experienced here, on my travels along the German Baltic shore. My understanding was shaped by *all* of my experiences. Of growing up in northern England. Of nearly fifteen years of living in Germany. Of being neither a local nor a complete outsider. Of being the father to a half-German daughter, for whom this history is *her* history in a way that it will never be mine.

I thought back to that afternoon in Travemünde, looking out over the Bay of Lübeck towards the spot where the *Cap Arcona* had been sunk by the pilots of the Royal Air Force. Standing at the lighthouse in Świnoujście I could look out now and imagine the survivors of the *Wilhelm Gustloff* being landed ashore, all but their lives lost, and work through the parallels between these wartime tragedies at either end of the Baltic shore. But there was no question that one hit me harder than the other, and it is only now that I begin to wonder whether it is the knowledge that the sinking of the *Cap Arcona* had been committed by British pilots that gave me greater pause for thought than the other ship, sunk by a Soviet submarine. Does a crime, even if it was an accidental crime, committed before you are born but in the name of a country whose passport you hold, still stain you in some way? Are the ghosts on the shore still our responsibility? That is the question long asked in my adopted home. That is the question of Germany.

That question of responsibility was why, on another day, I had felt uneasy at the new developments of Prora. It was not simply my knowledge of the place, my knowledge of who built it and why, but the fact that I could feel that, in that place of all places, history was being ignored. In Peenemünde, my reaction to a place where rockets of death were built was shaped as much by the skinheads in the car park as it was by the stories I was told in the museum. In Kühlungsborn, on the edge of town and in the snow, I had explored Katrin's old summer camp with her dad and felt the emotional pull of a time and a place that I never experienced and that was never coming back. Someone else would experience that collection of holiday apartments in a very different way, based on other memories perhaps, or as a blank slate.

A year after he wrote those words about *The Monk by the Sea*, Heinrich von Kleist committed suicide in a pact with his friend Henriette Vogel. They were buried in Wannsee, southern Berlin, roughly a mile from the villa where the Nazis planned out the Holocaust and not far from where

Philip Hoare went for his swim in the lake. As I stood by the Świnoujście lighthouse at the end of my journey I certainly did not feel alone on this particular stretch of coastline.

Katrin had moved on, down off the wall and on to the sands. It was time to make our way to the station to catch a train back across the border and into Germany. I took one last look at the Baltic in the rapidly fading light. If there were ghosts on this shore, here at the water's edge, it was because we had brought them with us. Those ghosts are indeed our responsibility, and they will live on in our memories of this place and others, and in the stories we choose to tell.

Sources

Select Bibliography

Note: I have selected the English-language edition of books and articles, where available

Blicke, Biermann, Faigle et al, 'Germany in Flames', *Zeit Online*, 4 December 2015

Hartmut Bornhoff, *Das Judenschloss am Meer*, website of Jüdische Gemeinde Berlin, 1 December 2010

Robert Cole, *Germany* (Northampton: Interlink, 2014)

Max Egremont, *Forgotten Land: Journeys among the Ghosts of East Prussia* (London: Picador, 2011)

Hebert Ewe, *Stralsund* (Rostock: Hinstorff Verlag, 1987)

Theodor Fontane, *Effi Briest* (London: Penguin Classics, 2001)

Mary Fulbrook, *The People's State* (New Haven: Yale University Press, 2008)

Timothy Garton Ash, *The File: A Personal History* (London: Atlantic Books, 2009)

Michael Gorra, *The Bells in Their Silence* (Princeton: Princeton University Press, 2004)

Günter Grass, *Crabwalk* (London: Faber & Faber, 2014)

Antony Grenville, 'The case of Gerhart Hauptmann', *AJR Journal*, July 2012

Hacker & Böttcher, *Hanseatic City of Stralsund* (Rostock: Hinstorff Verlag, 2000)

Nigel Hamilton, *The Brothers Mann* (New Haven: Yale University Press, 1979)

Kerstin Herrnkind, 'Der Arzt, der ins Wasser ging', *Stern Magazine*, 14 October 2009

Klaus-Dietmar Henke quoted in 'Paying with Life and Limb for the Crimes of Nazi Germany', *Der Spiegel*, 27 May 2011

Philip Hoare, 'The naming of the shrew: language, landscape and the new nature writing', *New Statesman*, 19 March 2015

Christopher Isherwood, *Goodbye to Berlin*
(London: Vintage, 1998)

Jonathan Jones, 'The ghosts of Germany's past', *The Guardian*, 19 February 2001

Klaus-Jürgen Liedtke, *The Lost Baltic Sea of German Literature*, The Baltic Sea Library, accessed online 1 February 2015

Heinrich Mann, *Man of Straw* (London: Penguin, 1984)

Thomas Mann, *Buddenbrooks* (London: Vintage, 1996)

Jan Morris, *Europe* (London: Faber & Faber, 2006)

Rick Noack, 'Germany's enthusiasm for refugees might not last. These maps explain why', *Washington Post*, 14 September 2015

Norman Page, *Auden and Isherwood: The Berlin Years* (Basingstoke: MacMillan, 2000)

Petra Schellin, 'Der Mann der dringend wegmusste', *TAZ*, 4 October 2009

Roswitha Schieb, *The Island of Rügen as Mythic Site in Germany,* Baltic Sea Library, accessed online 1 February 2015

W.G. Sebald, 'A Natural History of Destruction', *The New Yorker,* 4 November 2002

Julian Tompkin, 'Between a sea and a hard place', *Deutsche Welle,* 29 September 2015

Doktor Samuel Gottlieb Vogel, *Allgemeine Baderegeln* (Accessed online: http://www.lexikus.de/bibliothek/Allgemeine-Baderegeln)

Wernher von Braun, *Recollections of Childhood: Early Experiences of Rocketry, Marshall Space Flight Center* (Accessed online: https://history.msfc.nasa.gov/vonbraun/recollect-childhood.html)

Peter Watson, *The German Genius* (London: Simon & Schuster, 2010)

Jenny Williams, *More Lives Than One: A Biography of Hans Fallada* (London: Penguin, 2012)

RAF Pilot Allan Wyse, quoted in 'British error killed WW2 inmates', *China Daily*, 7 March 2000

Beat Wyss, 'The Whispering Zeitgeist', *Tate Etc*, Issue 14, Autumn 2008

Museums

Alte Nationalgalerie, Berlin
Buddenbrooks-Haus, Lübeck
Documentations Zentrum Prora, Rügen
Grenzturm Ausstellung, Kühlungsborn
Günter Grass-Haus, Lübeck
Hans Fallada-Museum, Carwitz
Historisch-Technisches Museum Peenemünde, Usedom
International Youth Meeting and Educational Centre, Golm

Films

The description of the anti-immigration 'stroll' through Stralsund came from a number of different online videos of similar events in 2015, including a video of the 12. MVGIDA walk through Stralsund-Grünhufe on 30 March 2015: https://www.youtube.com/watch?v=7aQglZnzQBo

Much of the history of events in Rostock-Lichtenhagen in 1992 was pieced together by a Channel 4 documentary team for their film *The Truth Lies in Rostock,* accessible online. The 2014 feature film *Wir sind jung. Wir sind stark* about the same events was directed by Burhan Qurbani (UFA Fiction, ZDF and Arte).

For a fascinating overview of the forest and German culture, see 'Into the Imagined Forest', a lecture from Dr Richard Hacking. Accessed online via Youtube: https://www.youtube.com/watch?v=SjUpktmyb3o

Other Sources

UNESCO inscription of Stralsund and Wismar onto the World Heritage List came in 2002: http://whc.unesco.org/en/list/1067

Statistics and other findings on East/West German attitudes from a 2015 study by The Berlin Institute for Population and Development, titled *So geht Einheit: Wie weit das einst geteilte Deutschland zusammengewachsen ist*, available online: http://www.berlin-institut.org/publikationen.html

Quotes from the promotional materials for New Prora come from the developers' website: http://www.neues-prora.de/en/history. Accessed online in January 2016

The Günter Grass Nobel Prize acceptance speech has been translated into English and is available on the Nobel Prize website

Acknowledgements

Thanks to Gary and Kit at Influx for all their support. I first had the idea for *Ghosts on the Shore* reading another of their books – *Marshland* by Gareth E. Rees – in an old GDR bungalow just a few hundred metres from the Baltic, so in reality, it could only have ever been Influx. Thanks also to Dan, Austin and Julia for all their work on the book.

Possibly the biggest thanks need to go to the Schönig family, and in particular Gabi and Fritz, for taking me to the Baltic and allowing me to tell some of their story in these pages. Others who have joined me on trips north or have helped or encouraged me as the project went along include, in no specific order: Jessi and Martin, Anja, Marcel and the rest of the springtime Baltic crew, Sean and Ailis, Mum and George, Dad and Deena, Andreas, Jim, Jared, Kenny, Paul, Marcel, Tim, Eymelt and Óli, Bine, Tobi and Anni, Tom and Jas. Some of the first pieces I wrote about the Baltic appeared on *Caught by the River*, and I will be forever grateful to Jeff, Robin, Andrew and Diva for all their support.

I start the book in Berlin, on a Saturday morning expedition to look at paintings with my daughter Lotte. She has been on many of the journeys told in these pages, and is a constant support and inspiration to me.

Finally, Katrin. You started it all on that rainy day in Warnemünde. Not long after I made a foolish promise to write you a song. I never did it. I hope this book will do instead.

About the author

Paul Scraton is a writer and editor based in Berlin. Born in Lancashire, he moved to the German capital in 2001 where he has lived ever since. He is the editor-in-chief of *Elsewhere: A Journal of Place* and his essays on place and memory have been published as the pocket book *The Idea of a River: Walking out of Berlin* by Readux Books in March 2015, and in *Mauerweg: Stories from the Berlin Wall Trail*, published by Slow Travel Berlin in 2014 to mark the 25th anniversary of the fall of the Berlin Wall. Among other publications, you can find more of Paul's writing on *Caught by the River* and in *hidden europe* magazine.

This book was made possible thanks to the support of the following people:

Greg Bowman
Steffi Fox
Katherine Hawes
Sam Jordison
Brian Lavelle
Gayle Lazda
Chris McCrudden
Toby Miller
Jim Mooney
Terri Mulholland
Kevin Mullen
Peter Nowell
Des O'Donoghue
Matt Petzny
Chris Power
Gareth Rees
John Rickets
Sheila Scraton
Ashley Stokes
Simon Wallace
Mary Warnemart
Sarah Wishart
Neil Young